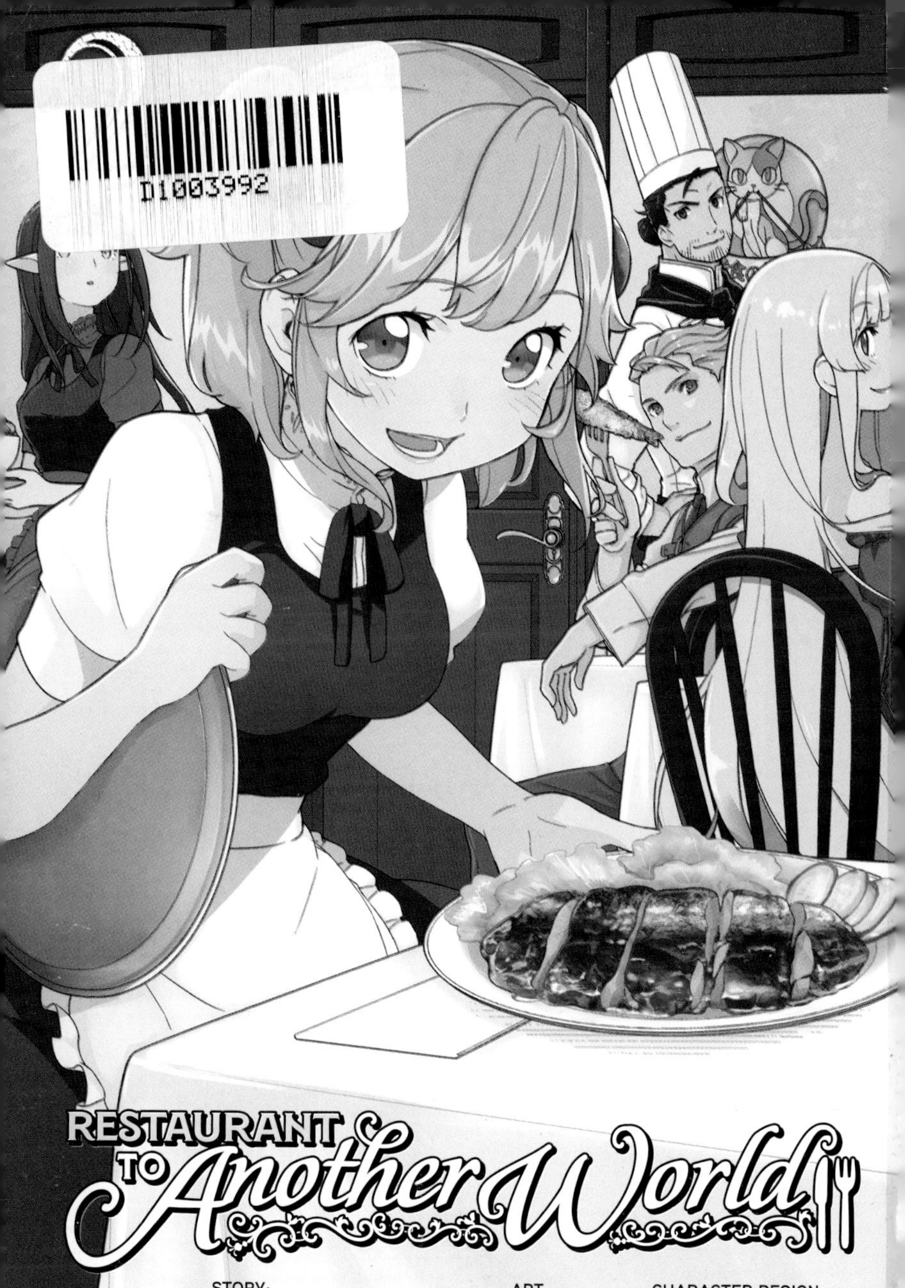

RESTAURANT TO Another World

STORY:
JUNPEI INUZUKA
(Shufunotomo Infos Co.,Ltd.)

ART:
TAKAAKI KUGATSU

CHARACTER DESIGN:
KATSUMI ENAMI

MENU

6th Dish Teriyaki

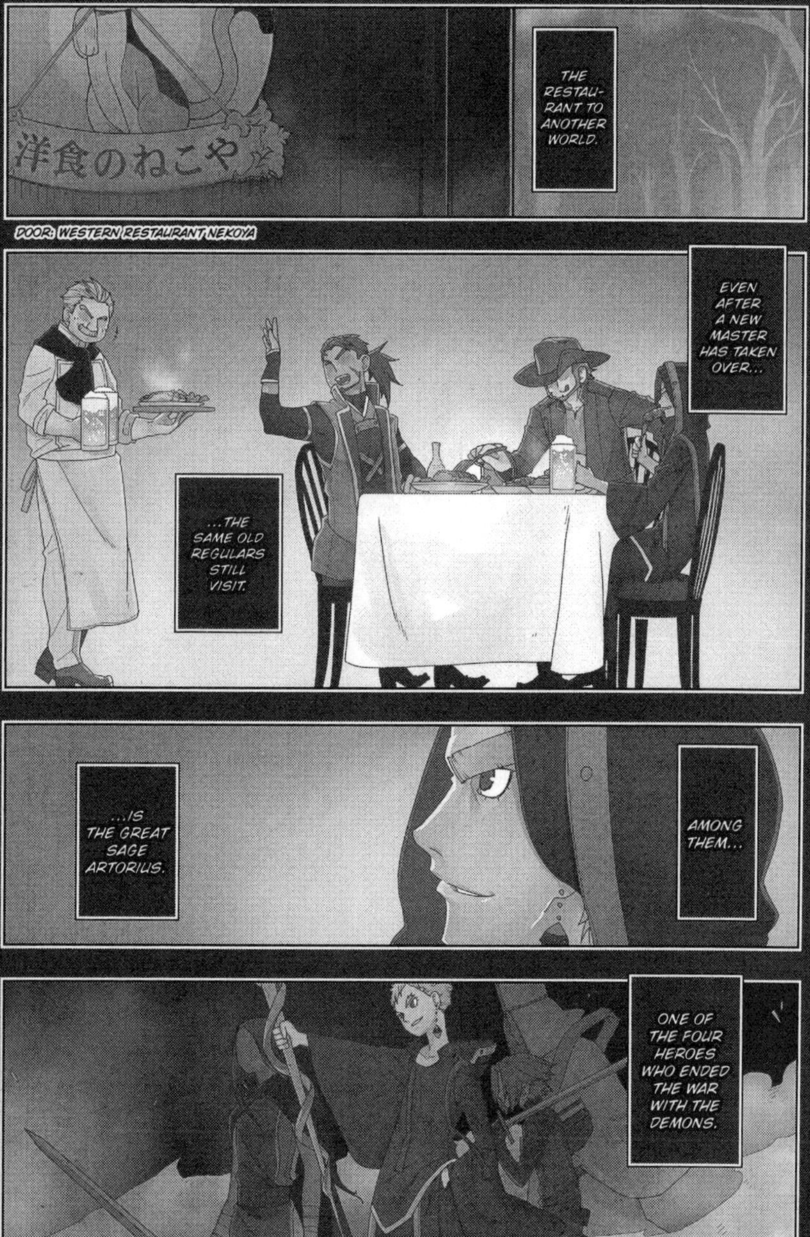
THE RESTAU-RANT TO ANOTHER WORLD.
洋食のねこや
DOOR: WESTERN RESTAURANT NEKOYA
EVEN AFTER A NEW MASTER HAS TAKEN OVER...
...THE SAME OLD REGULARS STILL VISIT.
AMONG THEM...
...IS THE GREAT SAGE ARTORIUS.
ONE OF THE FOUR HEROES WHO ENDED THE WAR WITH THE DEMONS.

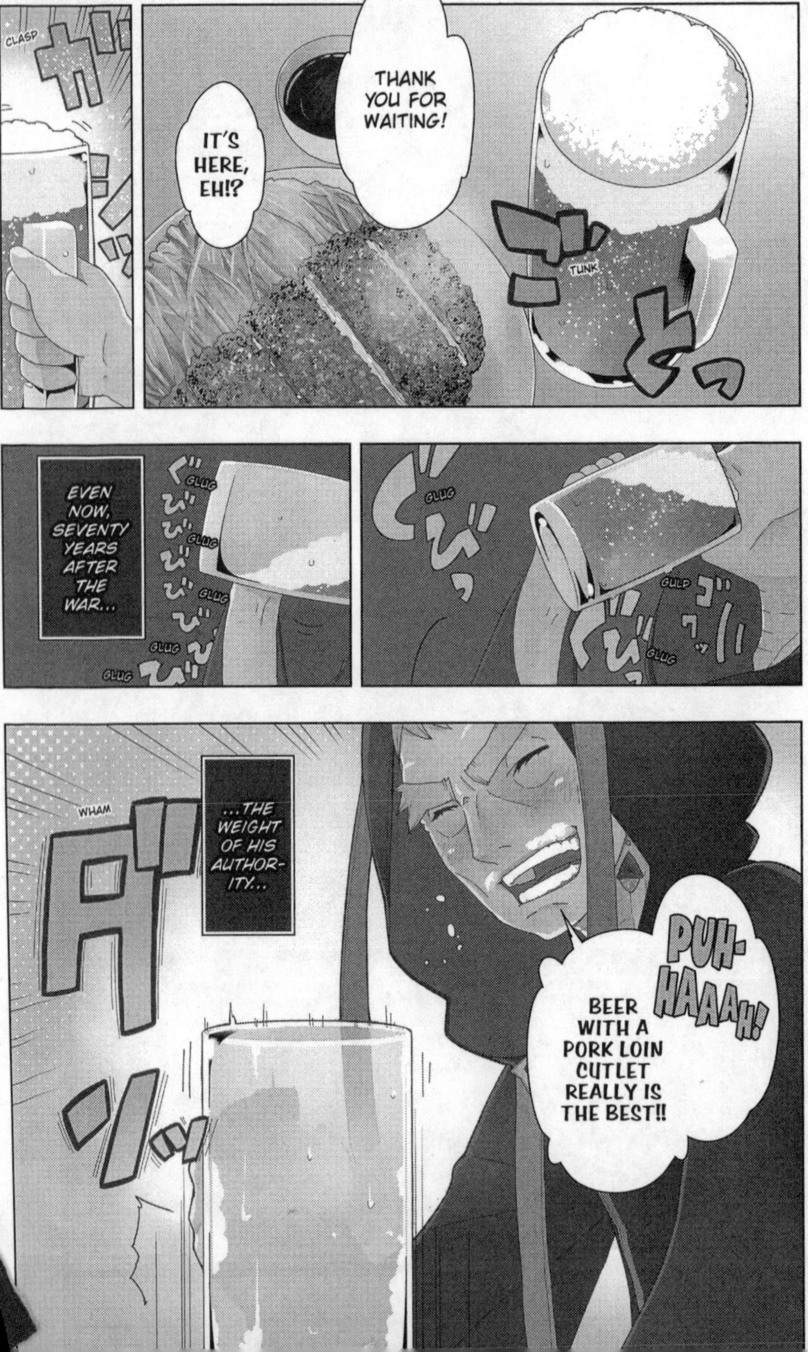
THANK YOU FOR WAITING!
IT'S HERE, EH!?
TUNK
CLASP
GLUG
GULP
GLUG
EVEN NOW, SEVENTY YEARS AFTER THE WAR...
GLUG
GLUG
GLUG
GLUG
GLUG
PUH-HAAAAH!
BEER WITH A PORK LOIN CUTLET REALLY IS THE BEST!!
...THE WEIGHT OF HIS AUTHORITY...
WHAM

CRUNCH

CHOMP

...HASN'T FADED...

SLOO

GLUG

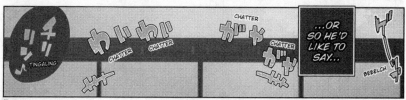
TINGALING

CHATTER

CHATTER

CHATTER

CHATTER

...OR SO HE'D LIKE TO SAY...

BEEELCH

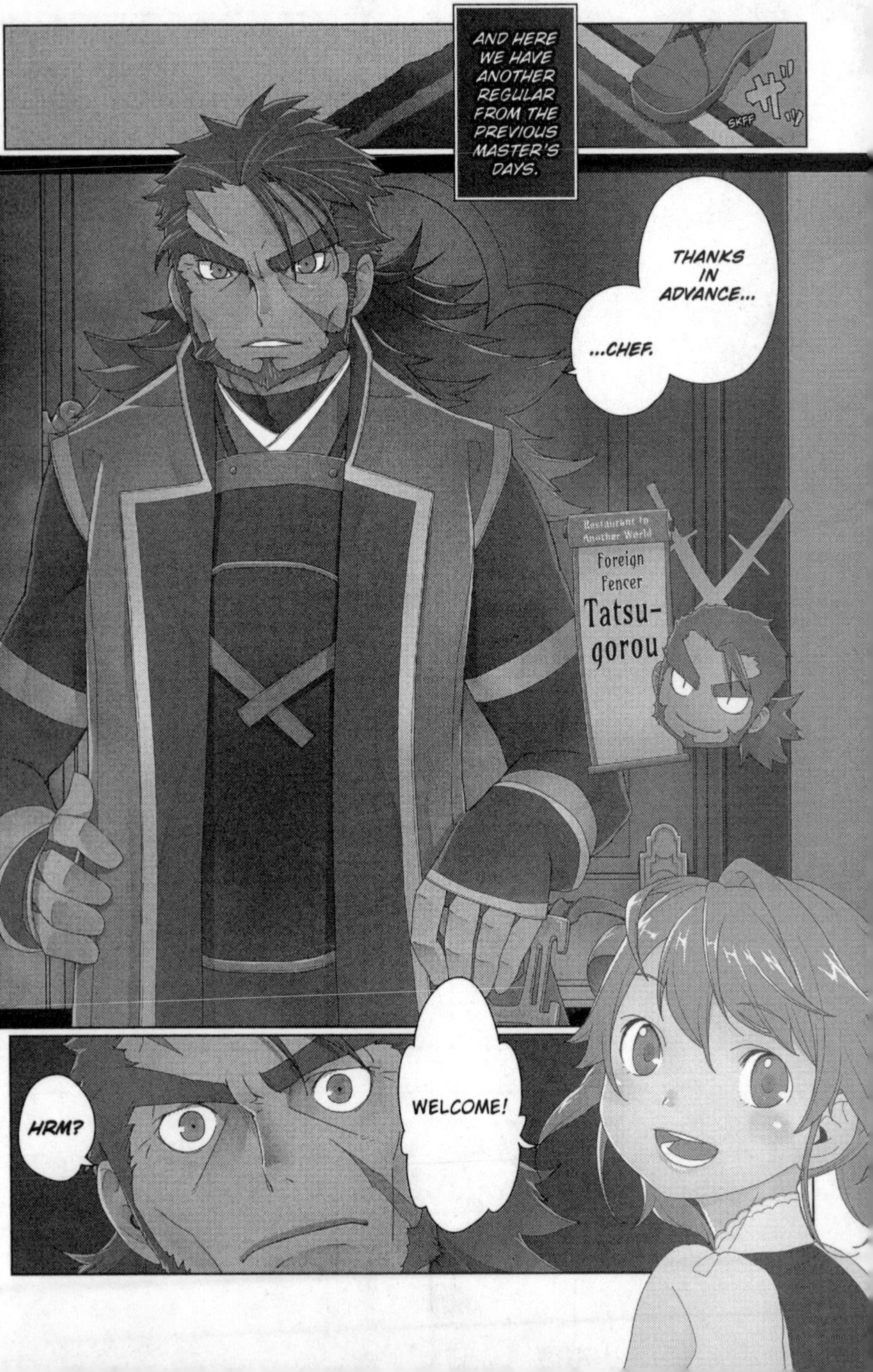
SKFF
AND HERE WE HAVE ANOTHER REGULAR FROM THE PREVIOUS MASTER'S DAYS.
THANKS IN ADVANCE...
...CHEF.
Restaurant to Another World
Foreign Fencer Tatsu-gorou
WELCOME!
HRM?

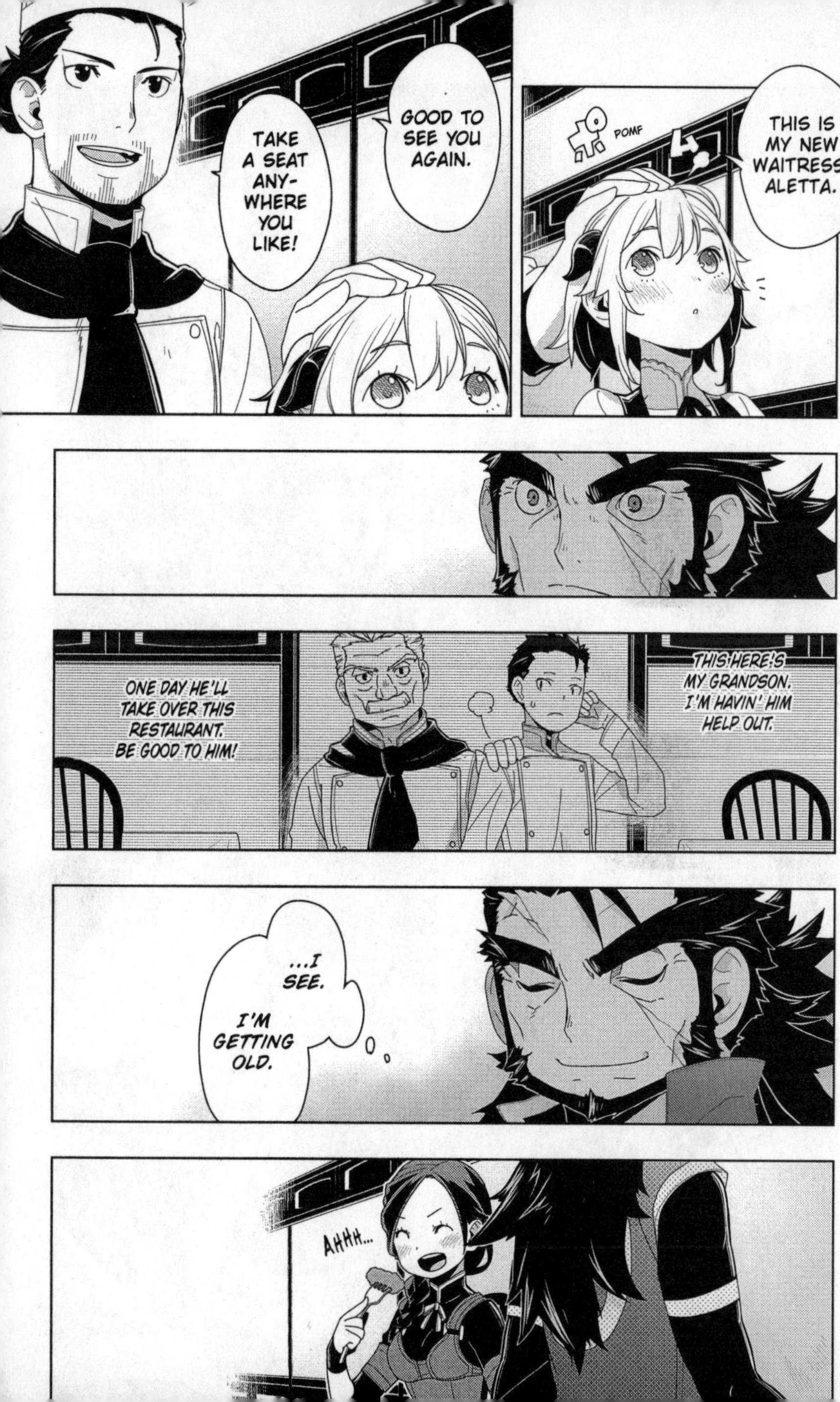
POMF
THIS IS MY NEW WAITRESS, ALETTA.
GOOD TO SEE YOU AGAIN.
TAKE A SEAT ANY-WHERE YOU LIKE!
THIS HERE'S MY GRANDSON. I'M HAVIN' HIM HELP OUT.
ONE DAY HE'LL TAKE OVER THIS RESTAURANT. BE GOOD TO HIM!
...I SEE.
I'M GETTING OLD.
AHHH...

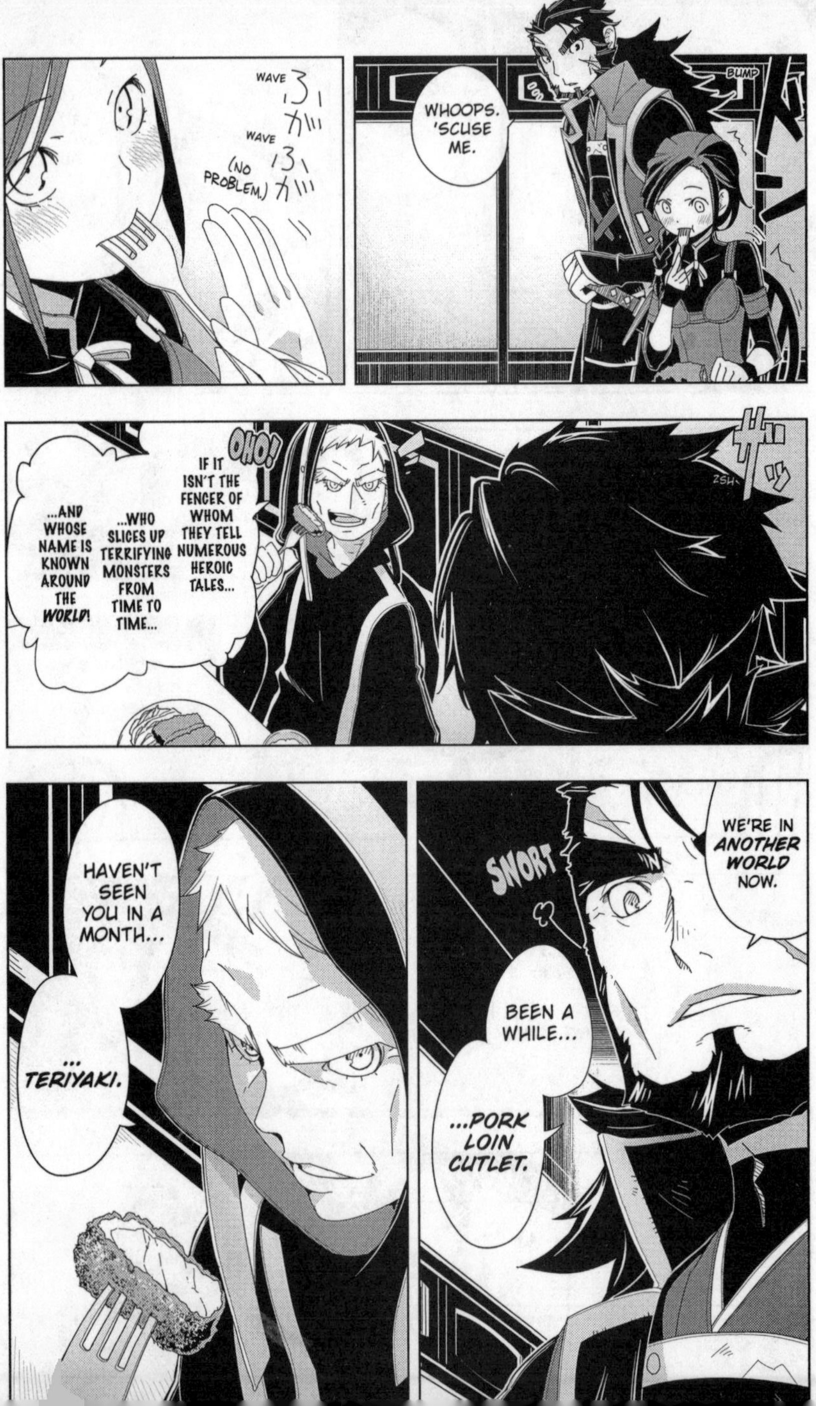
BUMP
WHOOPS. 'SCUSE ME.
WAVE
WAVE
(NO PROBLEM.)
ZSH
OHO!
IF IT ISN'T THE FENCER OF WHOM THEY TELL NUMEROUS HEROIC TALES...
...WHO SLICES UP TERRIFYING MONSTERS FROM TIME TO TIME...
...AND WHOSE NAME IS KNOWN AROUND THE *WORLD*!
WE'RE IN *ANOTHER WORLD* NOW.
SNORT
BEEN A WHILE...
...PORK LOIN CUTLET.
HAVEN'T SEEN YOU IN A MONTH...
... *TERIYAKI*.

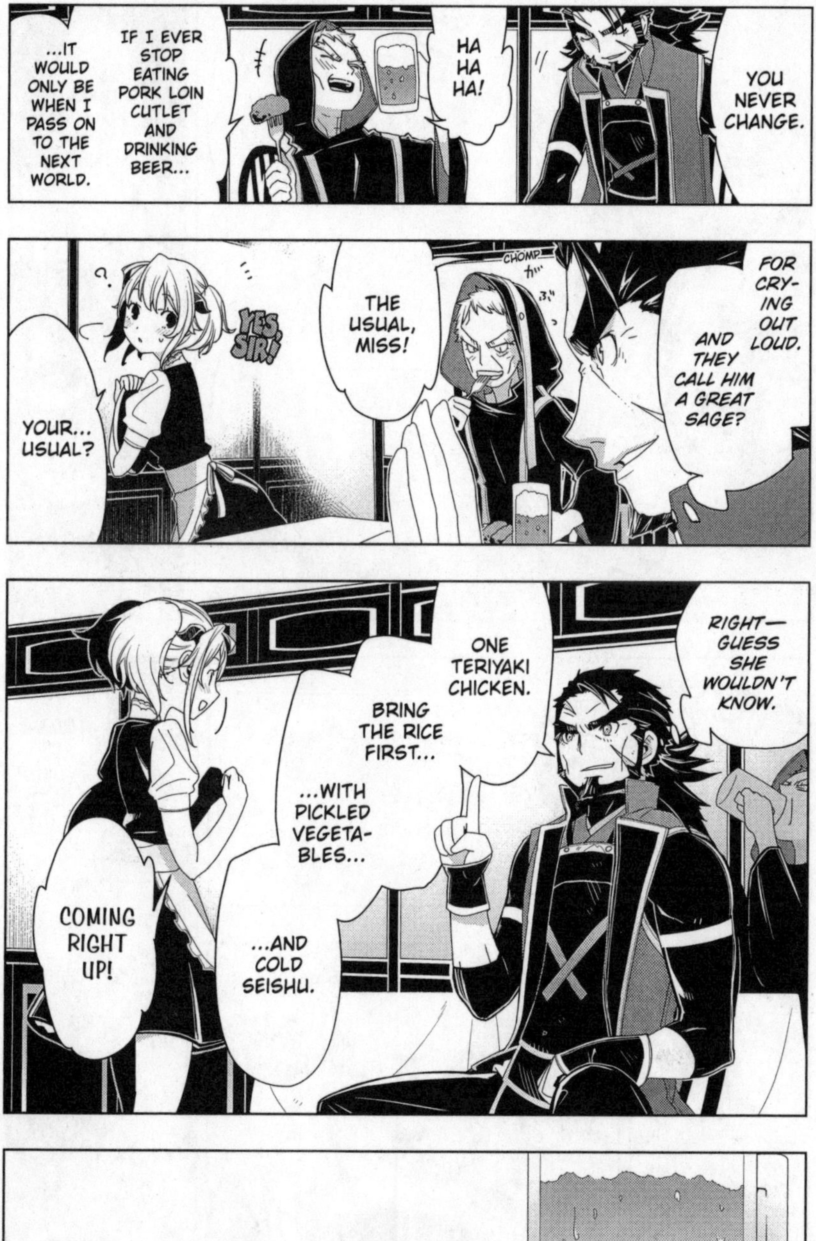
YOU NEVER CHANGE.
HA HA HA!
IF I EVER STOP EATING PORK LOIN CUTLET AND DRINKING BEER...
...IT WOULD ONLY BE WHEN I PASS ON TO THE NEXT WORLD.
FOR CRYING OUT LOUD.
AND THEY CALL HIM A GREAT SAGE?
CHOMP
THE USUAL, MISS!
YES, SIR!
YOUR... USUAL?
RIGHT—GUESS SHE WOULDN'T KNOW.
ONE TERIYAKI CHICKEN.
BRING THE RICE FIRST...
...WITH PICKLED VEGETABLES...
...AND COLD SEISHU.
COMING RIGHT UP!

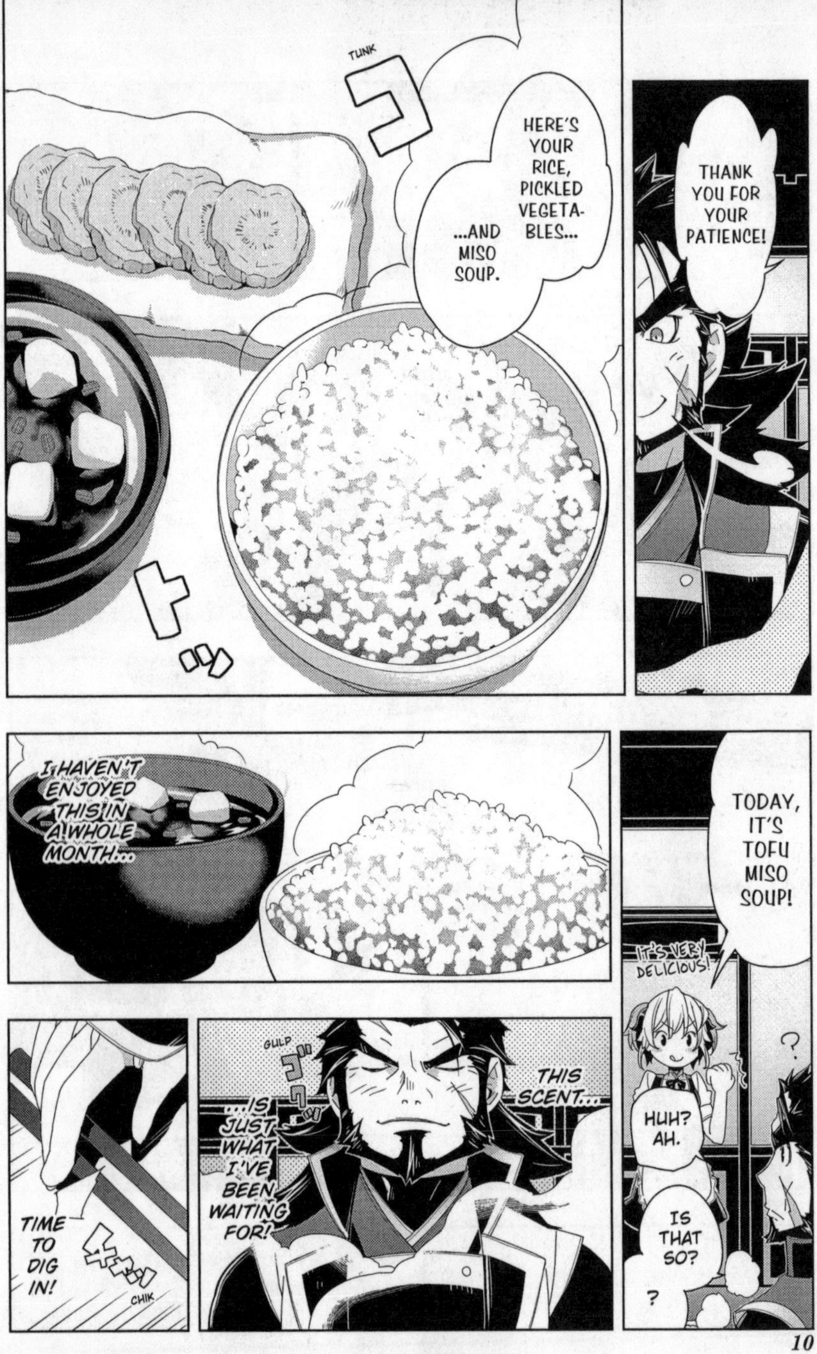
THANK YOU FOR YOUR PATIENCE!
TUNK
HERE'S YOUR RICE, PICKLED VEGETA-BLES...
...AND MISO SOUP.
TODAY, IT'S TOFU MISO SOUP!
IT'S VERY DELICIOUS!
?
HUH? AH.
IS THAT SO?
?
I HAVEN'T ENJOYED THIS IN A WHOLE MONTH...
GULP
THIS SCENT...
...IS JUST WHAT I'VE BEEN WAITING FOR!
TIME TO DIG IN!
CHIK

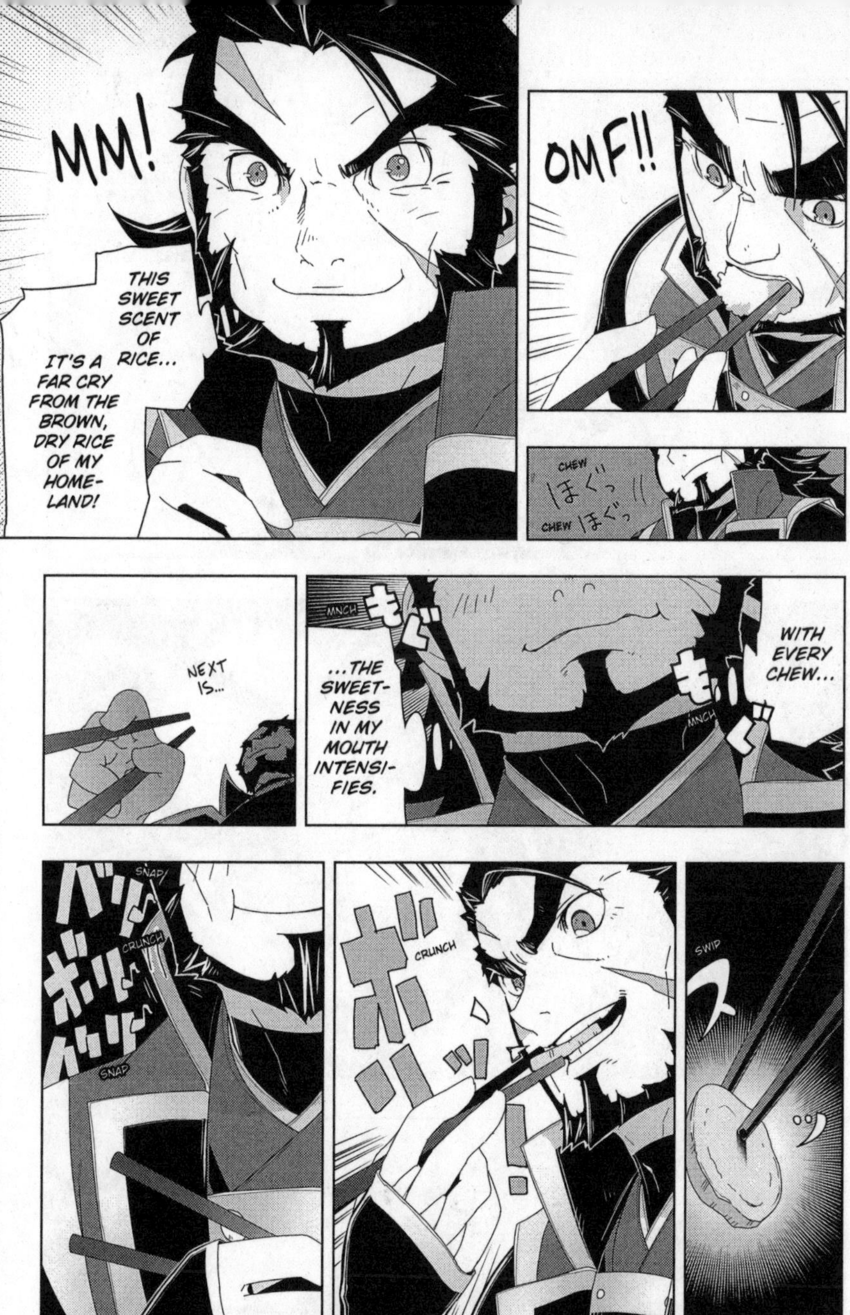
OMF!!
CHEW ほぐっ
CHEW ほぐっ
MM!
THIS SWEET SCENT OF RICE...
IT'S A FAR CRY FROM THE BROWN, DRY RICE OF MY HOMELAND!
WITH EVERY CHEW...
MNCH
MNCH
...THE SWEETNESS IN MY MOUTH INTENSIFIES.
NEXT IS...
SWIP
CRUNCH
SNAP
CRUNCH
SNAP

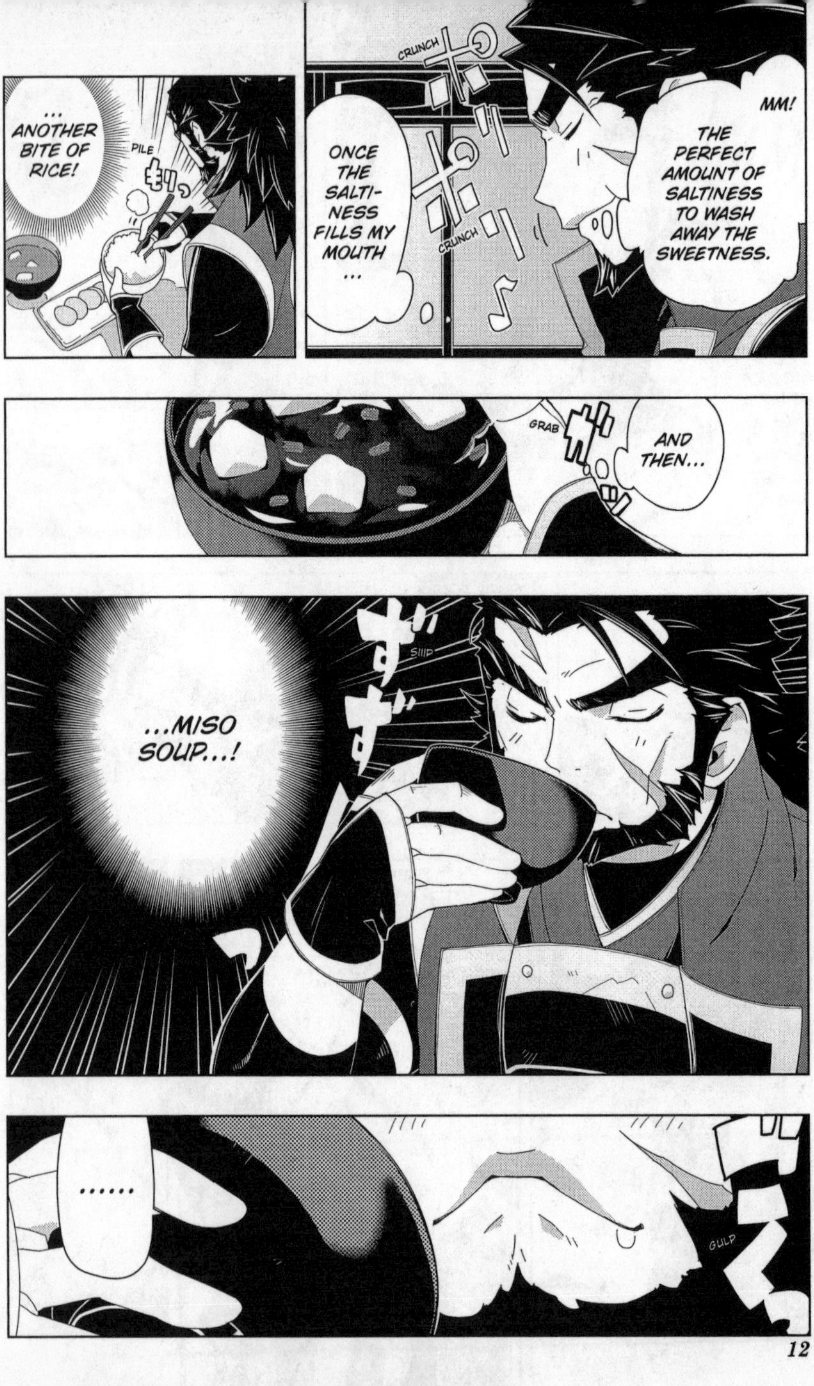
CRUNCH
MM!
THE PERFECT AMOUNT OF SALTINESS TO WASH AWAY THE SWEETNESS.
CRUNCH
ONCE THE SALTINESS FILLS MY MOUTH ...
... ANOTHER BITE OF RICE!
PILE
AND THEN...
GRAB
SIIIP
...MISO SOUP...!
GULP
......

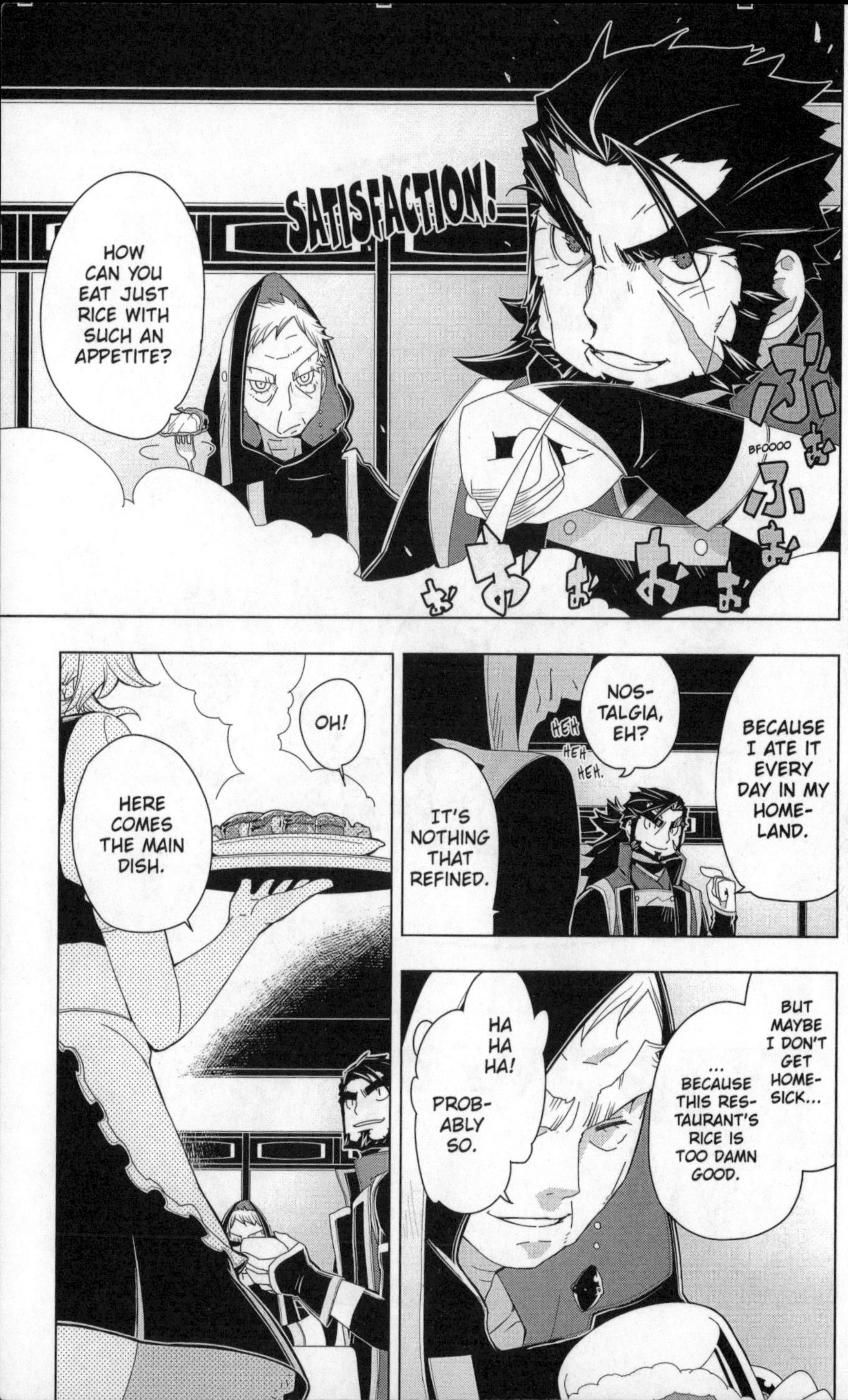
SATISFACTION!
HOW CAN YOU EAT JUST RICE WITH SUCH AN APPETITE?
BFOOOO
BECAUSE I ATE IT EVERY DAY IN MY HOME-LAND.
NOS-TALGIA, EH?
HEH HEH HEH.
IT'S NOTHING THAT REFINED.
BUT MAYBE I DON'T GET HOME-SICK...
... BECAUSE THIS RES-TAURANT'S RICE IS TOO DAMN GOOD.
HA HA HA!
PROB-ABLY SO.
OH!
HERE COMES THE MAIN DISH.

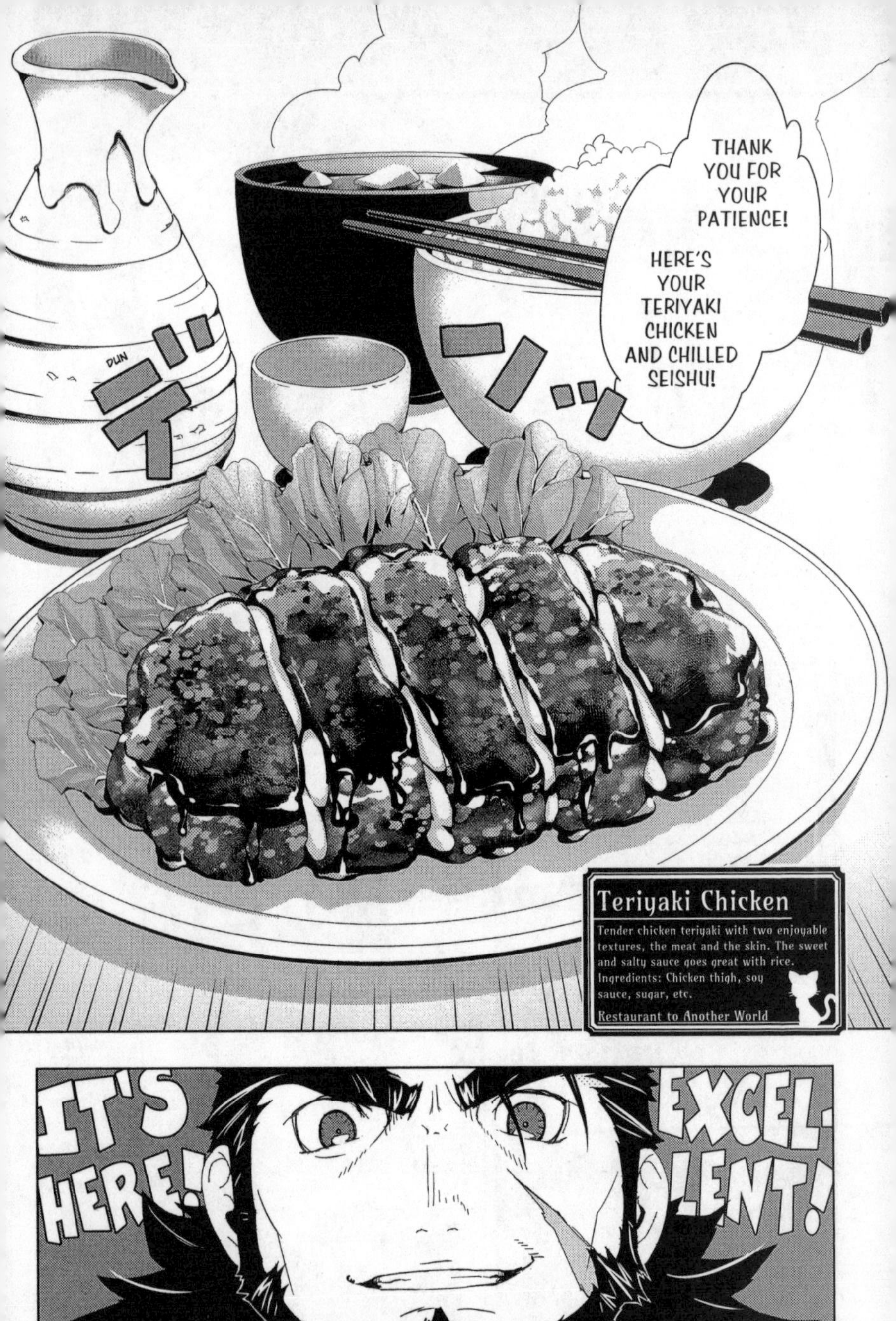
THANK YOU FOR YOUR PATIENCE!
HERE'S YOUR TERIYAKI CHICKEN AND CHILLED SEISHU!
DUN
Teriyaki Chicken
Tender chicken teriyaki with two enjoyable textures, the meat and the skin. The sweet and salty sauce goes great with rice.
Ingredients: Chicken thigh, soy sauce, sugar, etc.
Restaurant to Another World
EXCEL-LENT!
IT'S HERE!

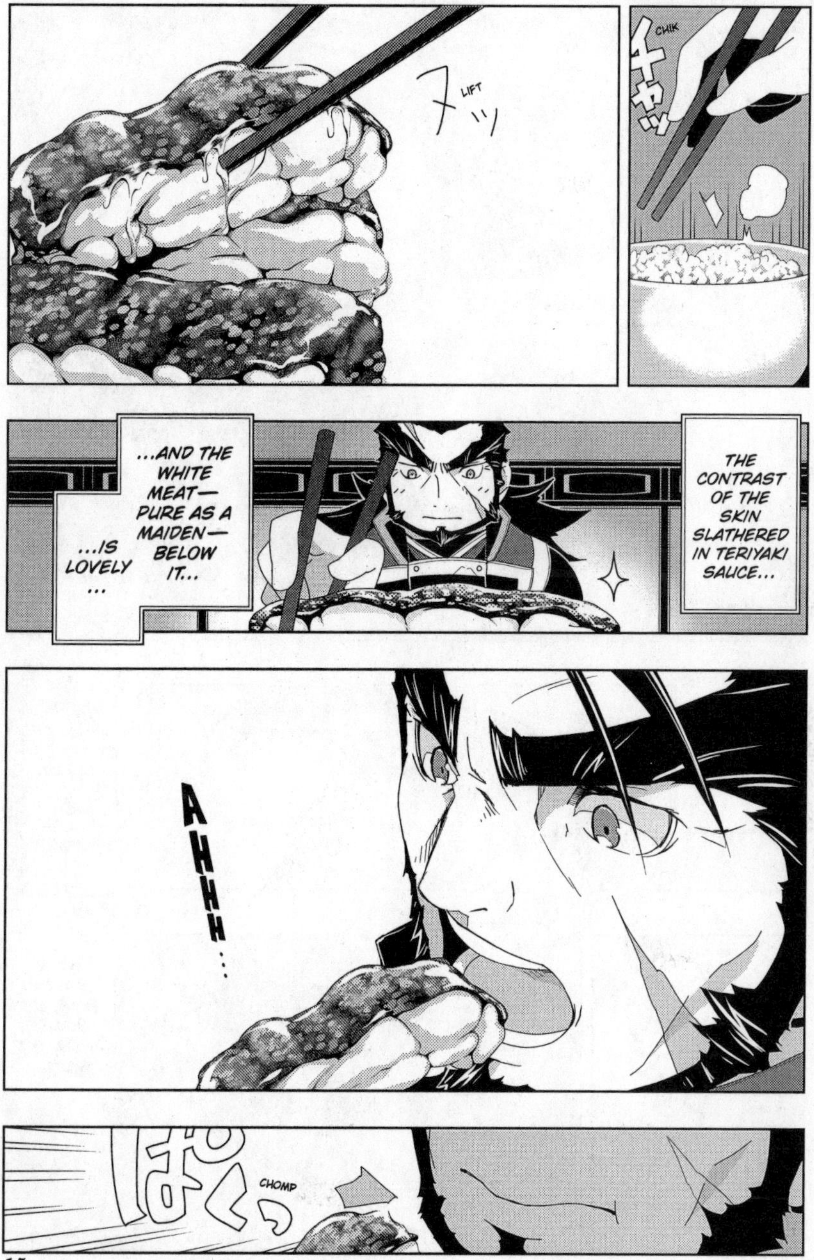
CHIK
ヌッ
LIFT
THE CONTRAST OF THE SKIN SLATHERED IN TERIYAKI SAUCE...
...AND THE WHITE MEAT—PURE AS A MAIDEN—BELOW IT...
...IS LOVELY...
AHHHH...
ぱくっ
CHOMP

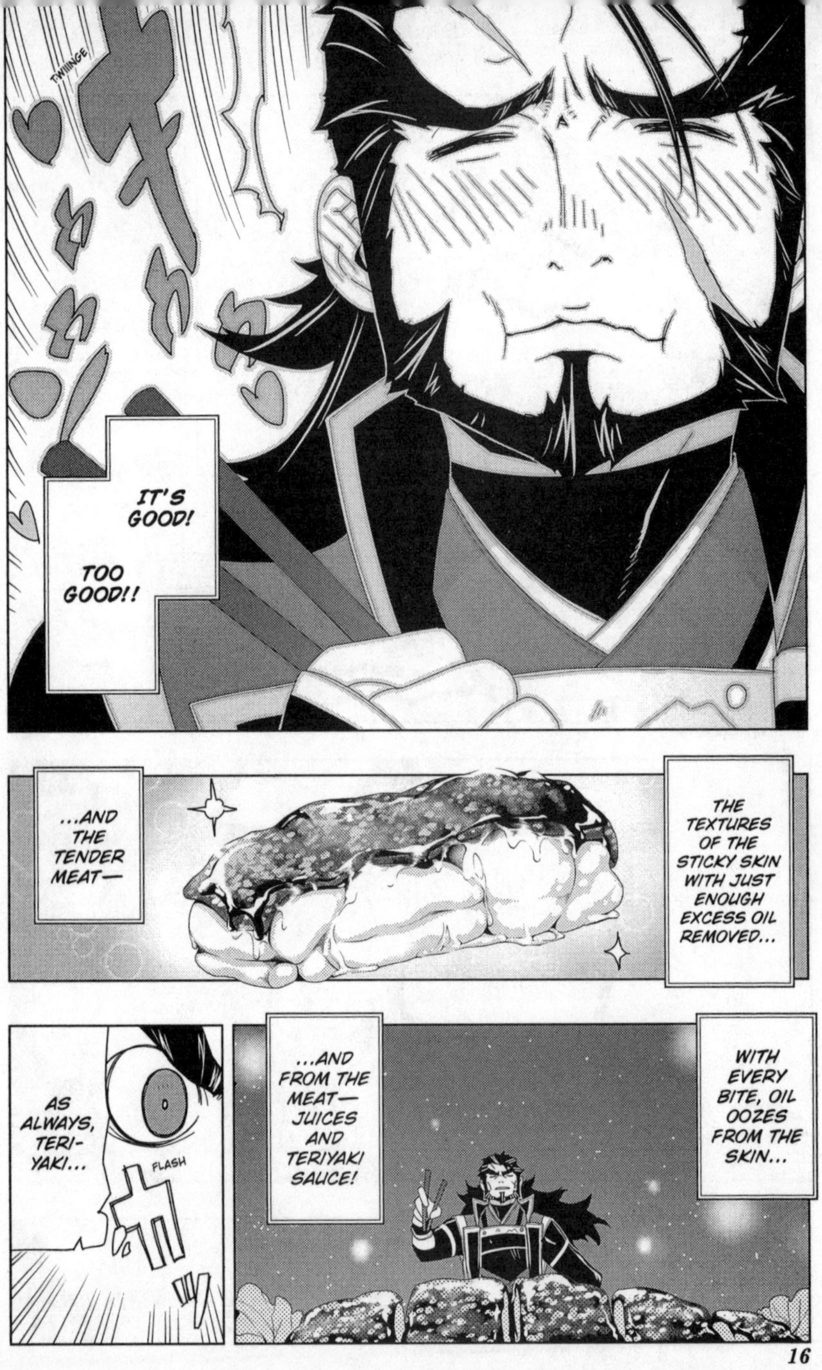
TWIIINGE
IT'S GOOD!
TOO GOOD!!
THE TEXTURES OF THE STICKY SKIN WITH JUST ENOUGH EXCESS OIL REMOVED...
...AND THE TENDER MEAT—
WITH EVERY BITE, OIL OOZES FROM THE SKIN...
...AND FROM THE MEAT— JUICES AND TERIYAKI SAUCE!
AS ALWAYS, TERI-YAKI...
FLASH

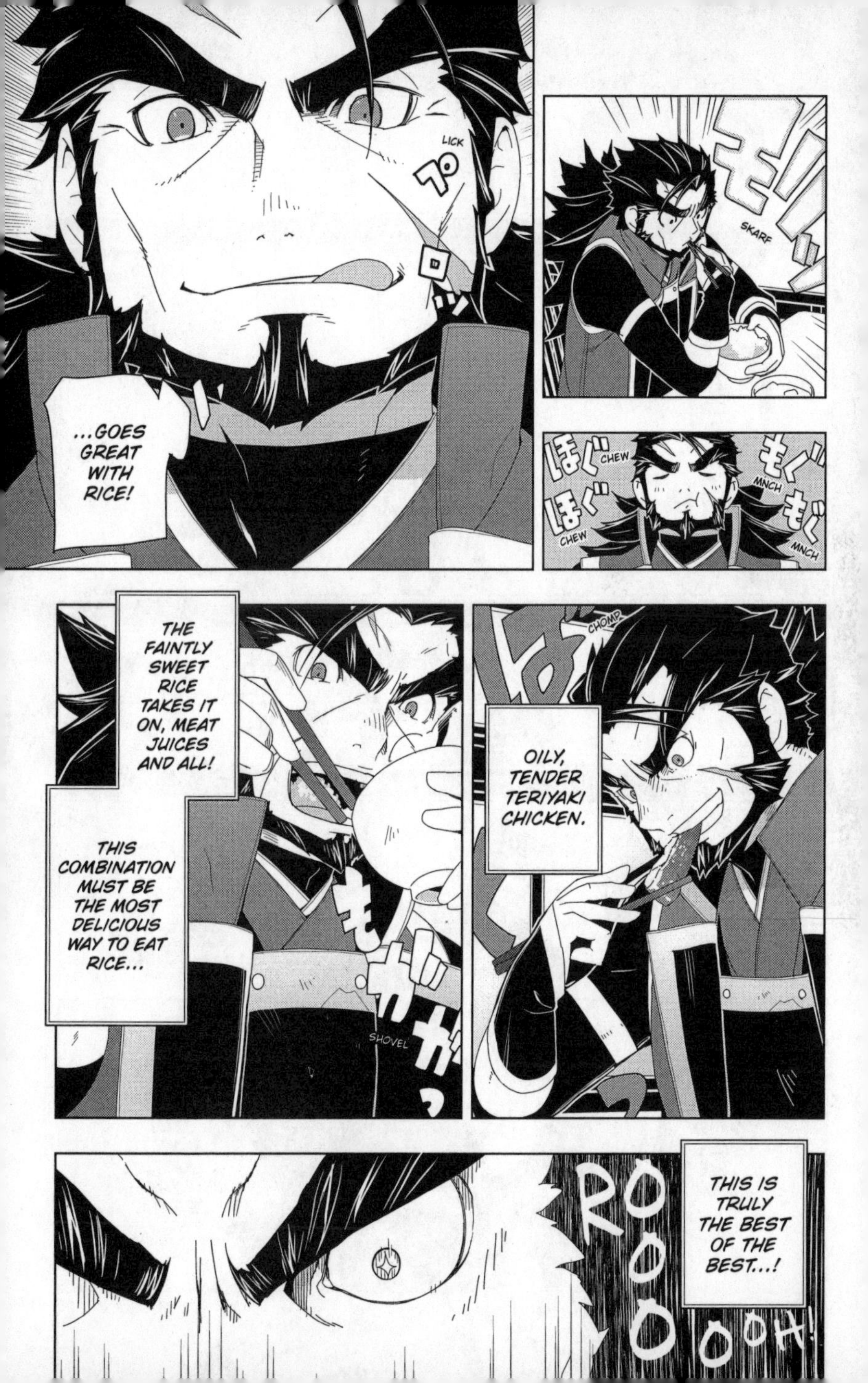
SKARF
CHEW
CHEW
MNCH
MNCH
LICK
...GOES GREAT WITH RICE!
CHOMP
OILY, TENDER TERIYAKI CHICKEN.
THE FAINTLY SWEET RICE TAKES IT ON, MEAT JUICES AND ALL!
THIS COMBINATION MUST BE THE MOST DELICIOUS WAY TO EAT RICE...
SHOVEL
THIS IS TRULY THE BEST OF THE BEST...!
ROOOOOOOH!

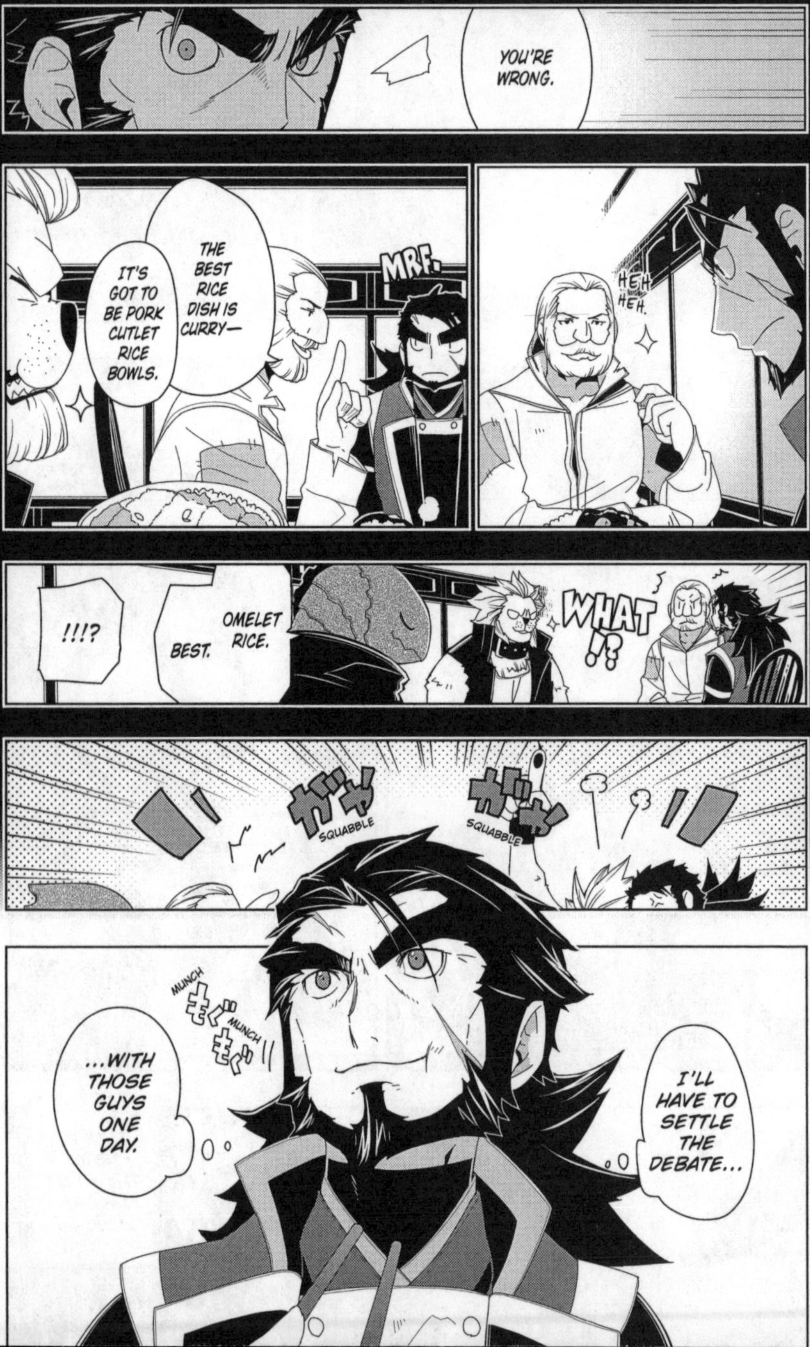
YOU'RE WRONG.
HEH HEH.
MRF.
THE BEST RICE DISH IS CURRY—
IT'S GOT TO BE PORK CUTLET RICE BOWLS.
WHAT!?
OMELET RICE.
BEST.
!!!?
がやSQUABBLE
がやSQUABBLE
I'LL HAVE TO SETTLE THE DEBATE...
MUNCH もぐ
MUNCH もぐ
...WITH THOSE GUYS ONE DAY.

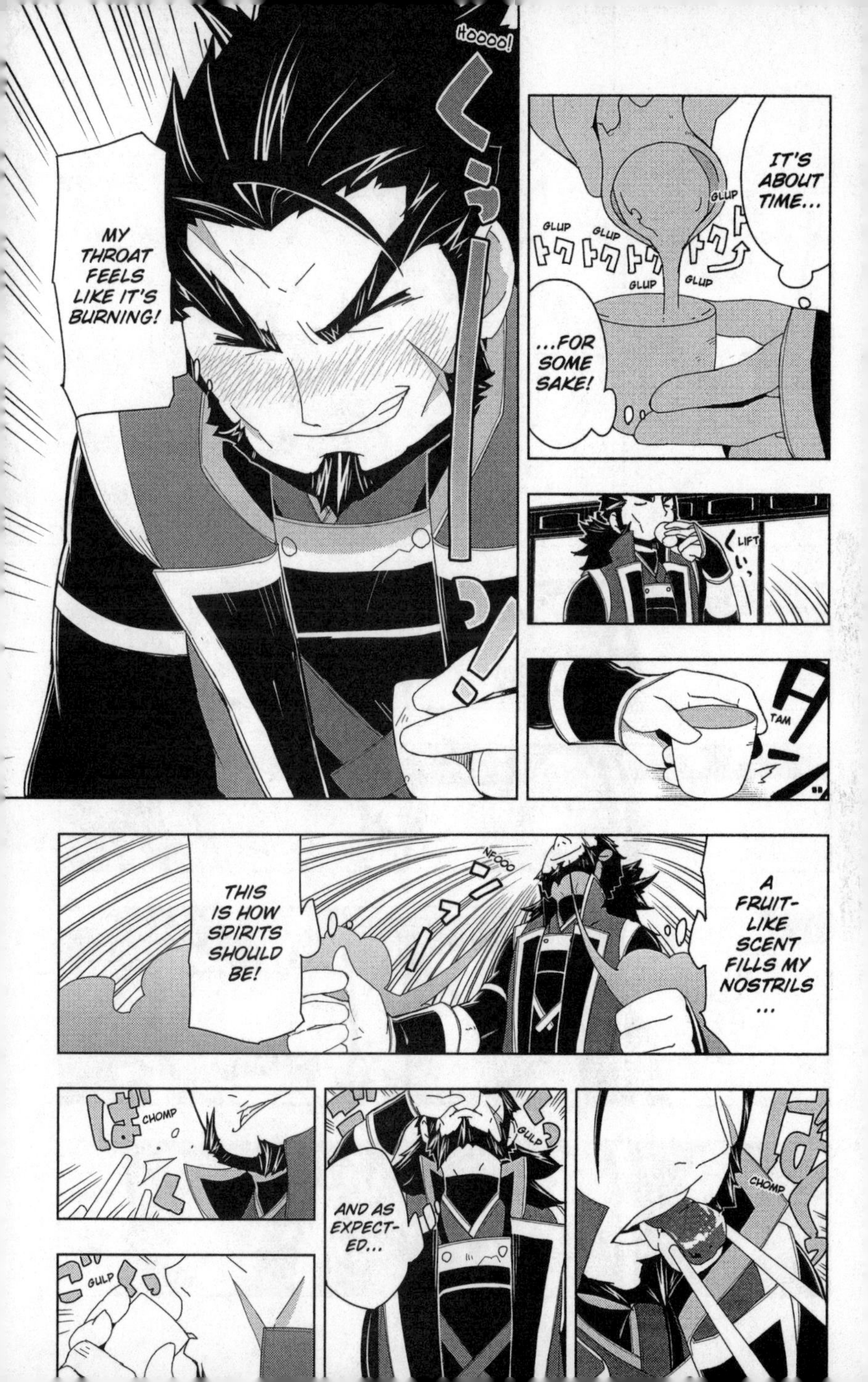
IT'S ABOUT TIME...
GLUP
GLUP
GLUP
GLUP
GLUP
...FOR SOME SAKE!
LIFT
TAM
HOOOO!
MY THROAT FEELS LIKE IT'S BURNING!
A FRUIT-LIKE SCENT FILLS MY NOSTRILS ...
NFOOO
THIS IS HOW SPIRITS SHOULD BE!
CHOMP
GULP
AND AS EXPECTED...
CHOMP
GULP

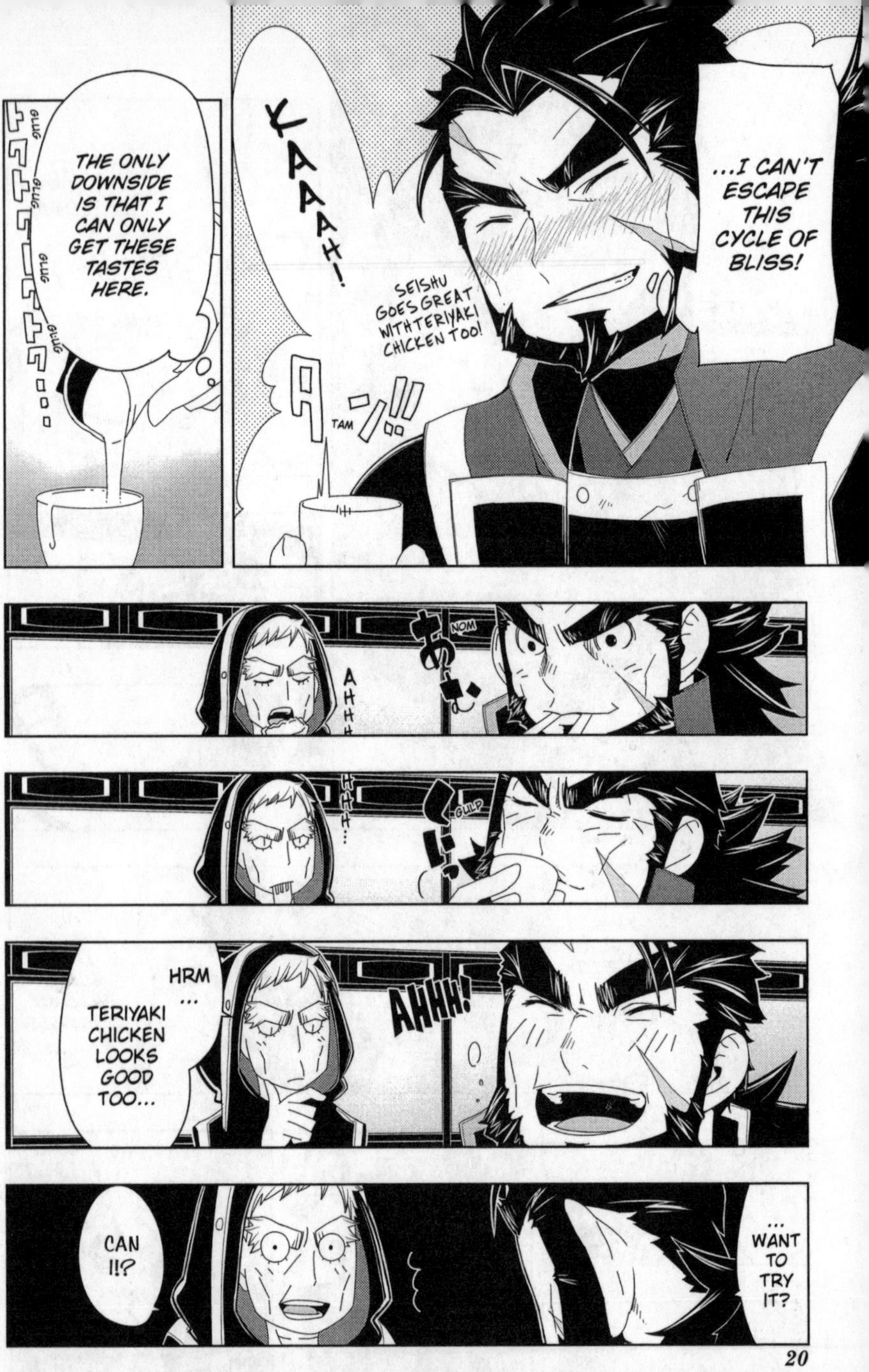
...I CAN'T ESCAPE THIS CYCLE OF BLISS!
KAAAAH!
SEISHU GOES GREAT WITH TERIYAKI CHICKEN TOO!
TAM
THE ONLY DOWNSIDE IS THAT I CAN ONLY GET THESE TASTES HERE.
GLUG GLUG GLUG GLUG
NOM
AHHHHHH...
GULP
AHHH!
HRM ... TERIYAKI CHICKEN LOOKS GOOD TOO...
...WANT TO TRY IT?
CAN I!?

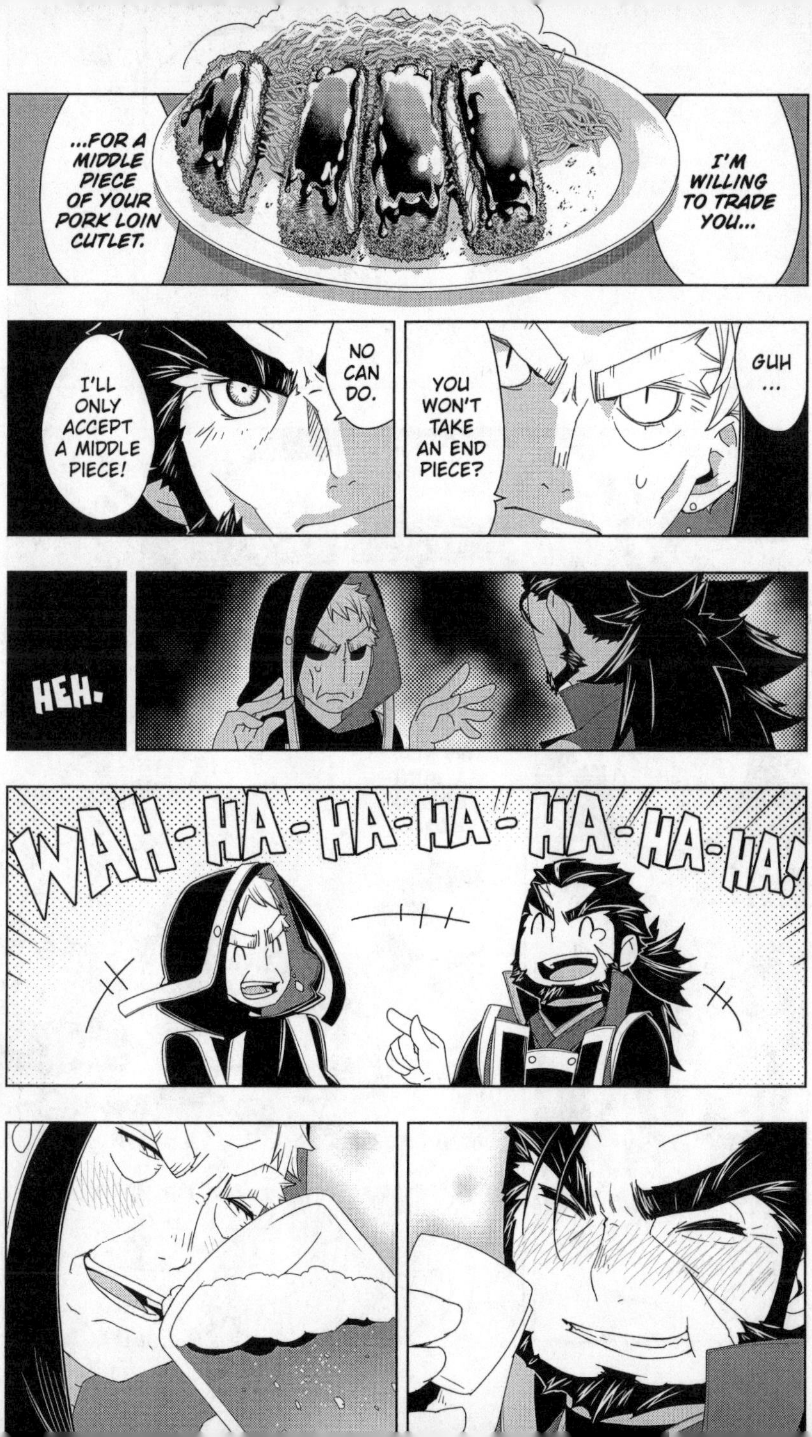
I'M WILLING TO TRADE YOU...
...FOR A MIDDLE PIECE OF YOUR PORK LOIN CUTLET.
GUH ...
YOU WON'T TAKE AN END PIECE?
NO CAN DO.
I'LL ONLY ACCEPT A MIDDLE PIECE!
HEH.
WAH-HA-HA-HA-HA-HA-HA!

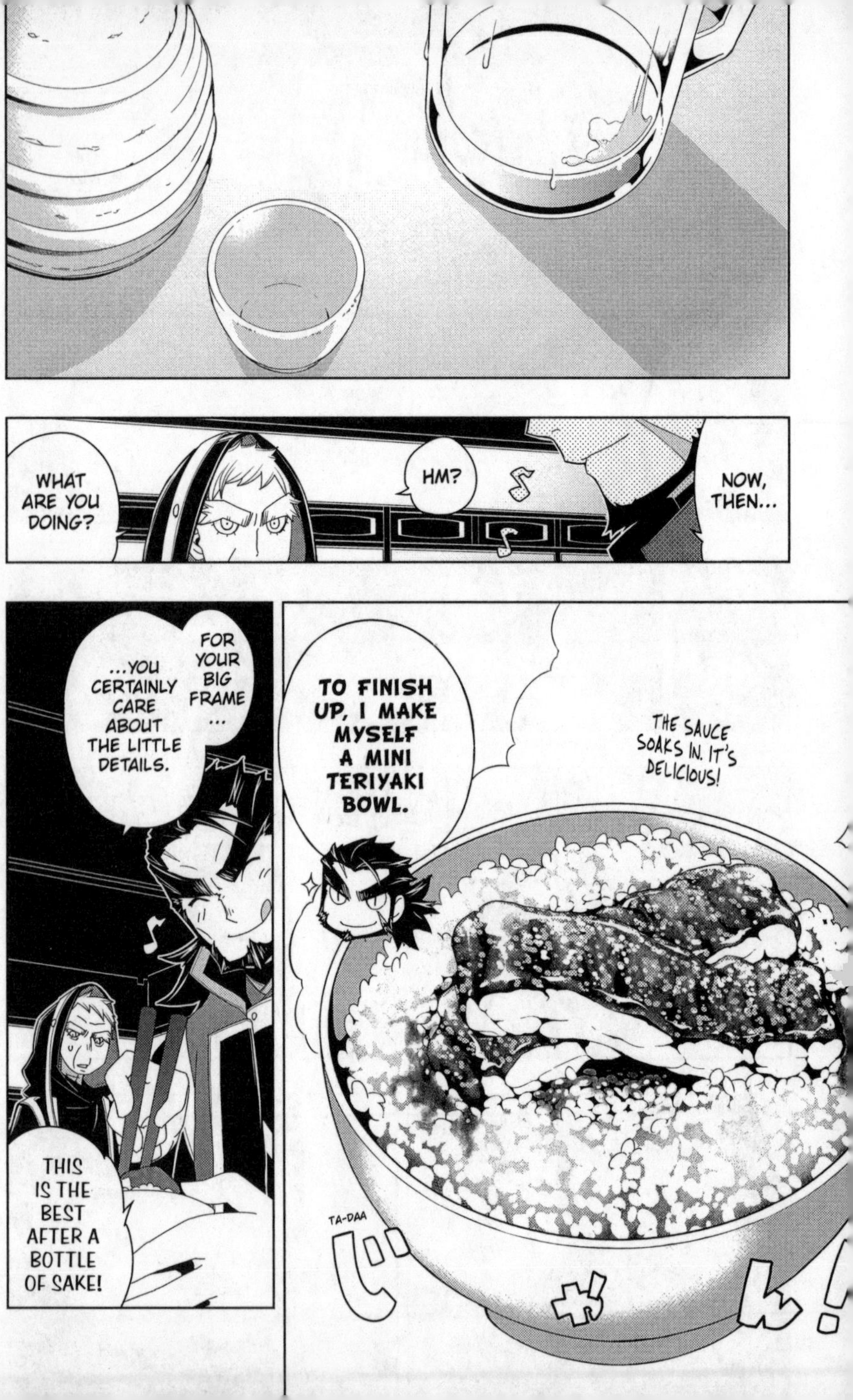
NOW, THEN...
HM?
WHAT ARE YOU DOING?
TO FINISH UP, I MAKE MYSELF A MINI TERIYAKI BOWL.
THE SAUCE SOAKS IN. IT'S DELICIOUS!
TA-DAA
FOR YOUR BIG FRAME...
...YOU CERTAINLY CARE ABOUT THE LITTLE DETAILS.
THIS IS THE BEST AFTER A BOTTLE OF SAKE!

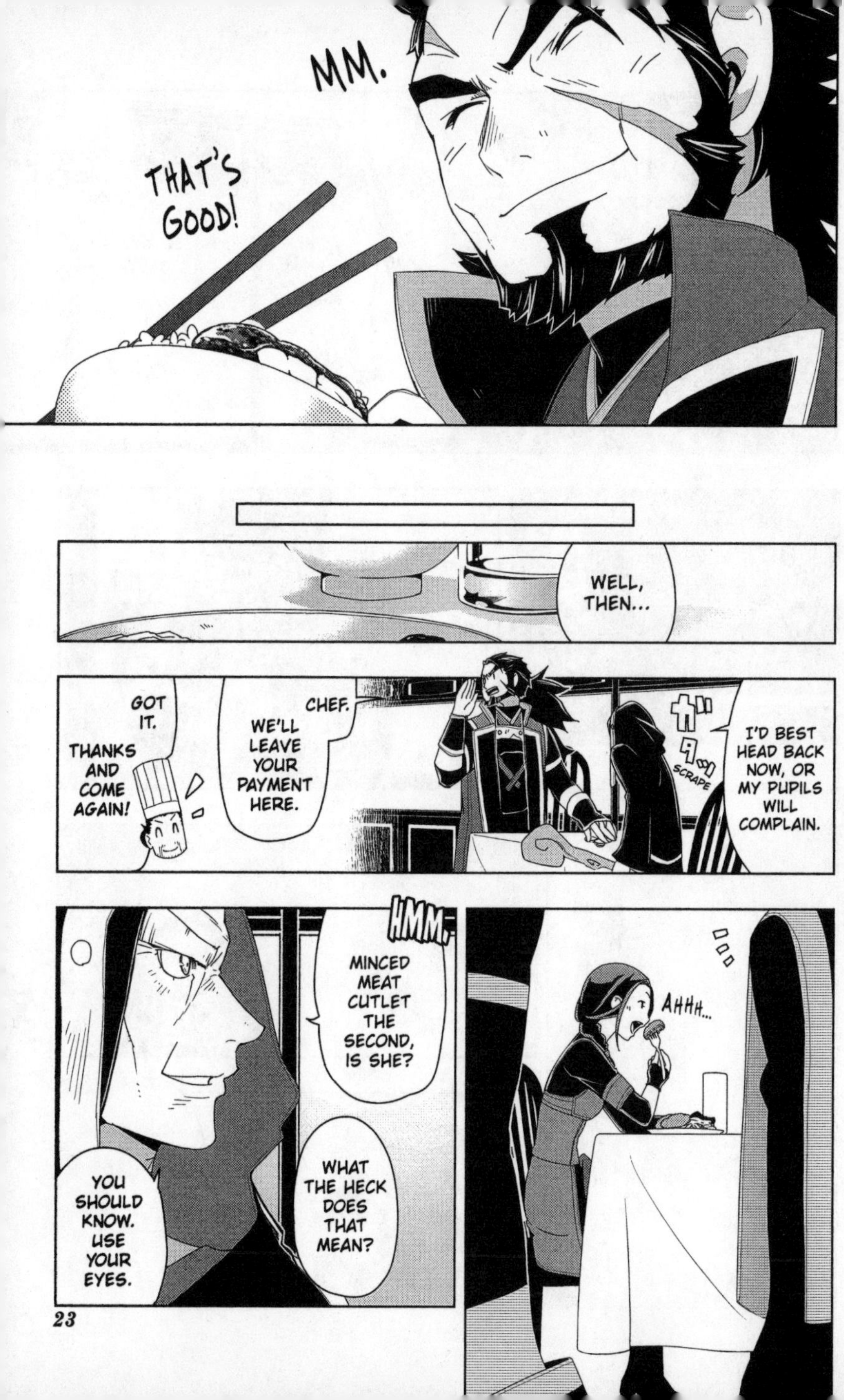
MM.
THAT'S GOOD!
WELL, THEN...
I'D BEST HEAD BACK NOW, OR MY PUPILS WILL COMPLAIN.
SCRAPE
CHEF.
WE'LL LEAVE YOUR PAYMENT HERE.
GOT IT.
THANKS AND COME AGAIN!
AHHH...
HMM.
MINCED MEAT CUTLET THE SECOND, IS SHE?
WHAT THE HECK DOES THAT MEAN?
YOU SHOULD KNOW. USE YOUR EYES.

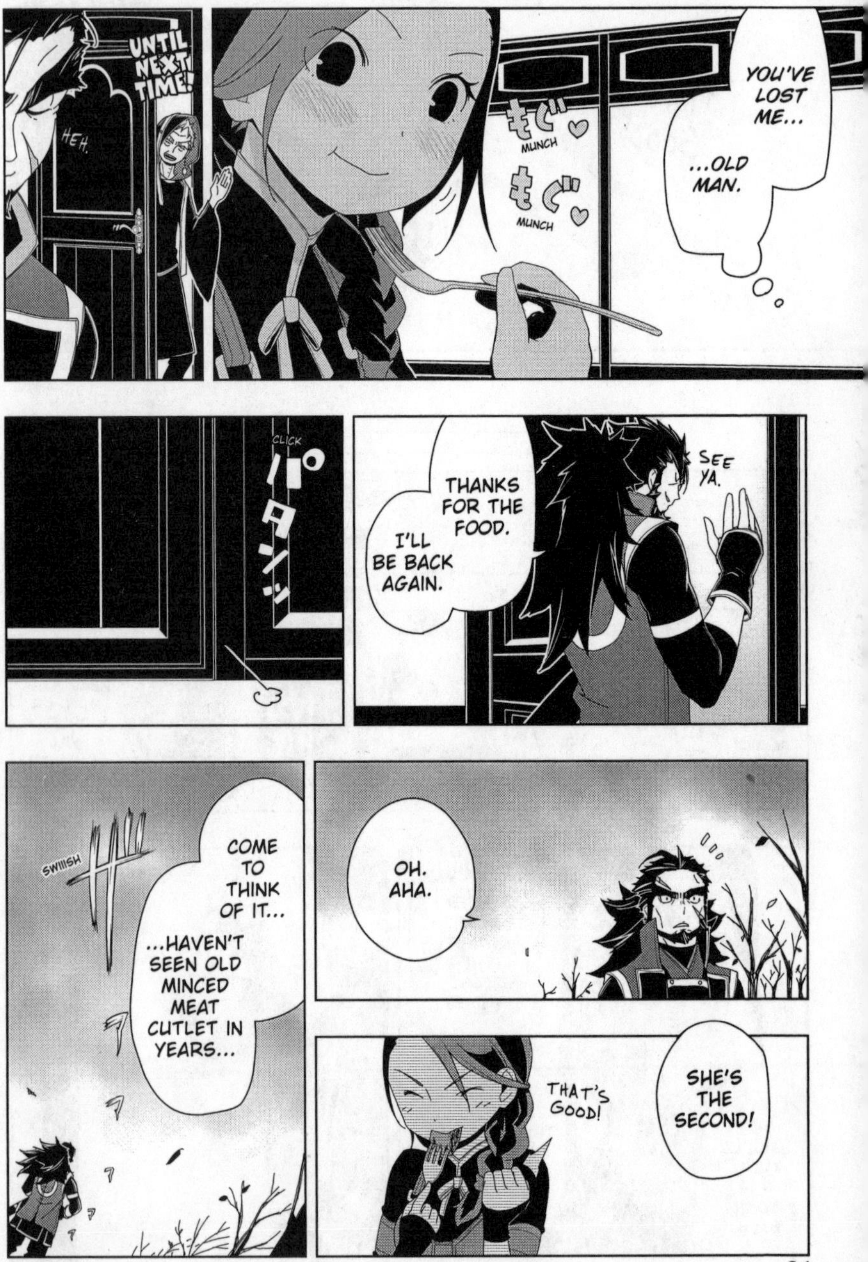
YOU'VE LOST ME...
...OLD MAN.
もぐ MUNCH
もぐ MUNCH
UNTIL NEXT TIME!
HEH.
SEE YA.
THANKS FOR THE FOOD.
I'LL BE BACK AGAIN.
CLICK パタン
OH. AHA.
SHE'S THE SECOND!
THAT'S GOOD!
SWIIISH
COME TO THINK OF IT...
...HAVEN'T SEEN OLD MINCED MEAT CUTLET IN YEARS...

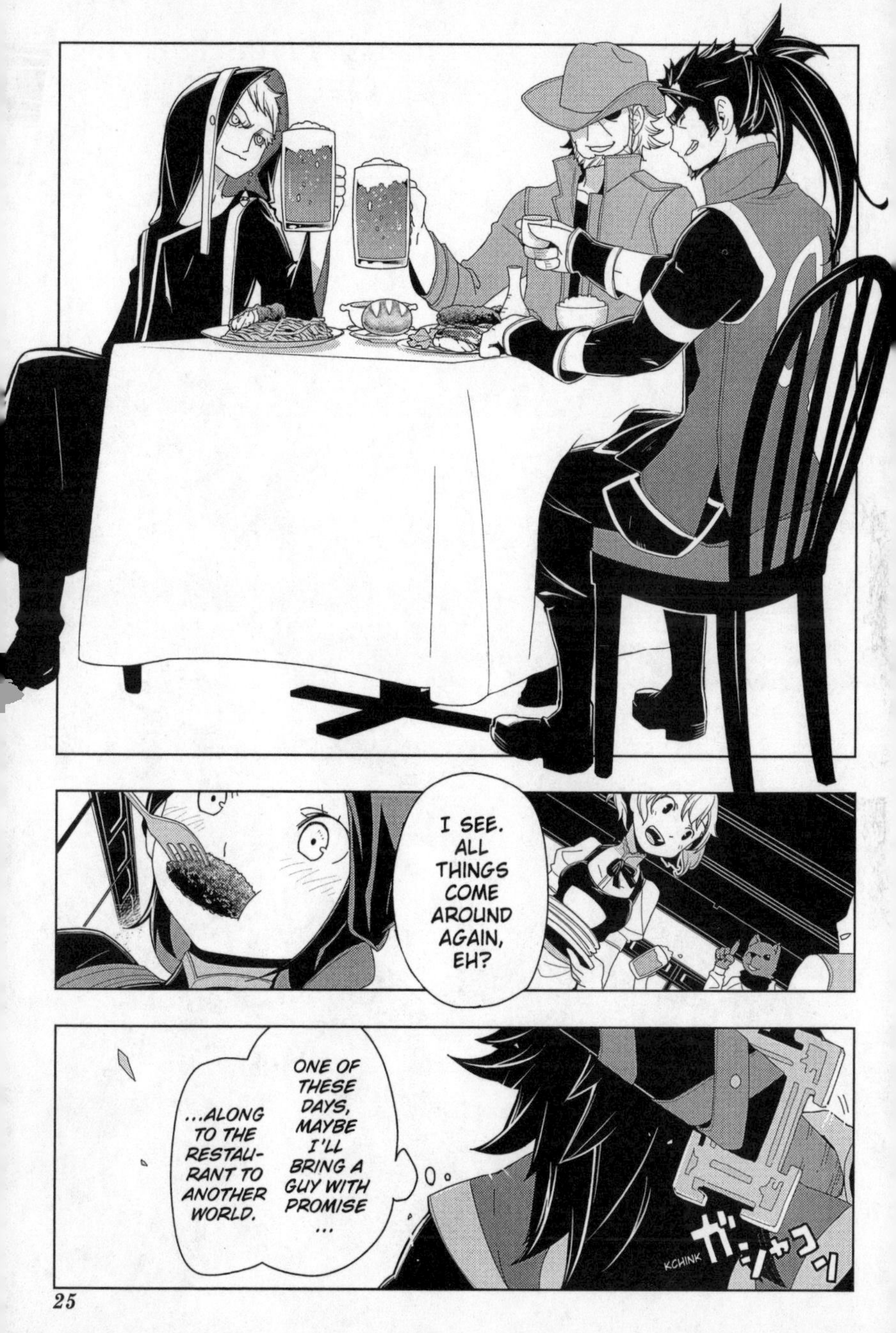
I SEE. ALL THINGS COME AROUND AGAIN, EH?
ONE OF THESE DAYS, MAYBE I'LL BRING A GUY WITH PROMISE...
...ALONG TO THE RESTAURANT TO ANOTHER WORLD.
KCHINK

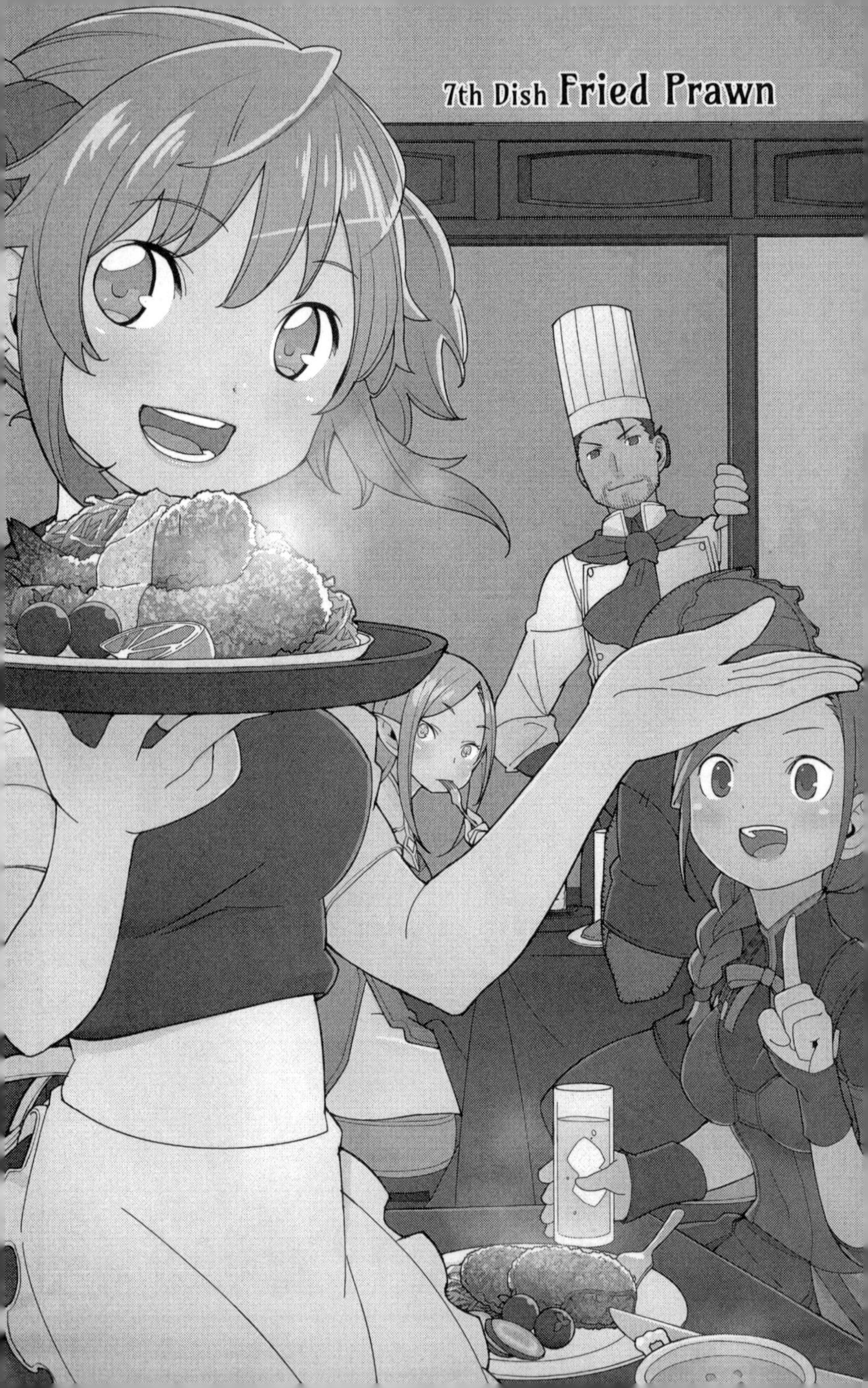
7th Dish Fried Prawn

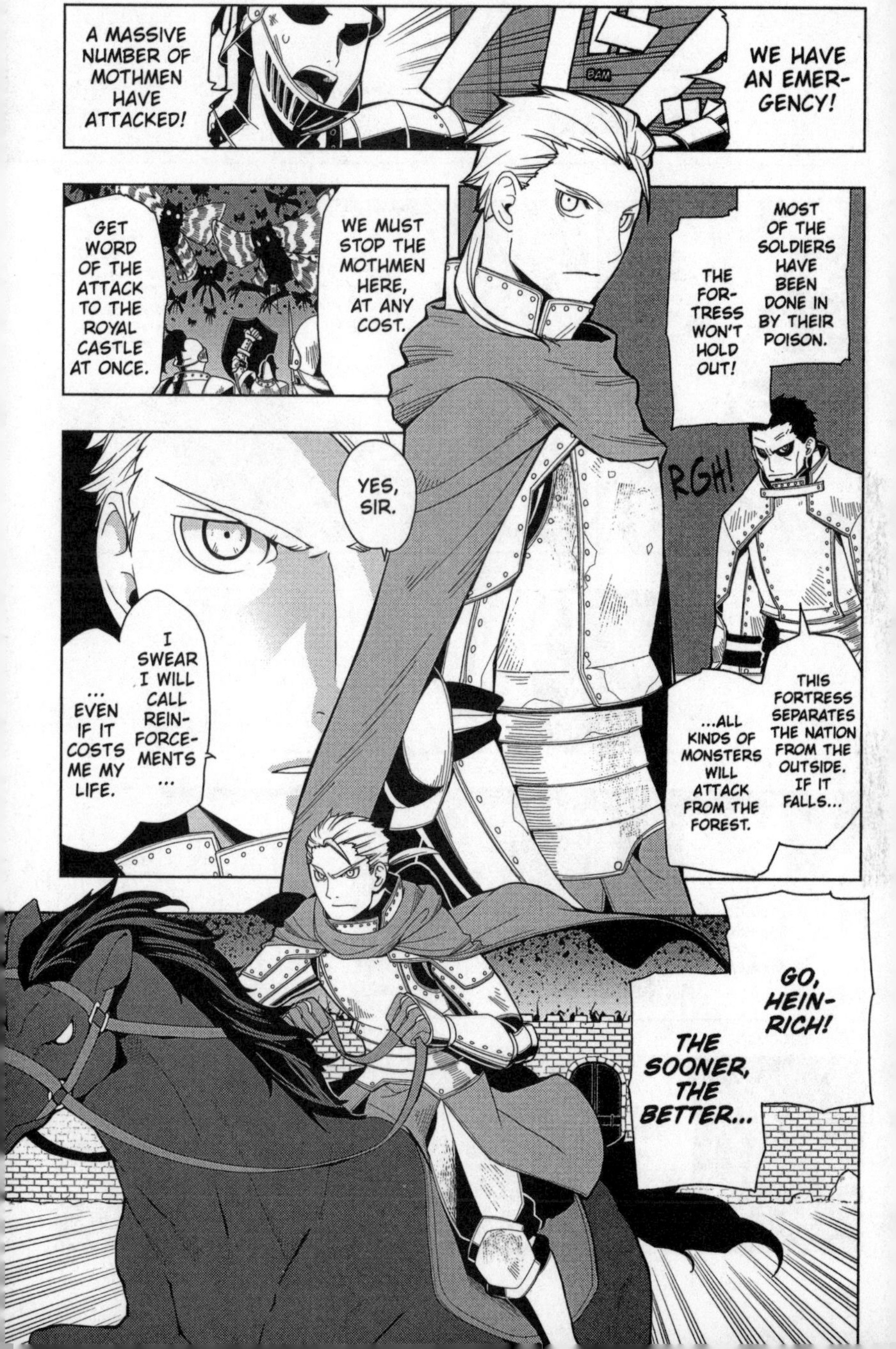
WE HAVE AN EMERGENCY!
BAM
A MASSIVE NUMBER OF MOTHMEN HAVE ATTACKED!
MOST OF THE SOLDIERS HAVE BEEN DONE IN BY THEIR POISON.
THE FORTRESS WON'T HOLD OUT!
WE MUST STOP THE MOTHMEN HERE, AT ANY COST.
GET WORD OF THE ATTACK TO THE ROYAL CASTLE AT ONCE.
RGH!
THIS FORTRESS SEPARATES THE NATION FROM THE OUTSIDE. IF IT FALLS...
...ALL KINDS OF MONSTERS WILL ATTACK FROM THE FOREST.
YES, SIR.
I SWEAR I WILL CALL REINFORCEMENTS...
...EVEN IF IT COSTS ME MY LIFE.
GO, HEINRICH!
THE SOONER, THE BETTER...

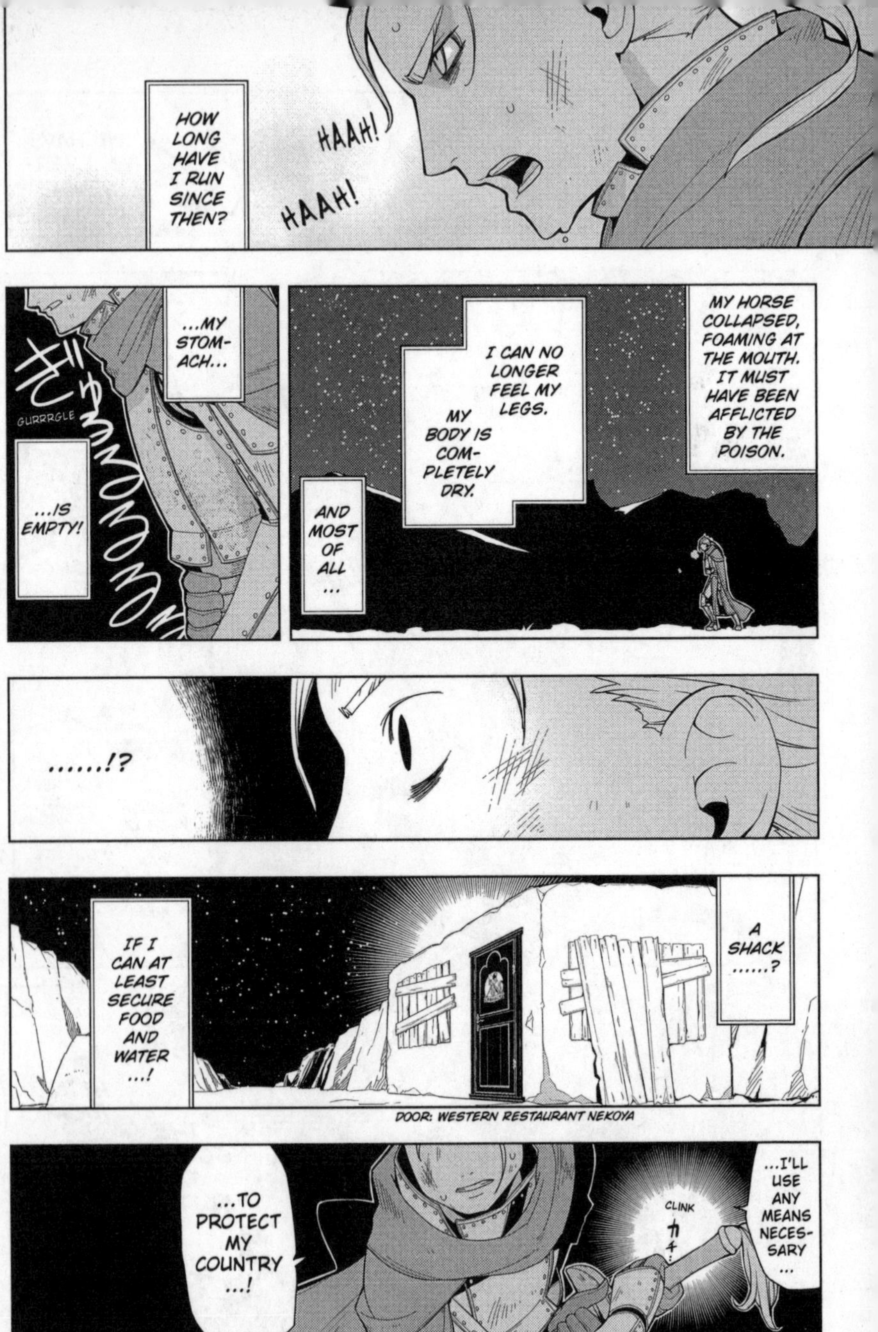
HAAAH!
HAAAH!
HOW LONG HAVE I RUN SINCE THEN?
MY HORSE COLLAPSED, FOAMING AT THE MOUTH. IT MUST HAVE BEEN AFFLICTED BY THE POISON.
I CAN NO LONGER FEEL MY LEGS.
MY BODY IS COMPLETELY DRY.
AND MOST OF ALL...
...MY STOMACH...
GURRRGLE
...IS EMPTY!
......!?
A SHACK......?
IF I CAN AT LEAST SECURE FOOD AND WATER...!
DOOR: WESTERN RESTAURANT NEKOYA
...I'LL USE ANY MEANS NECESSARY...
CLINK
...TO PROTECT MY COUNTRY...!

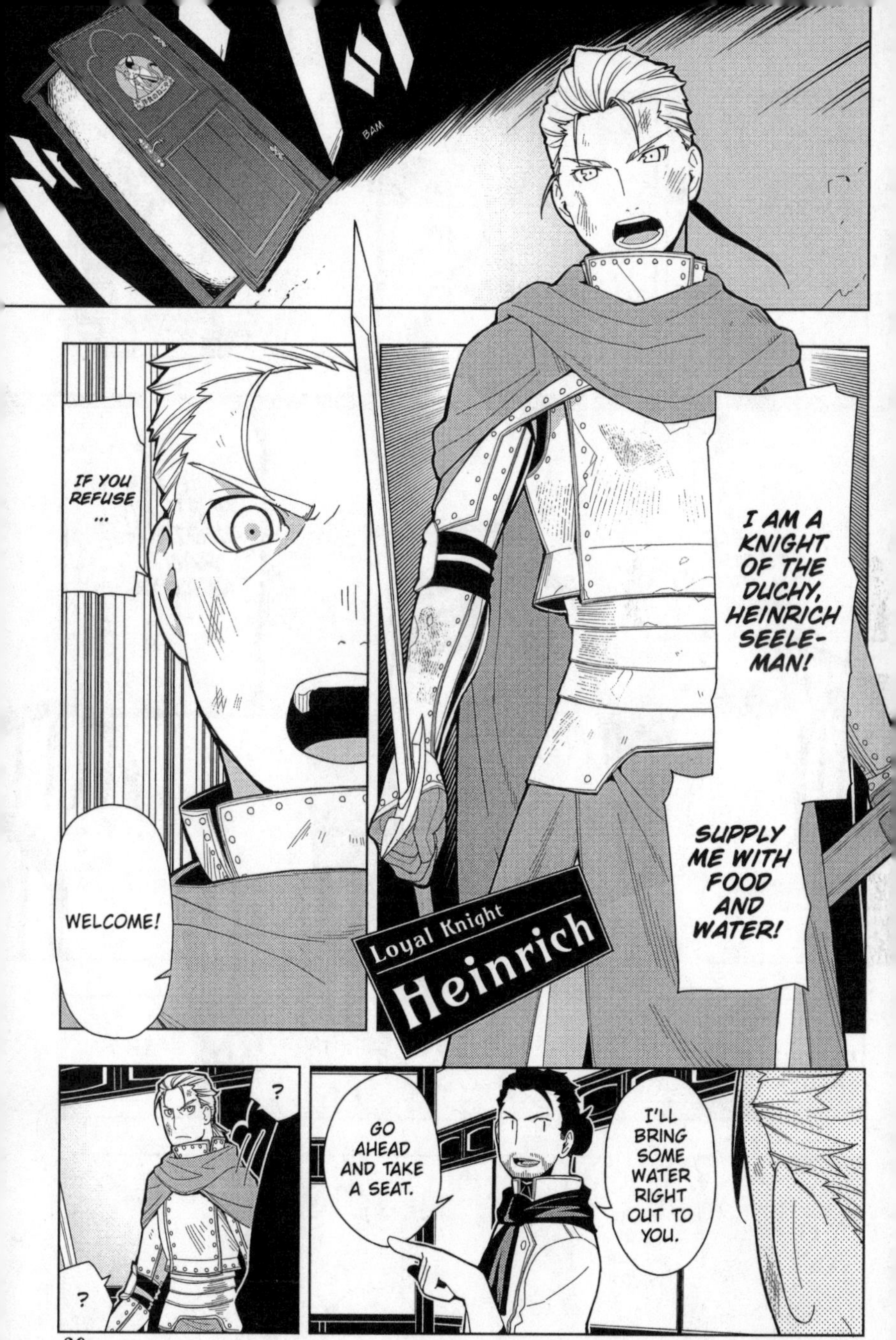
BAM
I AM A KNIGHT OF THE DUCHY, HEINRICH SEELE-MAN!
SUPPLY ME WITH FOOD AND WATER!
Loyal Knight
Heinrich
IF YOU REFUSE ...
WELCOME!
I'LL BRING SOME WATER RIGHT OUT TO YOU.
GO AHEAD AND TAKE A SEAT.
?
?

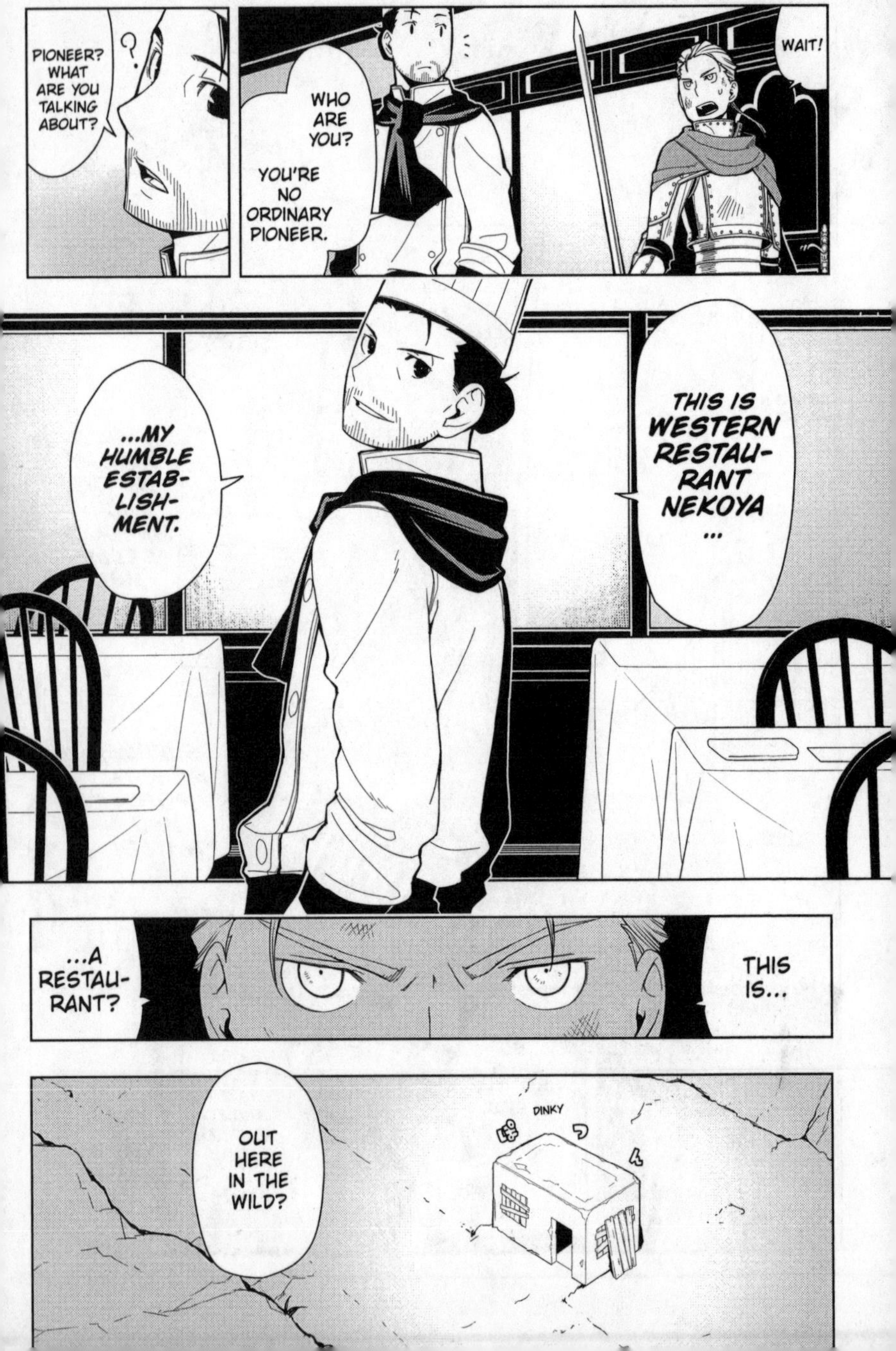
WAIT!
WHO ARE YOU?
YOU'RE NO ORDINARY PIONEER.
PIONEER? WHAT ARE YOU TALKING ABOUT?
THIS IS WESTERN RESTAURANT NEKOYA...
...MY HUMBLE ESTABLISHMENT.
THIS IS...
...A RESTAURANT?
DINKY
OUT HERE IN THE WILD?

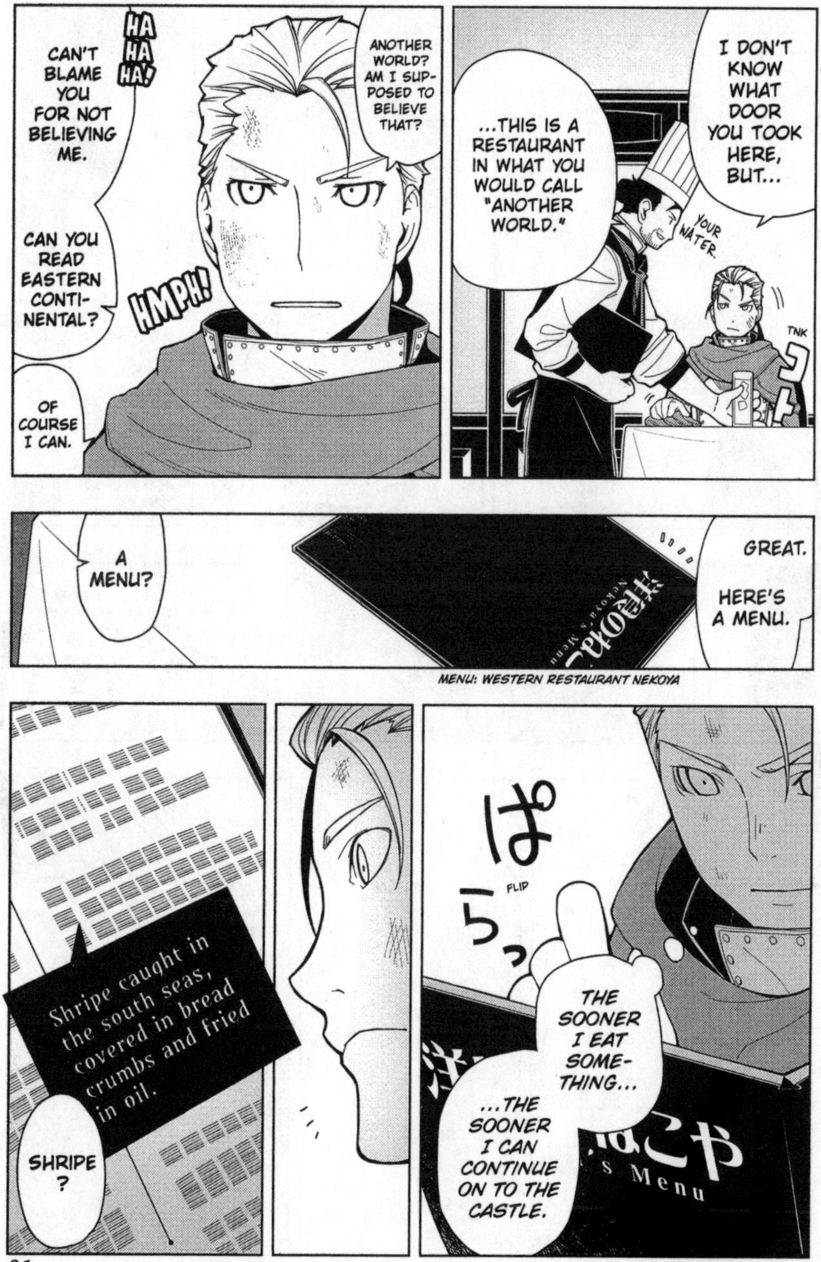
I DON'T KNOW WHAT DOOR YOU TOOK HERE, BUT...
...THIS IS A RESTAURANT IN WHAT YOU WOULD CALL "ANOTHER WORLD."
YOUR WATER.
TNK
ANOTHER WORLD? AM I SUP-POSED TO BELIEVE THAT?
HA HA HA!
CAN'T BLAME YOU FOR NOT BELIEVING ME.
HMPH!
CAN YOU READ EASTERN CONTI-NENTAL?
OF COURSE I CAN.
GREAT.
HERE'S A MENU.
A MENU?
MENU: WESTERN RESTAURANT NEKOYA
ぱらっ
FLIP
THE SOONER I EAT SOME-THING...
...THE SOONER I CAN CONTINUE ON TO THE CASTLE.
Shripe caught in the south seas, covered in bread crumbs and fried in oil.
SHRIPE?

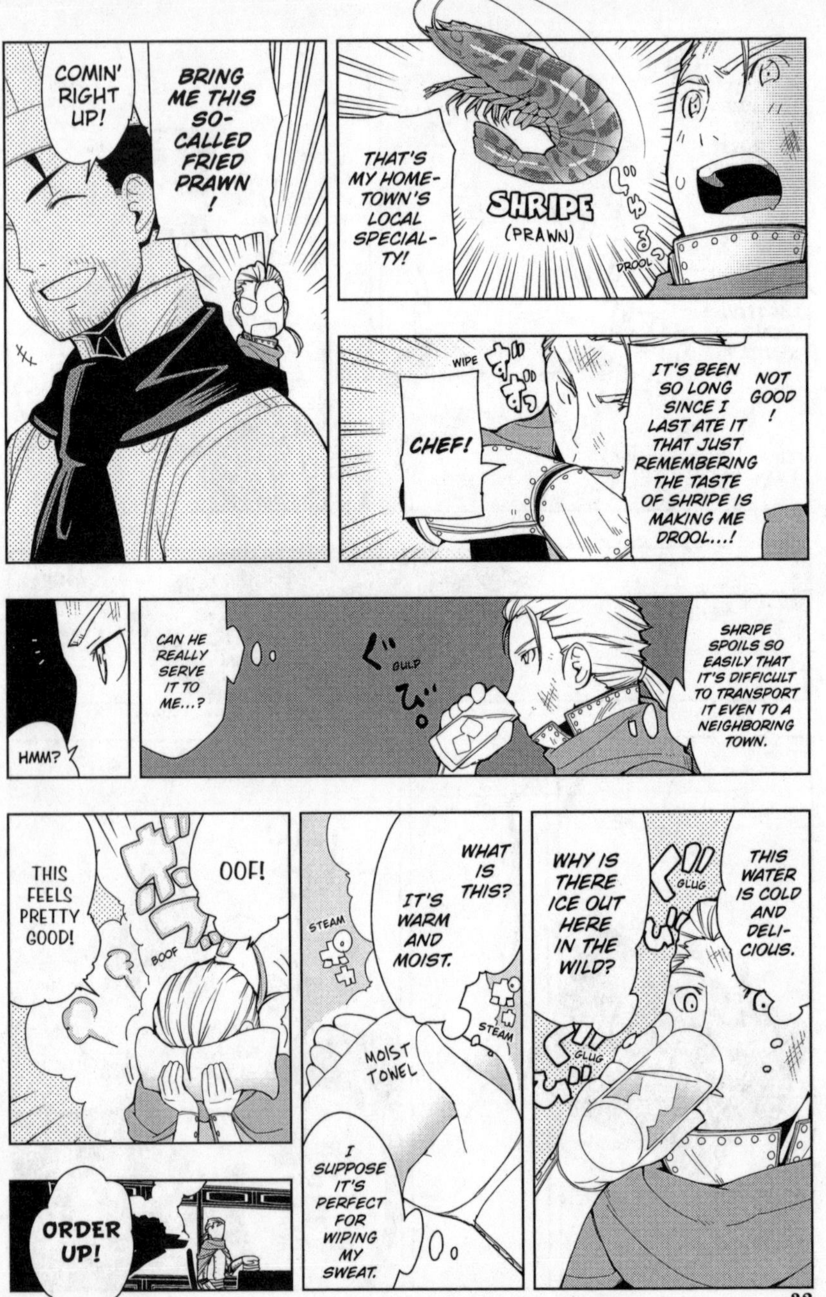
THAT'S MY HOME-TOWN'S LOCAL SPECIAL-TY!
SHRIPE
(PRAWN)
DROOL
NOT GOOD!
IT'S BEEN SO LONG SINCE I LAST ATE IT THAT JUST REMEMBERING THE TASTE OF SHRIPE IS MAKING ME DROOL...!
WIPE
CHEF!
BRING ME THIS SO-CALLED FRIED PRAWN!
COMIN' RIGHT UP!
SHRIPE SPOILS SO EASILY THAT IT'S DIFFICULT TO TRANSPORT IT EVEN TO A NEIGHBORING TOWN.
GULP
CAN HE REALLY SERVE IT TO ME...?
HMM?
THIS WATER IS COLD AND DELI-CIOUS.
GLUG
WHY IS THERE ICE OUT HERE IN THE WILD?
GLUG
WHAT IS THIS?
IT'S WARM AND MOIST.
STEAM
STEAM
MOIST TOWEL
I SUPPOSE IT'S PERFECT FOR WIPING MY SWEAT.
OOF!
BOOF
THIS FEELS PRETTY GOOD!
ORDER UP!

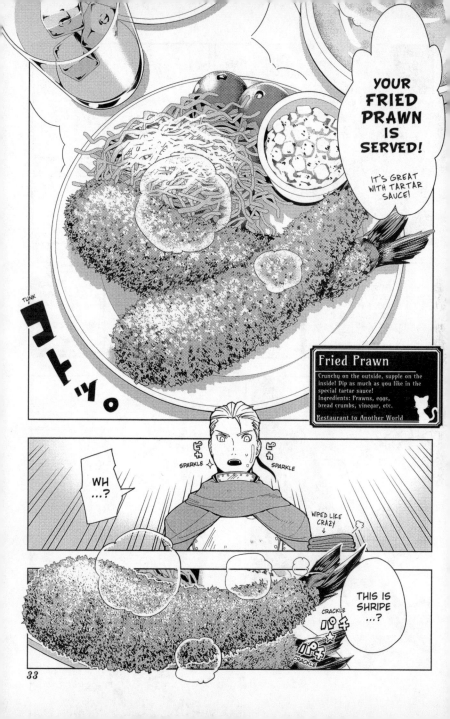

YOUR FRIED PRAWN IS SERVED!

IT'S GREAT WITH TARTAR SAUCE!

TUNK

Fried Prawn

Crunchy on the outside, supple on the inside! Dip as much as you like in the special tartar sauce!
Ingredients: Prawns, eggs, bread crumbs, vinegar, etc.

Restaurant to Another World

SPARKLE

SPARKLE

WH ...?

WIPED LIKE CRAZY
↓

THIS IS SHRIPE ...?

CRACKLE

CRACKLE

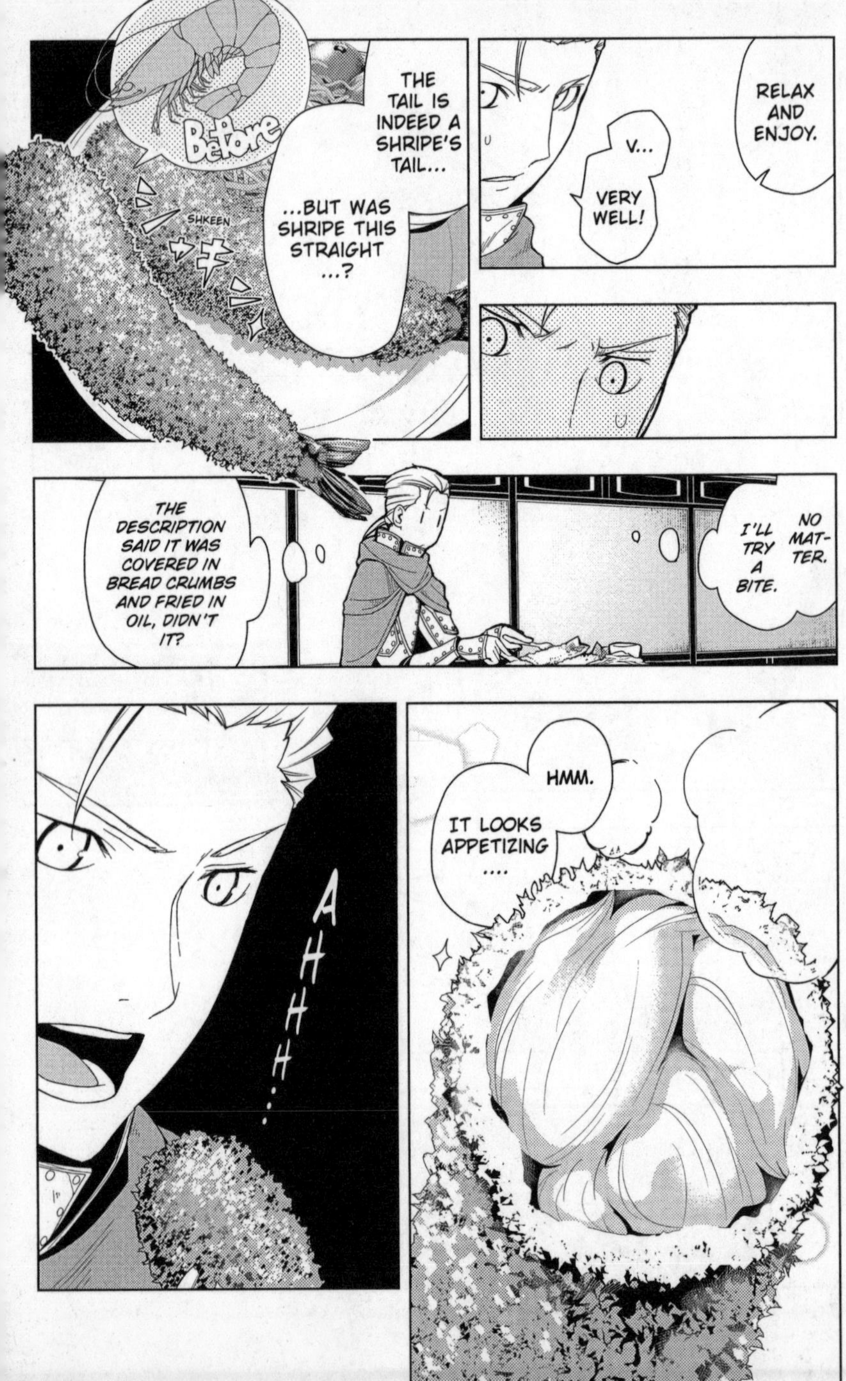
RELAX AND ENJOY.
V...
VERY WELL!
THE TAIL IS INDEED A SHRIPE'S TAIL...
Before
...BUT WAS SHRIPE THIS STRAIGHT ...?
SHKEEN
NO MATTER.
I'LL TRY A BITE.
THE DESCRIPTION SAID IT WAS COVERED IN BREAD CRUMBS AND FRIED IN OIL, DIDN'T IT?
HMM.
IT LOOKS APPETIZING ....
AHHHH...

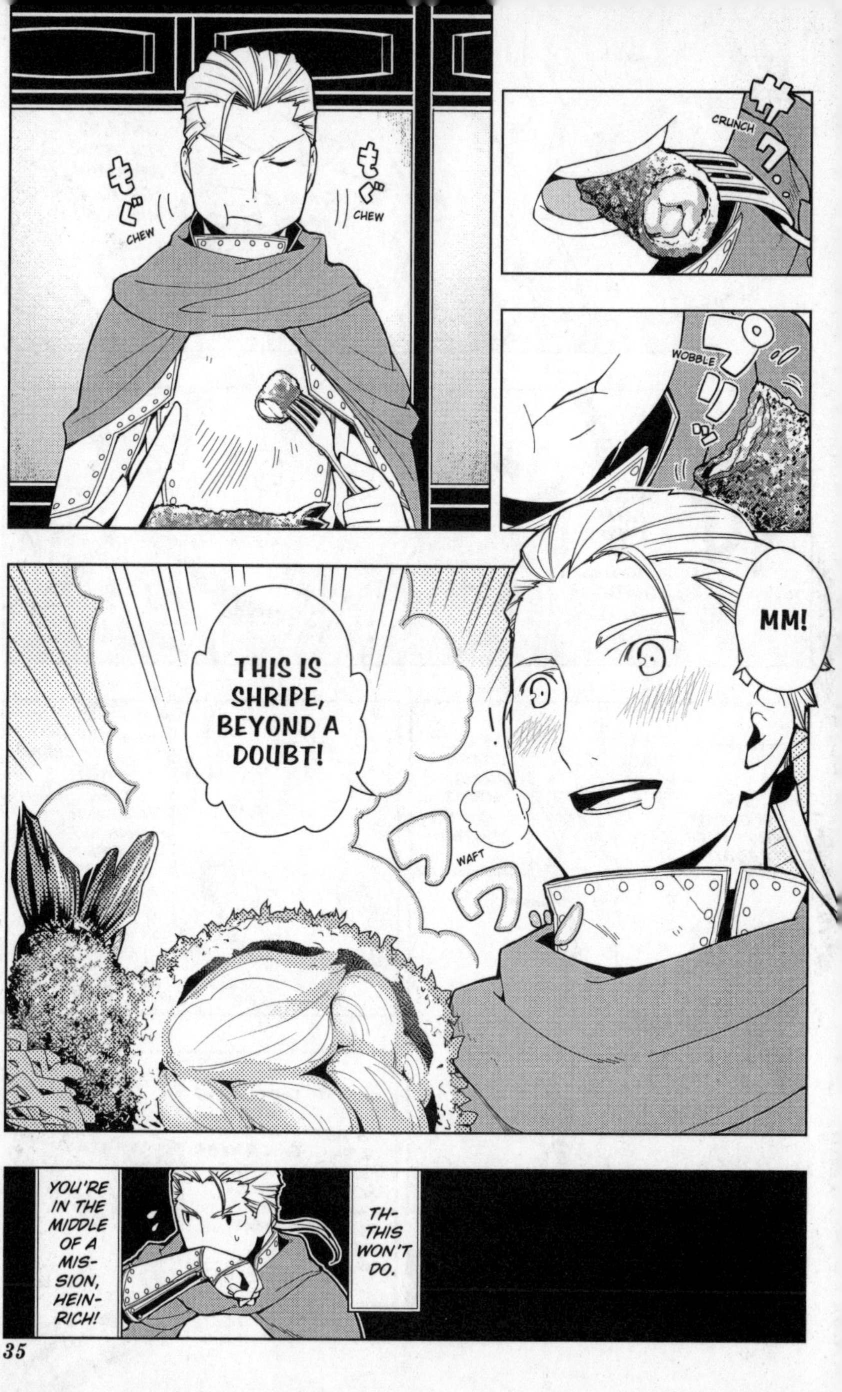
CRUNCH
WOBBLE
CHEW
CHEW
MM!
THIS IS SHRIPE, BEYOND A DOUBT!
WAFT
TH- THIS WON'T DO.
YOU'RE IN THE MIDDLE OF A MIS- SION, HEIN- RICH!

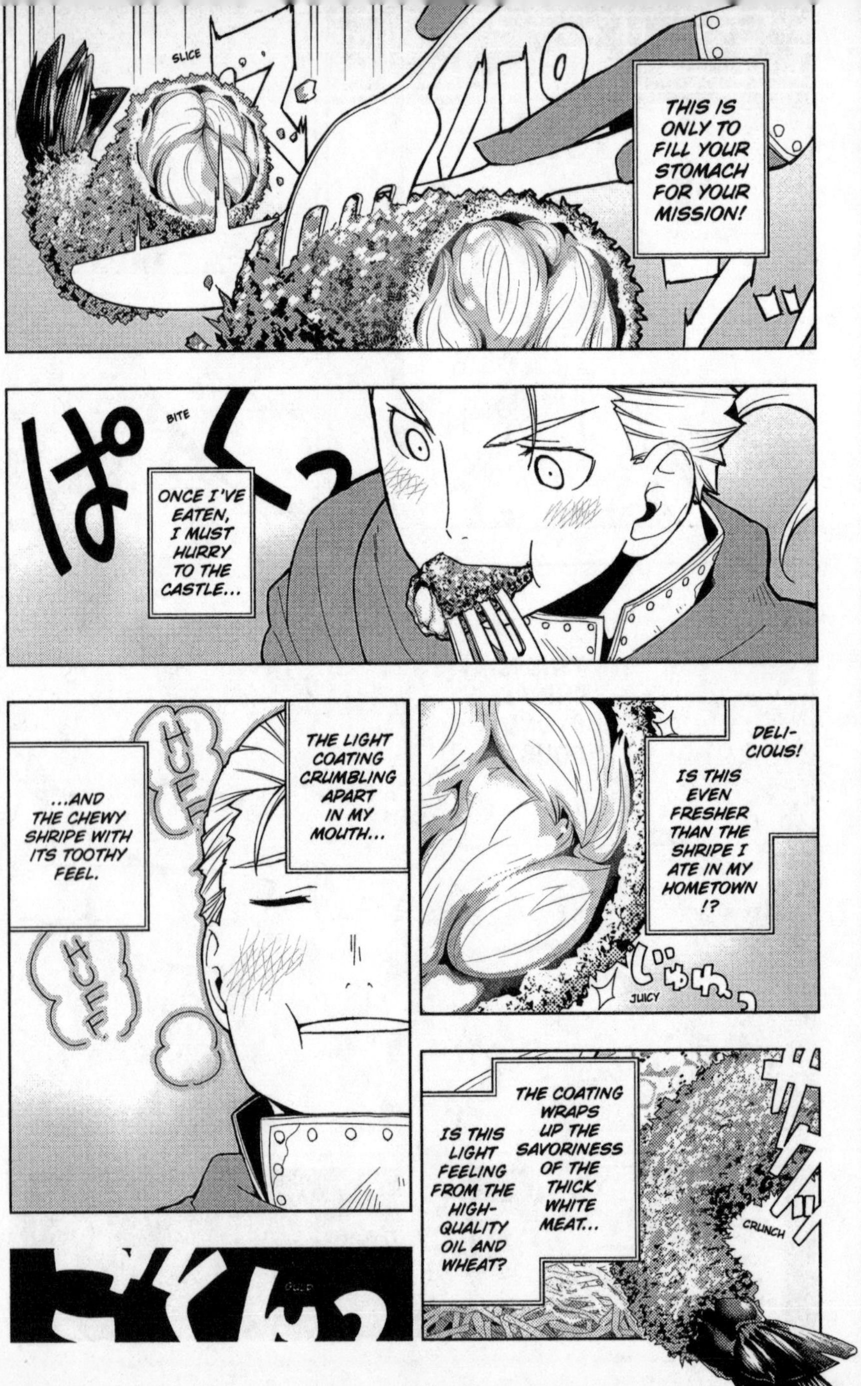
THIS IS ONLY TO FILL YOUR STOMACH FOR YOUR MISSION!
SLICE
ONCE I'VE EATEN, I MUST HURRY TO THE CASTLE...
ぱくっ
BITE
DELI-CIOUS! IS THIS EVEN FRESHER THAN THE SHRIPE I ATE IN MY HOMETOWN!?
JUICY
CRUNCH
THE COATING WRAPS UP THE SAVORINESS OF THE THICK WHITE MEAT...
IS THIS LIGHT FEELING FROM THE HIGH-QUALITY OIL AND WHEAT?
THE LIGHT COATING CRUMBLING APART IN MY MOUTH...
...AND THE CHEWY SHRIPE WITH ITS TOOTHY FEEL.
HUFF
HUFF
GULP

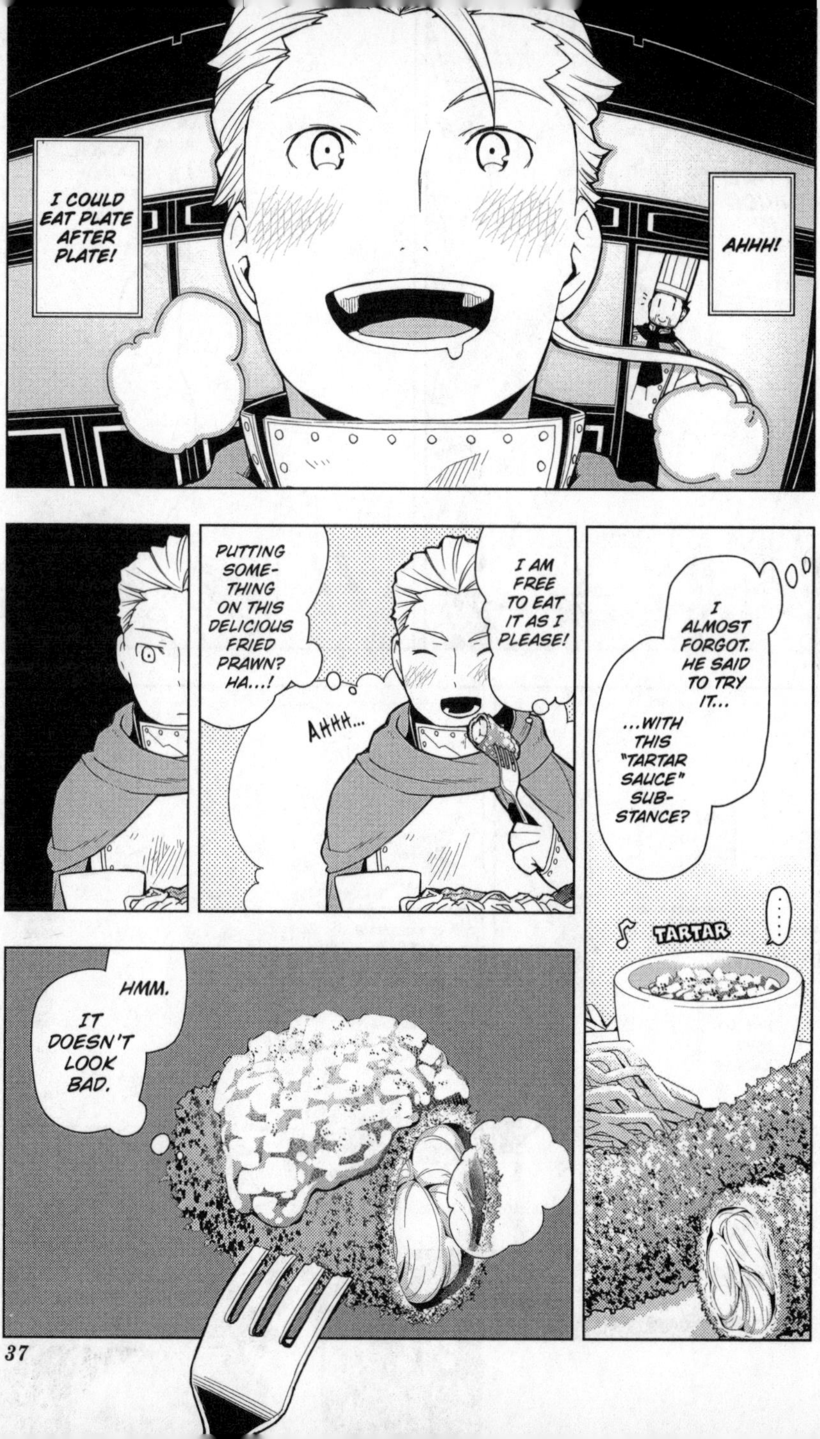
AHHH!
I COULD EAT PLATE AFTER PLATE!
I ALMOST FORGOT. HE SAID TO TRY IT...
...WITH THIS "TARTAR SAUCE" SUB-STANCE?
......
TARTAR
I AM FREE TO EAT IT AS I PLEASE!
PUTTING SOME-THING ON THIS DELICIOUS FRIED PRAWN? HA...!
AHHH...
HMM.
IT DOESN'T LOOK BAD.

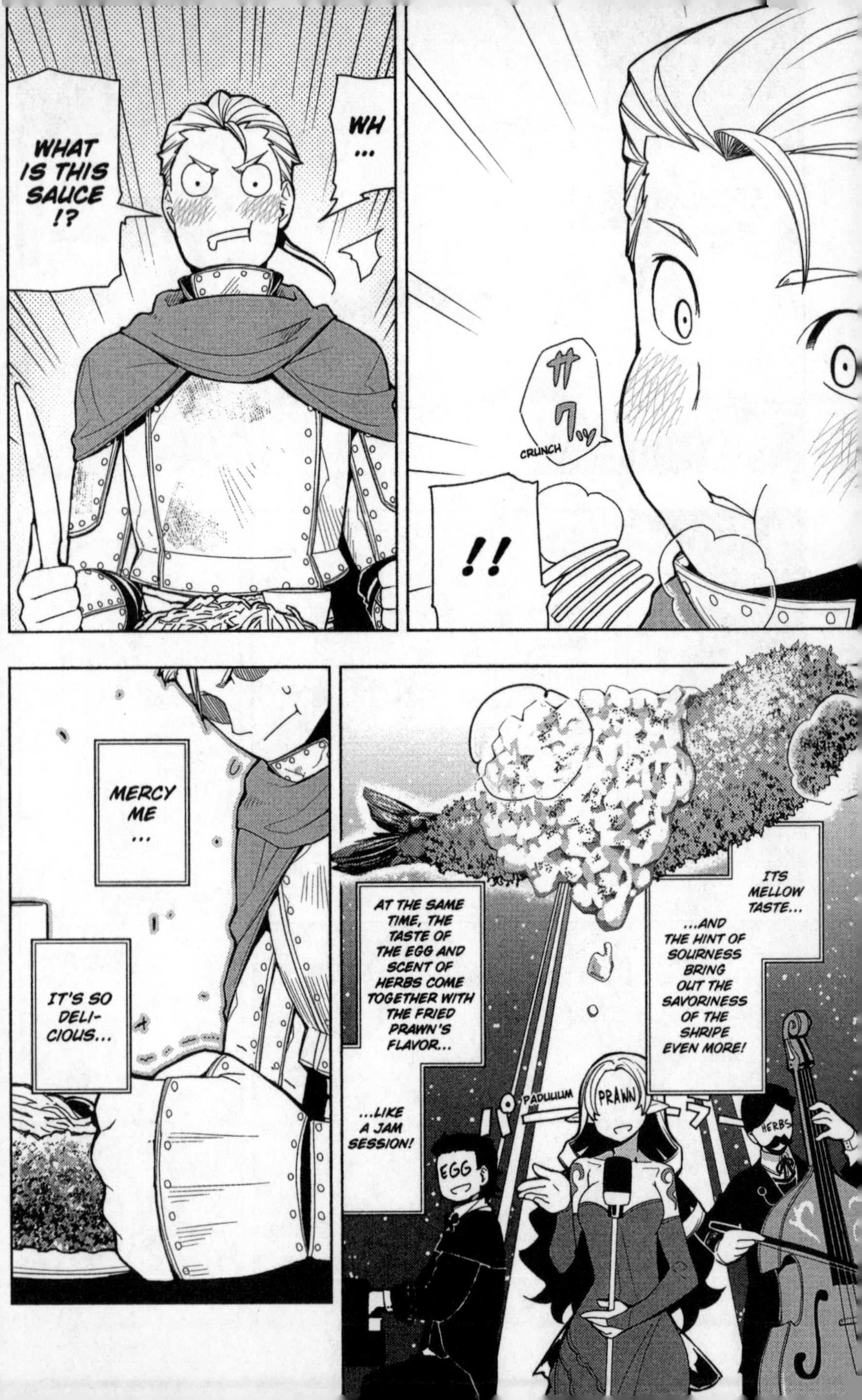

サクッ
CRUNCH
!!
WH...
WHAT IS THIS SAUCE!?
ITS MELLOW TASTE...
...AND THE HINT OF SOURNESS BRING OUT THE SAVORINESS OF THE SHRIPE EVEN MORE!
AT THE SAME TIME, THE TASTE OF THE EGG AND SCENT OF HERBS COME TOGETHER WITH THE FRIED PRAWN'S FLAVOR...
...LIKE A JAM SESSION!
PADUUUM
PRAWN
HERBS
EGG
MERCY ME...
IT'S SO DELICIOUS...

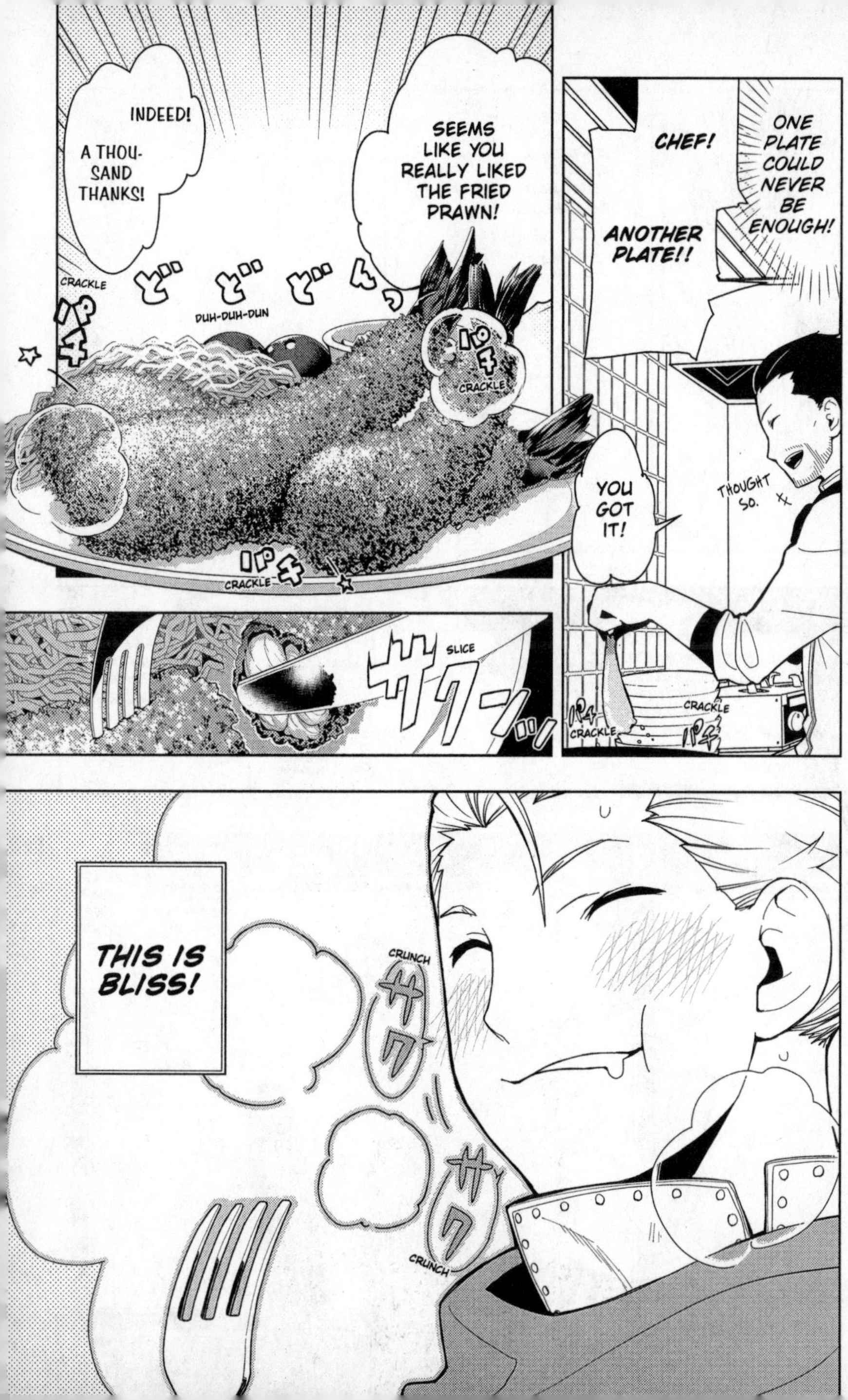
ONE PLATE COULD NEVER BE ENOUGH!
CHEF!
ANOTHER PLATE!!
THOUGHT SO.
YOU GOT IT!
CRACKLE
CRACKLE
SEEMS LIKE YOU REALLY LIKED THE FRIED PRAWN!
INDEED!
A THOU-SAND THANKS!
DUH-DUH-DUN
CRACKLE
CRACKLE
CRACKLE
SLICE
CRUNCH
CRUNCH
THIS IS BLISS!

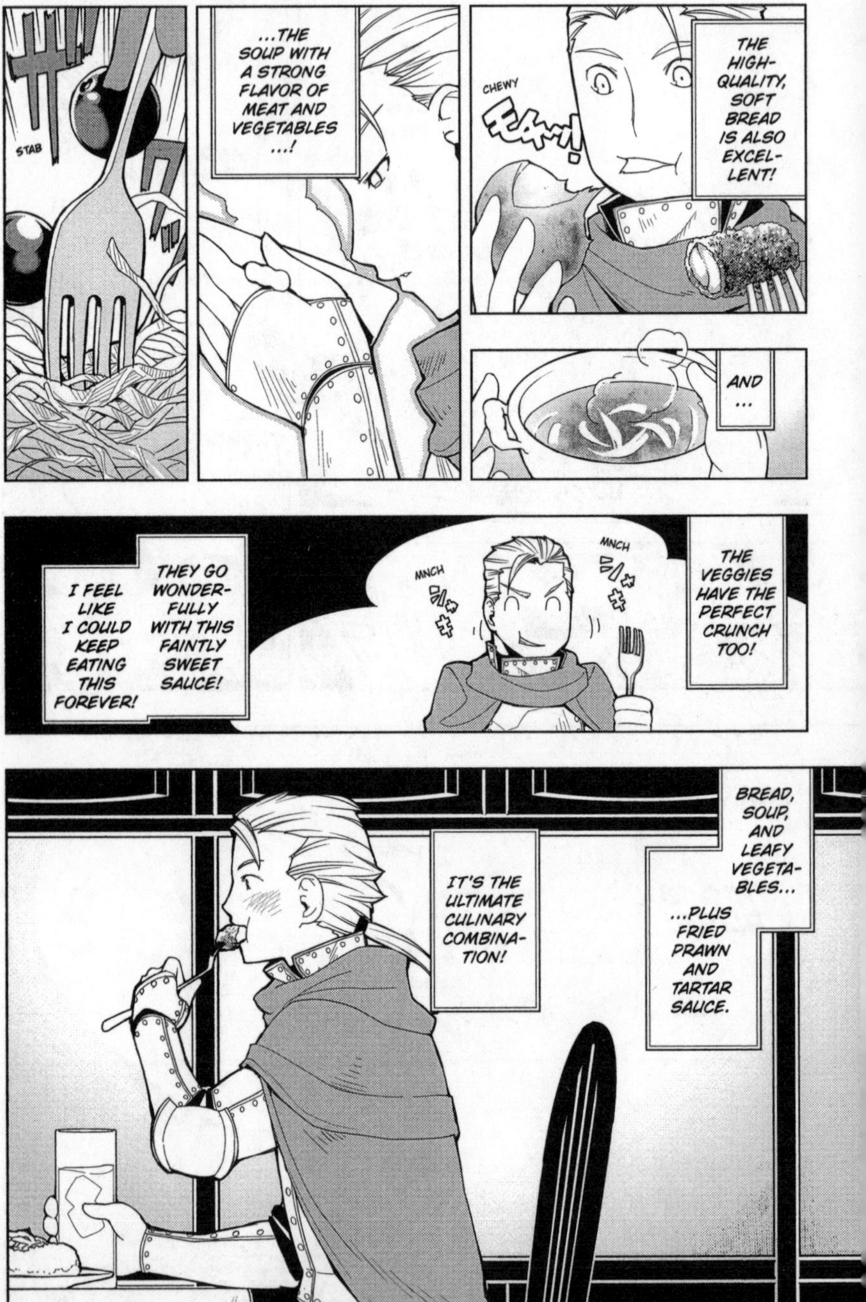
CHEWY
THE HIGH-QUALITY, SOFT BREAD IS ALSO EXCELLENT!
AND...
...THE SOUP WITH A STRONG FLAVOR OF MEAT AND VEGETABLES...!
STAB
THE VEGGIES HAVE THE PERFECT CRUNCH TOO!
MNCH
MNCH
THEY GO WONDERFULLY WITH THIS FAINTLY SWEET SAUCE!
I FEEL LIKE I COULD KEEP EATING THIS FOREVER!
BREAD, SOUP, AND LEAFY VEGETABLES...
...PLUS FRIED PRAWN AND TARTAR SAUCE.
IT'S THE ULTIMATE CULINARY COMBINATION!

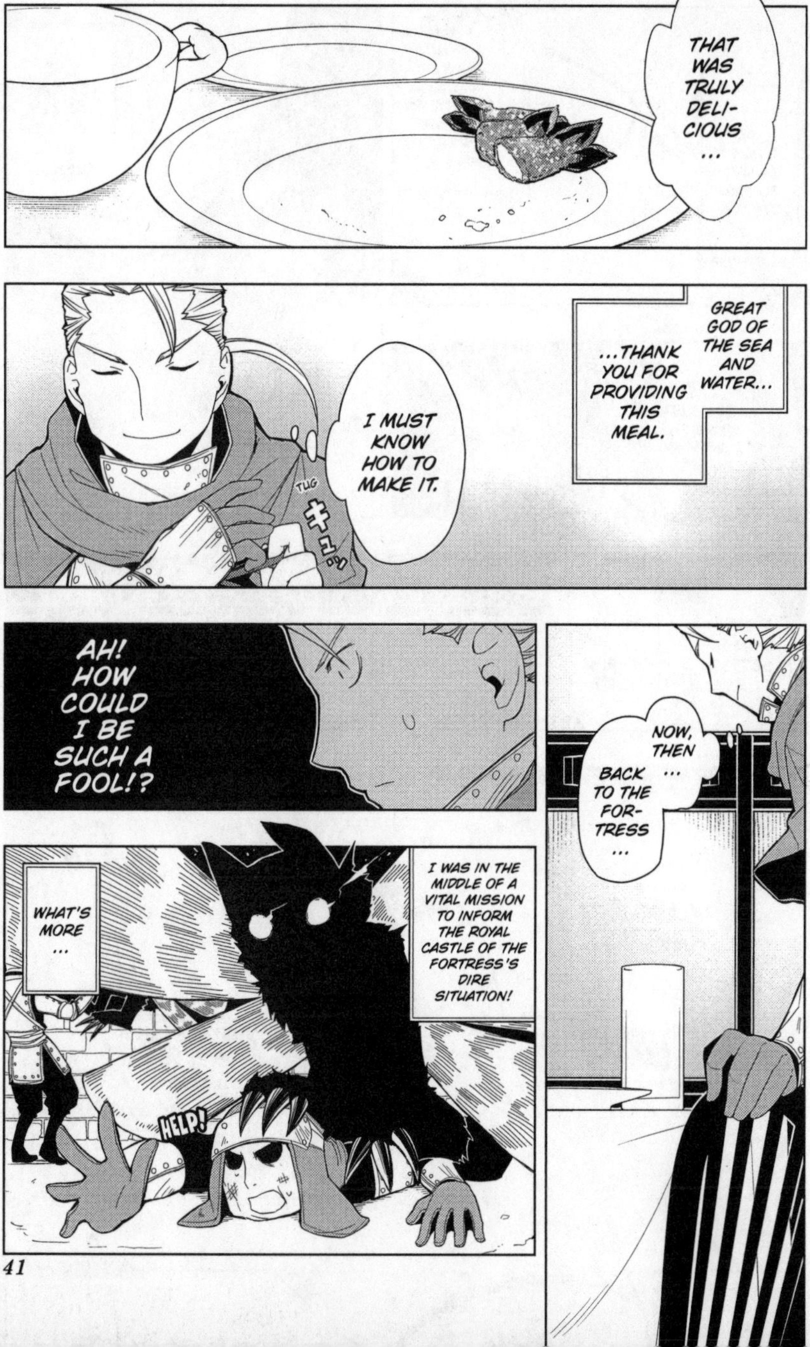
THAT WAS TRULY DELI-CIOUS ...
GREAT GOD OF THE SEA AND WATER...
...THANK YOU FOR PROVIDING THIS MEAL.
I MUST KNOW HOW TO MAKE IT.
TUG
キュッ
NOW, THEN ...
BACK TO THE FOR-TRESS ...
AH! HOW COULD I BE SUCH A FOOL!?
I WAS IN THE MIDDLE OF A VITAL MISSION TO INFORM THE ROYAL CASTLE OF THE FORTRESS'S DIRE SITUATION!
WHAT'S MORE ...
HELP!

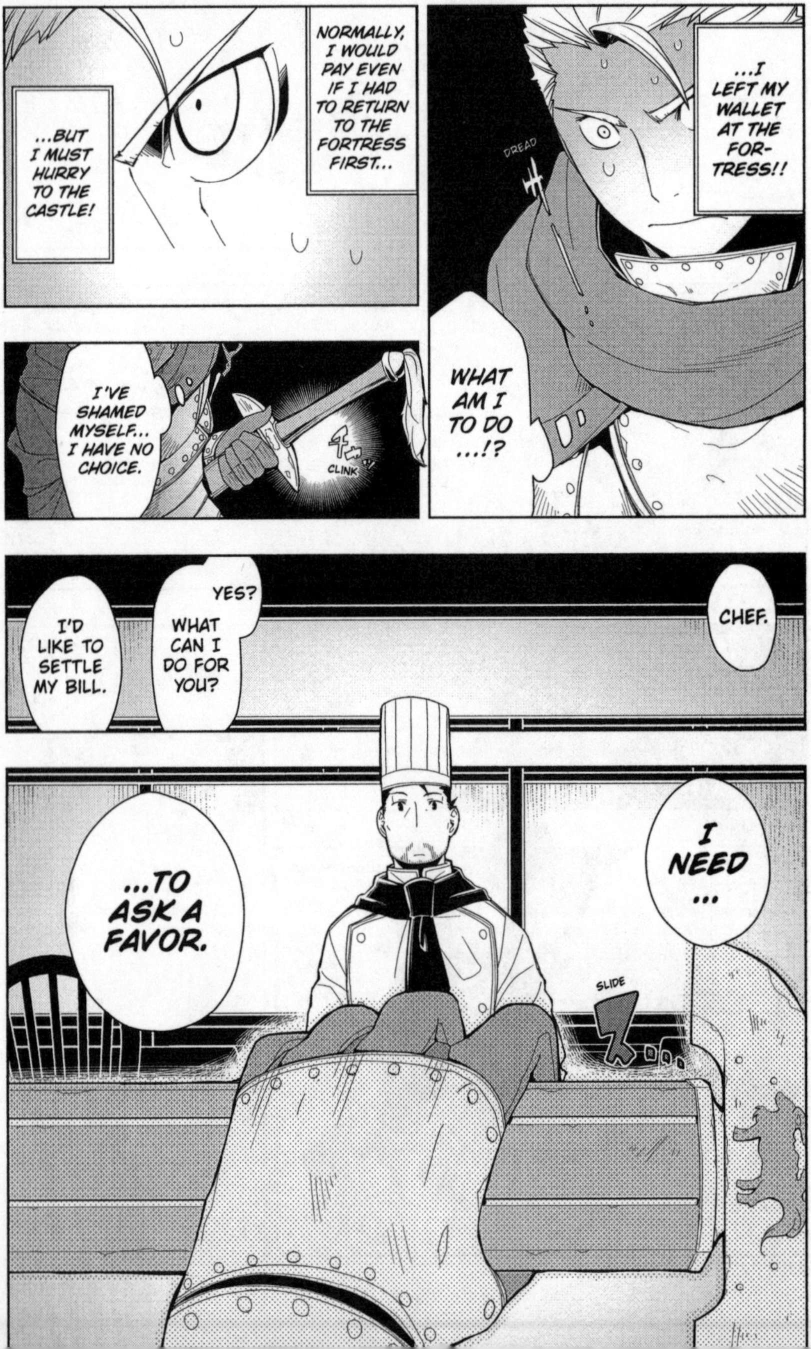
...I LEFT MY WALLET AT THE FOR-TRESS!!
DREAD
WHAT AM I TO DO ...!?
NORMALLY, I WOULD PAY EVEN IF I HAD TO RETURN TO THE FORTRESS FIRST...
...BUT I MUST HURRY TO THE CASTLE!
I'VE SHAMED MYSELF... I HAVE NO CHOICE.
CLINK
CHEF.
YES? WHAT CAN I DO FOR YOU?
I'D LIKE TO SETTLE MY BILL.
I NEED...
SLIDE
...TO ASK A FAVOR.

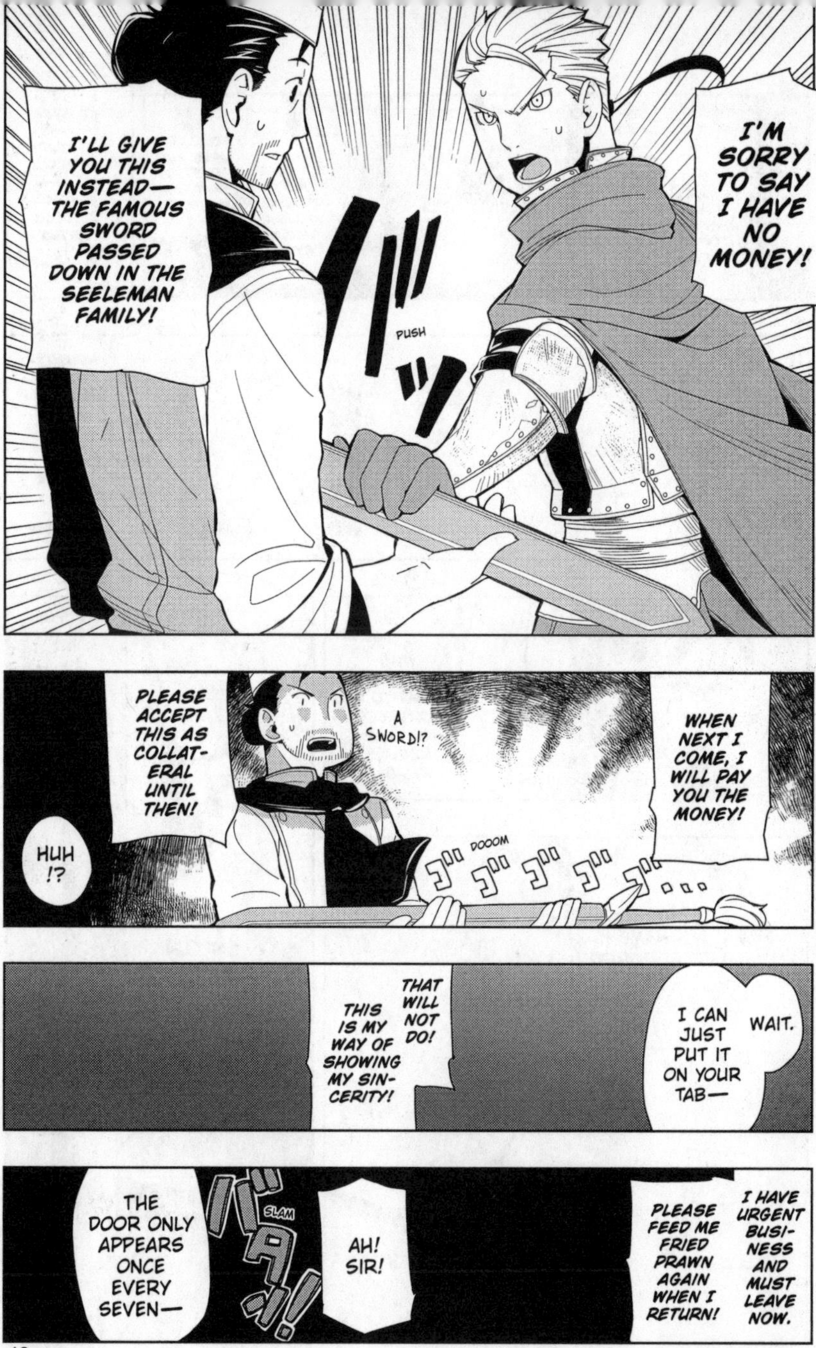

I'M SORRY TO SAY I HAVE NO MONEY!
PUSH
I'LL GIVE YOU THIS INSTEAD—THE FAMOUS SWORD PASSED DOWN IN THE SEELEMAN FAMILY!
WHEN NEXT I COME, I WILL PAY YOU THE MONEY!
A SWORD!?
PLEASE ACCEPT THIS AS COLLAT-ERAL UNTIL THEN!
DOOOM
HUH!?
WAIT.
I CAN JUST PUT IT ON YOUR TAB—
THAT WILL NOT DO!
THIS IS MY WAY OF SHOWING MY SIN-CERITY!
I HAVE URGENT BUSI-NESS AND MUST LEAVE NOW.
PLEASE FEED ME FRIED PRAWN AGAIN WHEN I RETURN!
AH! SIR!
SLAM
THE DOOR ONLY APPEARS ONCE EVERY SEVEN—

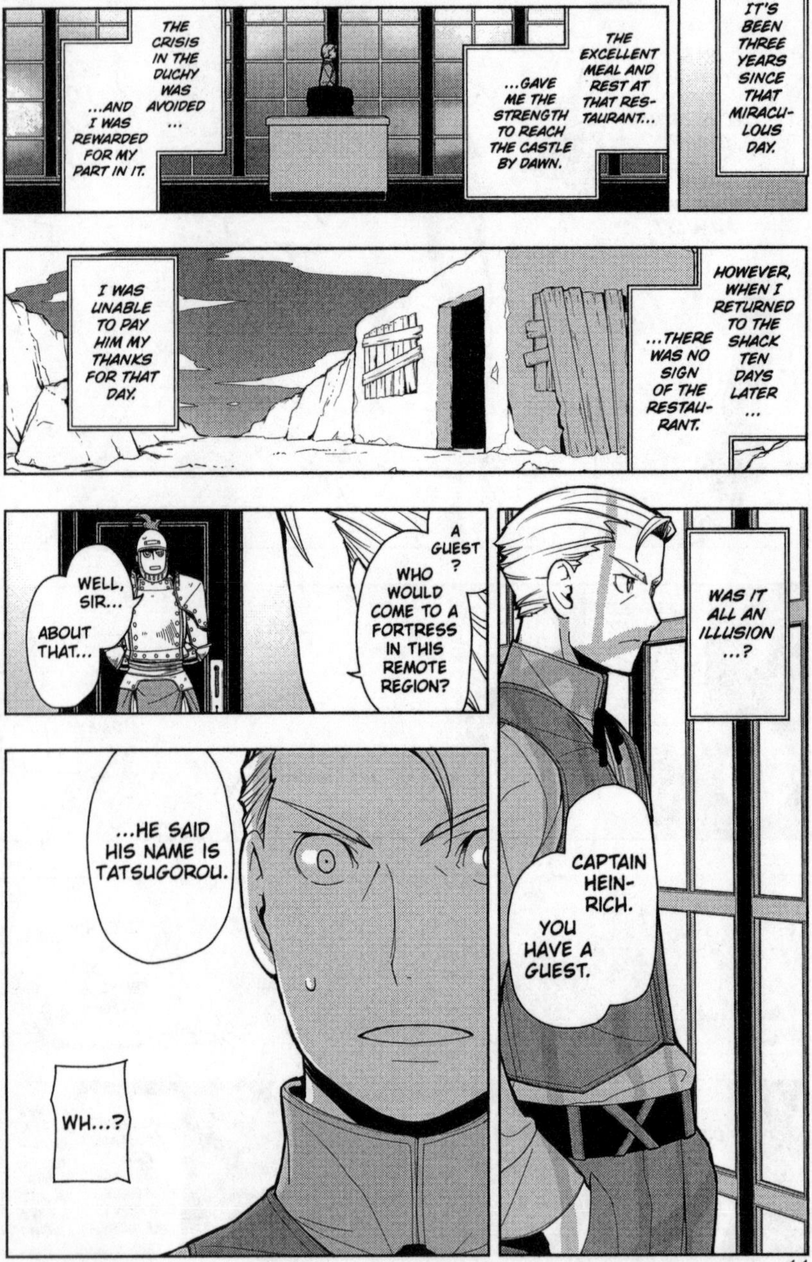
IT'S BEEN THREE YEARS SINCE THAT MIRACULOUS DAY.
THE EXCELLENT MEAL AND REST AT THAT RESTAURANT...
...GAVE ME THE STRENGTH TO REACH THE CASTLE BY DAWN.
THE CRISIS IN THE DUCHY WAS AVOIDED...
...AND I WAS REWARDED FOR MY PART IN IT.
HOWEVER, WHEN I RETURNED TO THE SHACK TEN DAYS LATER...
...THERE WAS NO SIGN OF THE RESTAURANT.
I WAS UNABLE TO PAY HIM MY THANKS FOR THAT DAY.
WAS IT ALL AN ILLUSION...?
CAPTAIN HEINRICH. YOU HAVE A GUEST.
A GUEST? WHO WOULD COME TO A FORTRESS IN THIS REMOTE REGION?
WELL, SIR... ABOUT THAT...
...HE SAID HIS NAME IS TATSUGOROU.
WH...?

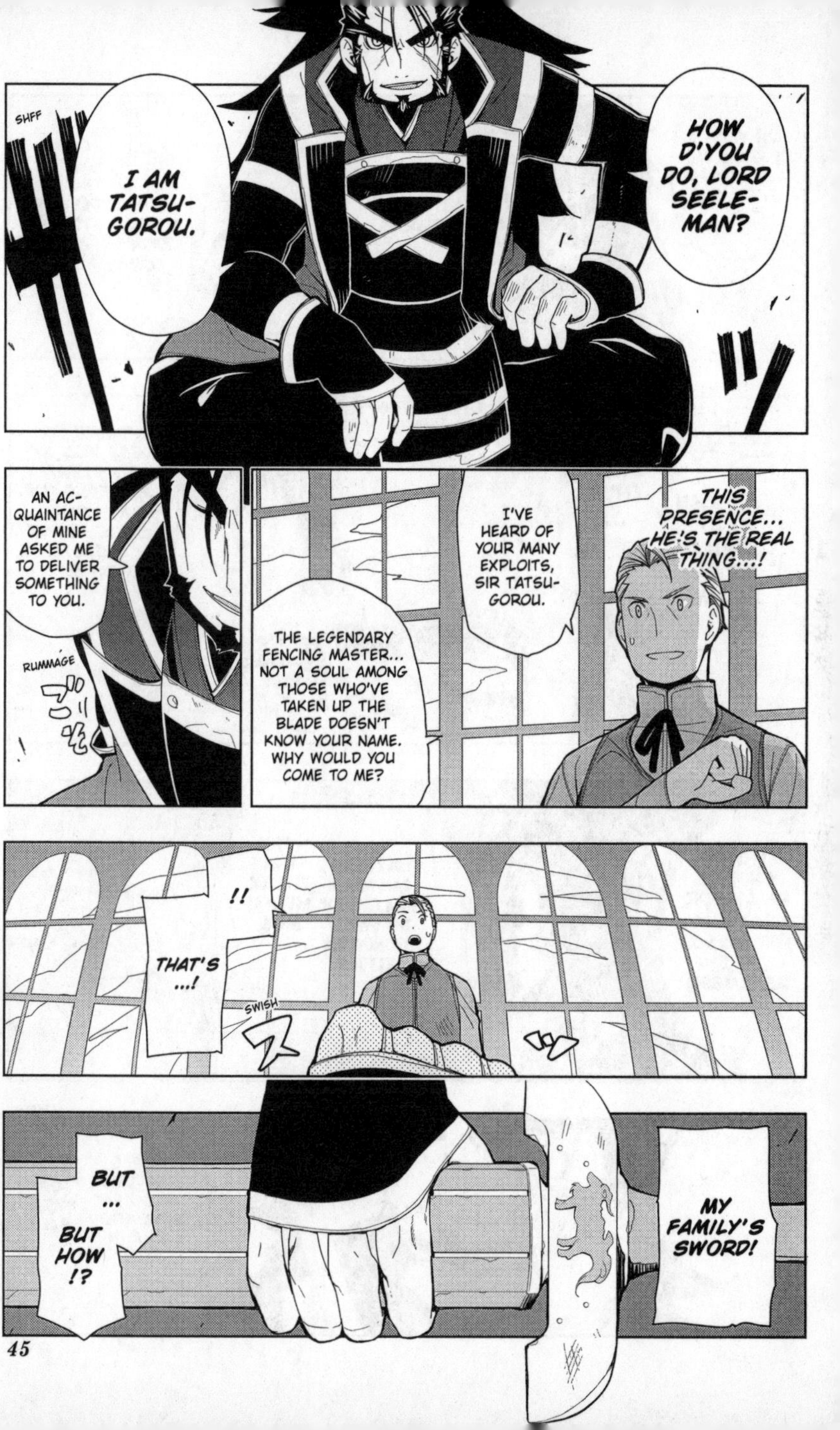
HOW D'YOU DO, LORD SEELE-MAN?
I AM TATSU-GOROU.
SHFF
THIS PRESENCE... HE'S THE REAL THING...!
I'VE HEARD OF YOUR MANY EXPLOITS, SIR TATSU-GOROU.
THE LEGENDARY FENCING MASTER... NOT A SOUL AMONG THOSE WHO'VE TAKEN UP THE BLADE DOESN'T KNOW YOUR NAME. WHY WOULD YOU COME TO ME?
AN AC-QUAINTANCE OF MINE ASKED ME TO DELIVER SOMETHING TO YOU.
RUMMAGE
!!
THAT'S ...!
SWISH
MY FAMILY'S SWORD!
BUT ... BUT HOW !?

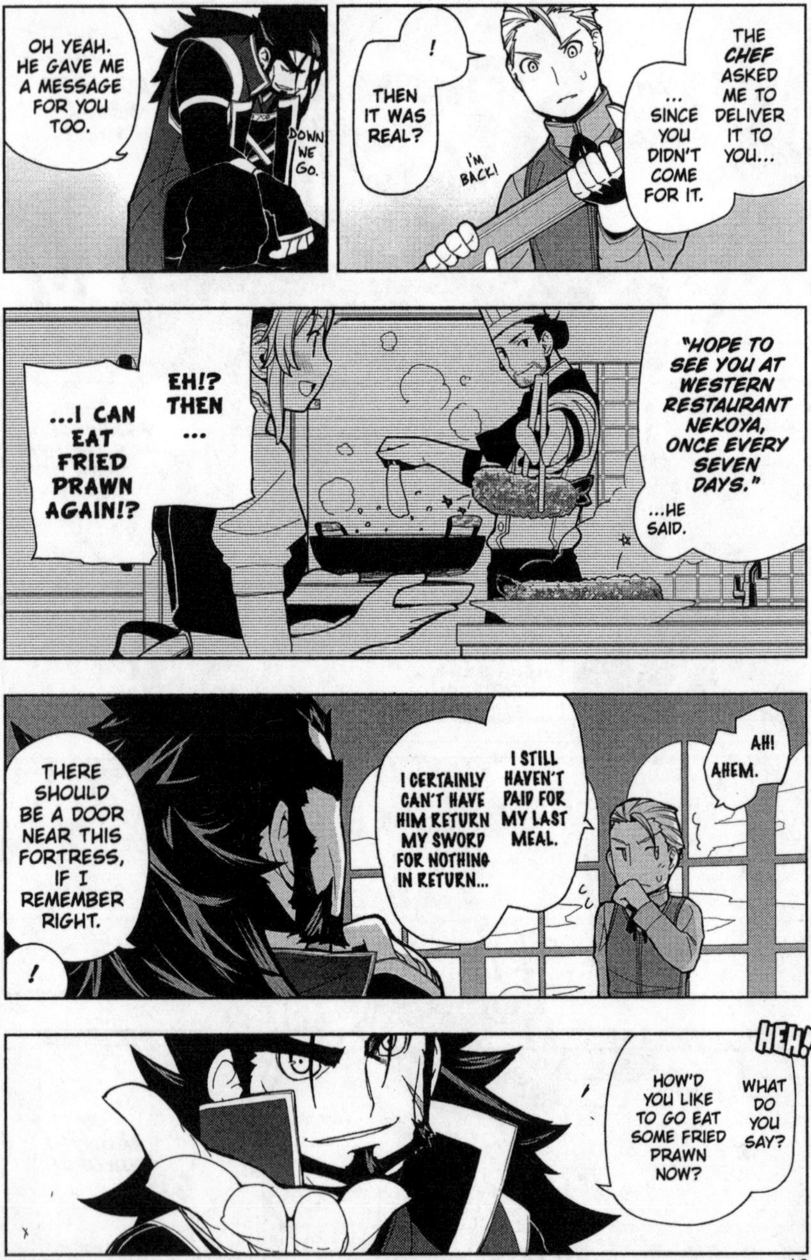
THE *CHEF* ASKED ME TO DELIVER IT TO YOU...
... SINCE YOU DIDN'T COME FOR IT.
!
THEN IT WAS REAL?
I'M BACK!
DOWN WE GO.
OH YEAH. HE GAVE ME A MESSAGE FOR YOU TOO.
"HOPE TO SEE YOU AT WESTERN RESTAURANT NEKOYA, ONCE EVERY SEVEN DAYS."
...HE SAID.
EH!? THEN ...
...I CAN EAT FRIED PRAWN AGAIN!?
AH! AHEM.
I STILL HAVEN'T PAID FOR MY LAST MEAL.
I CERTAINLY CAN'T HAVE HIM RETURN MY SWORD FOR NOTHING IN RETURN...
THERE SHOULD BE A DOOR NEAR THIS FORTRESS, IF I REMEMBER RIGHT.
!
HEH!
WHAT DO YOU SAY?
HOW'D YOU LIKE TO GO EAT SOME FRIED PRAWN NOW?

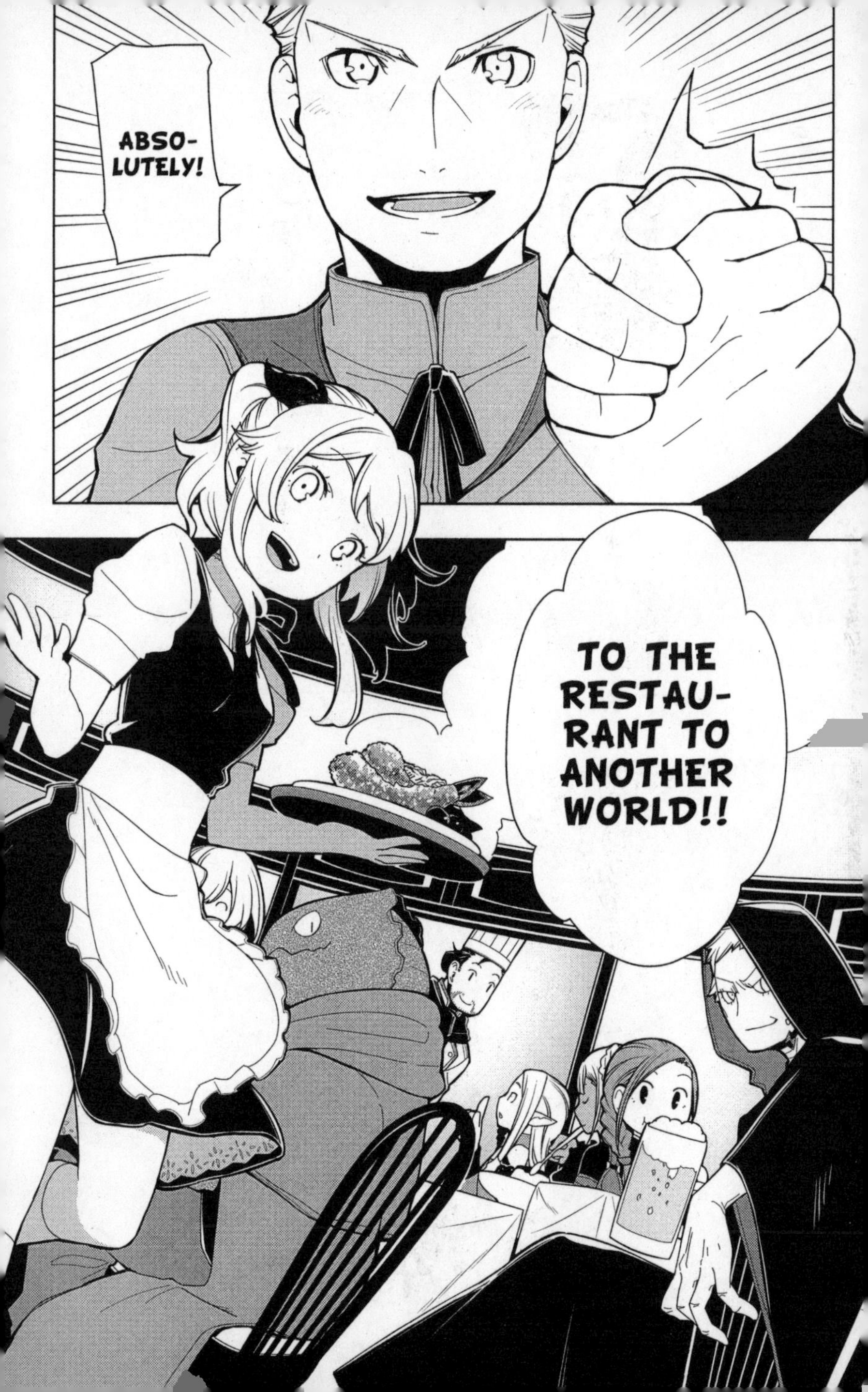
ABSO-LUTELY!
TO THE RESTAU-RANT TO ANOTHER WORLD!!

RESTAURANT TO Another World

8th Dish Chocolate Parfait

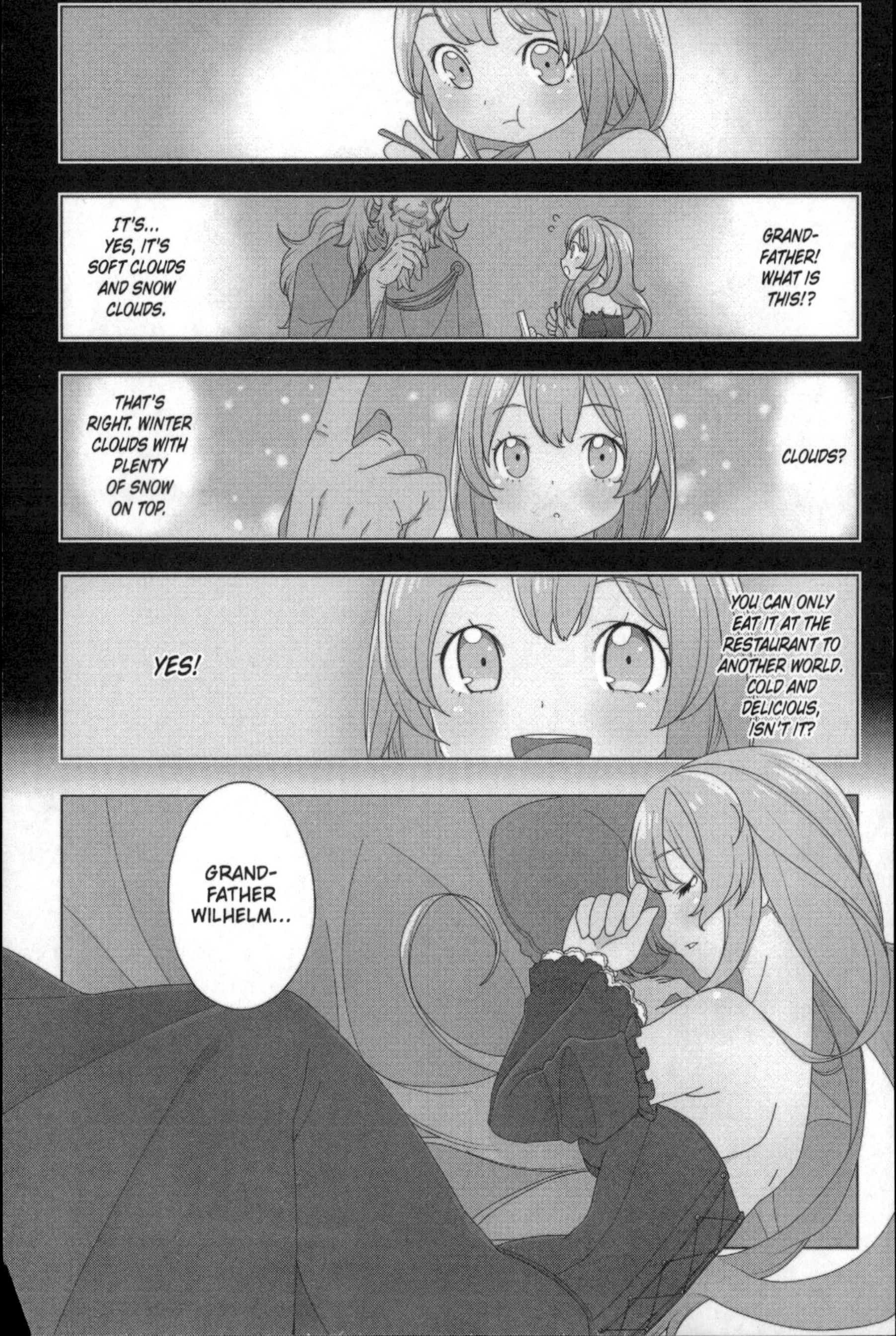
GRAND-FATHER! WHAT IS THIS!?
IT'S... YES, IT'S SOFT CLOUDS AND SNOW CLOUDS.
CLOUDS?
THAT'S RIGHT. WINTER CLOUDS WITH PLENTY OF SNOW ON TOP.
YOU CAN ONLY EAT IT AT THE RESTAURANT TO ANOTHER WORLD. COLD AND DELICIOUS, ISN'T IT?
YES!
GRAND-FATHER WILHELM...

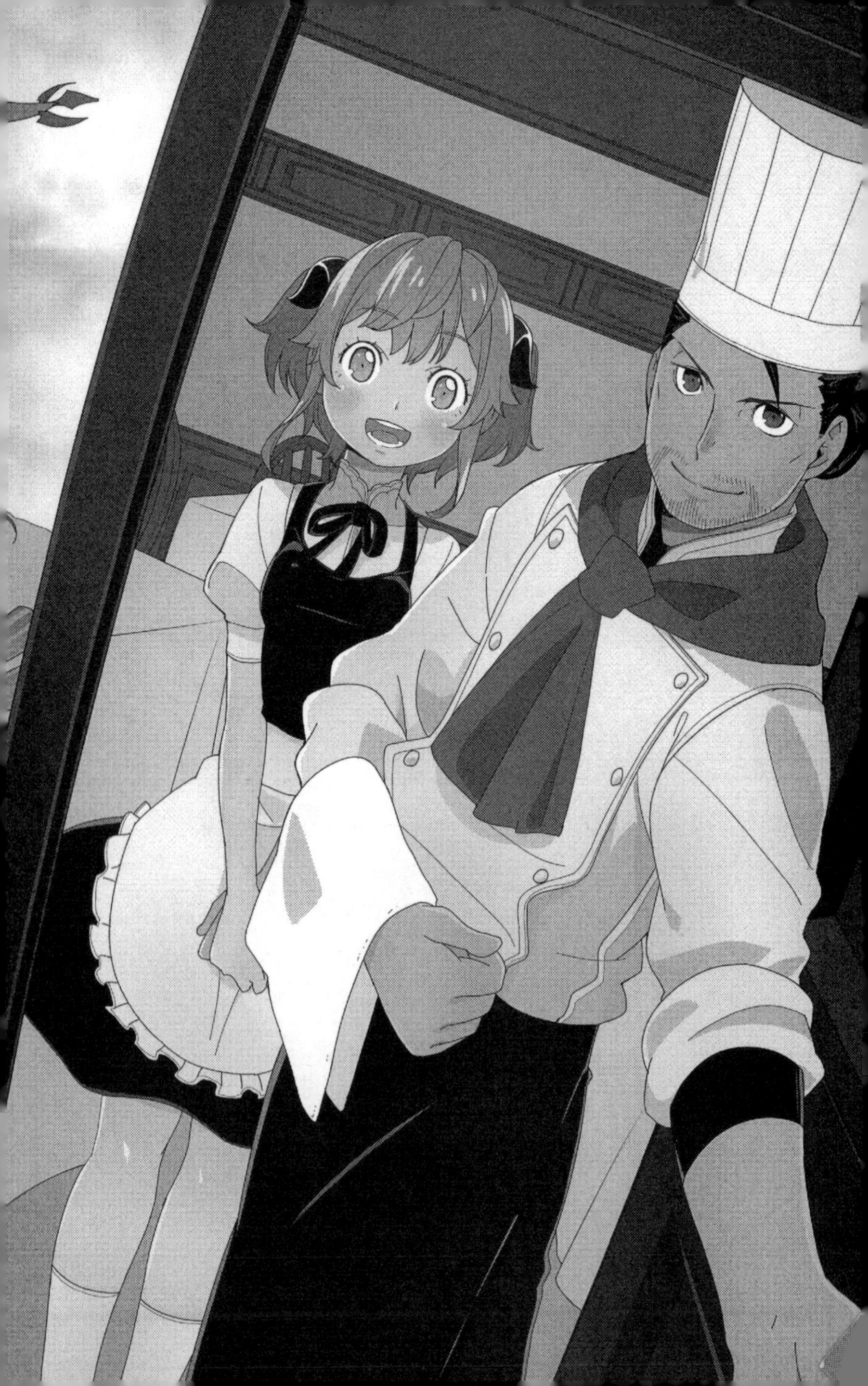

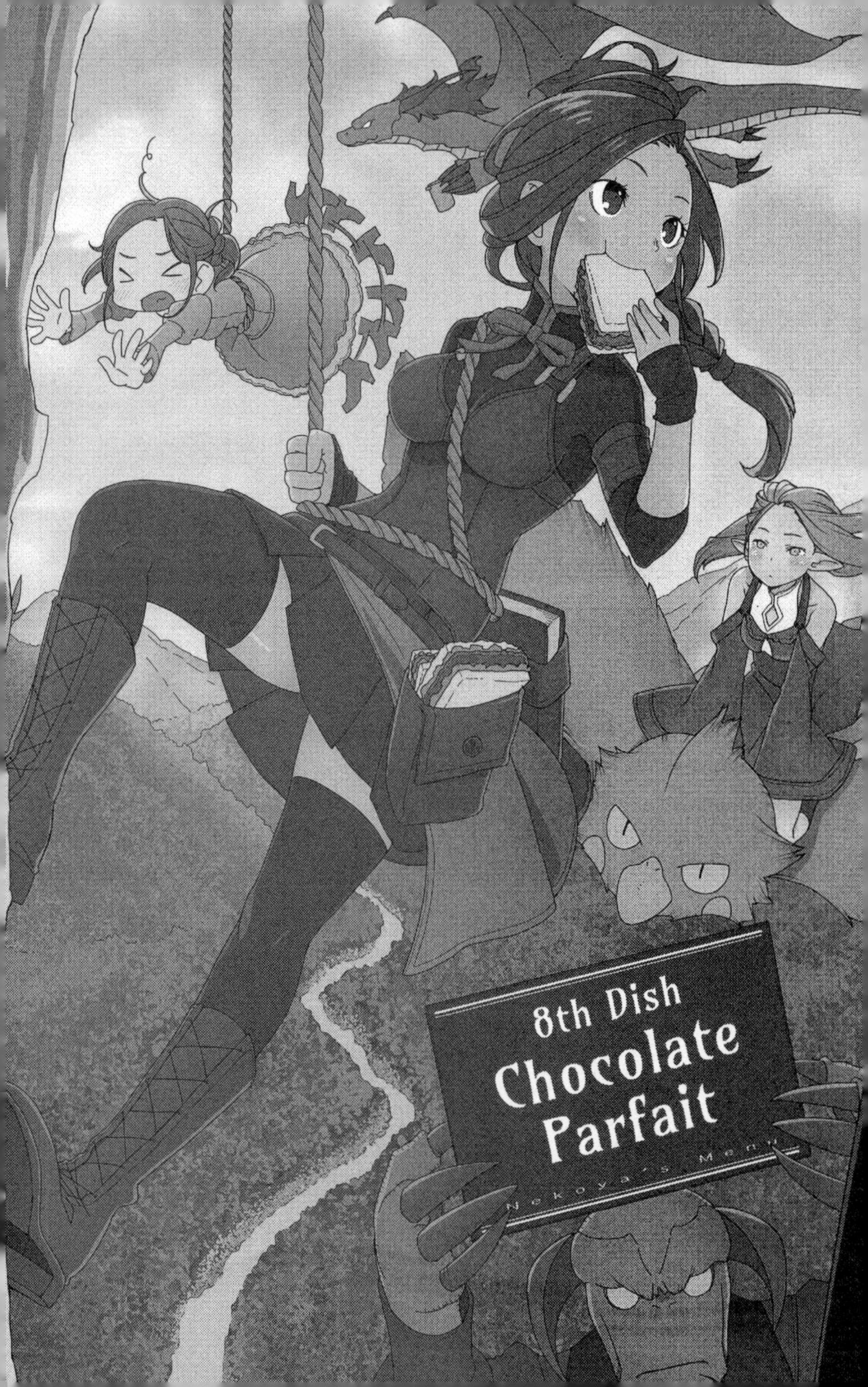
8th Dish
Chocolate Parfait
Nekoya's Menu

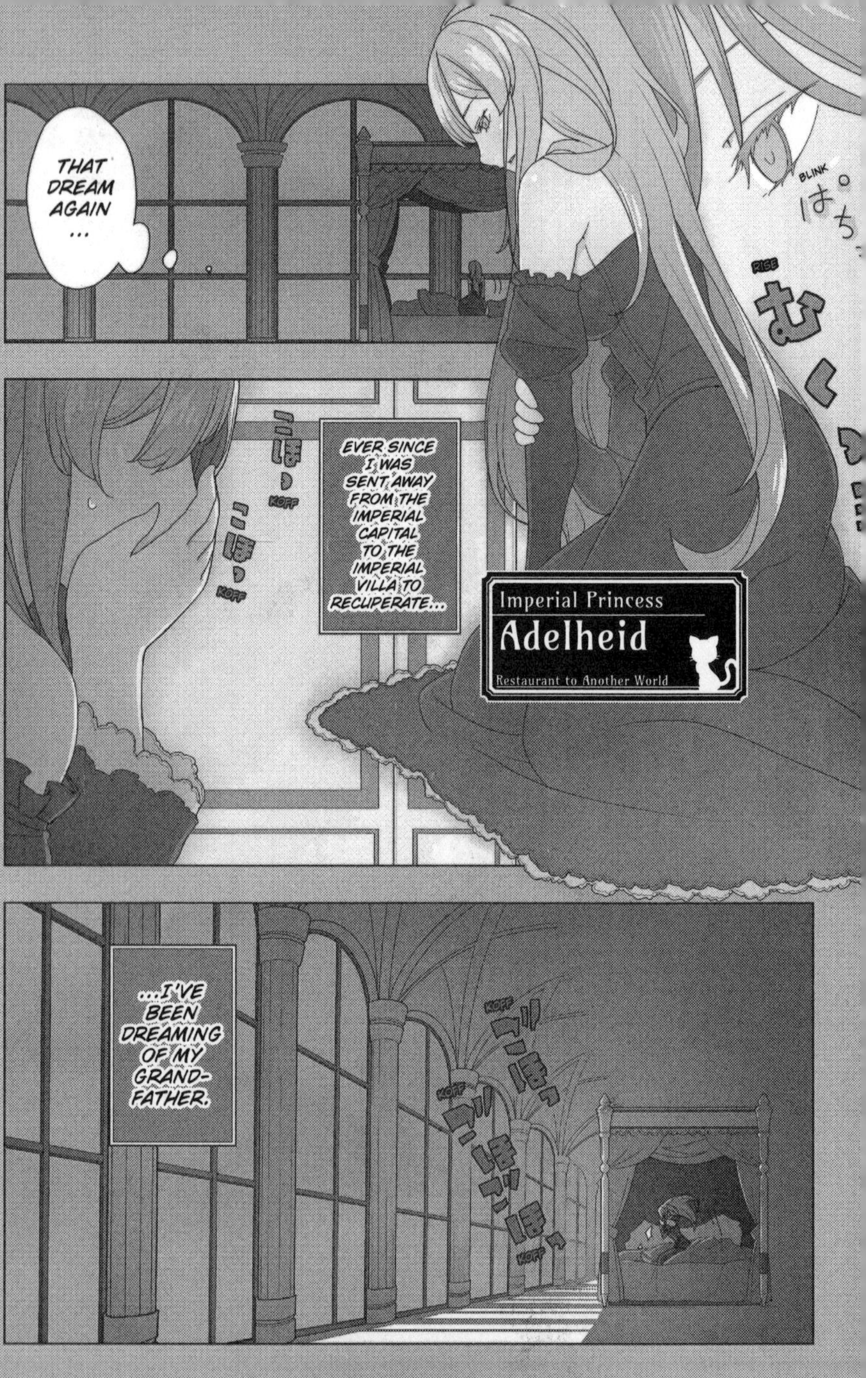

BLINK
RISE
THAT DREAM AGAIN ...
Imperial Princess
Adelheid
Restaurant to Another World
EVER SINCE I WAS SENT AWAY FROM THE IMPERIAL CAPITAL TO THE IMPERIAL VILLA TO RECUPERATE...
KOFF
KOFF
...I'VE BEEN DREAMING OF MY GRAND-FATHER.
KOFF
KOFF
KOFF

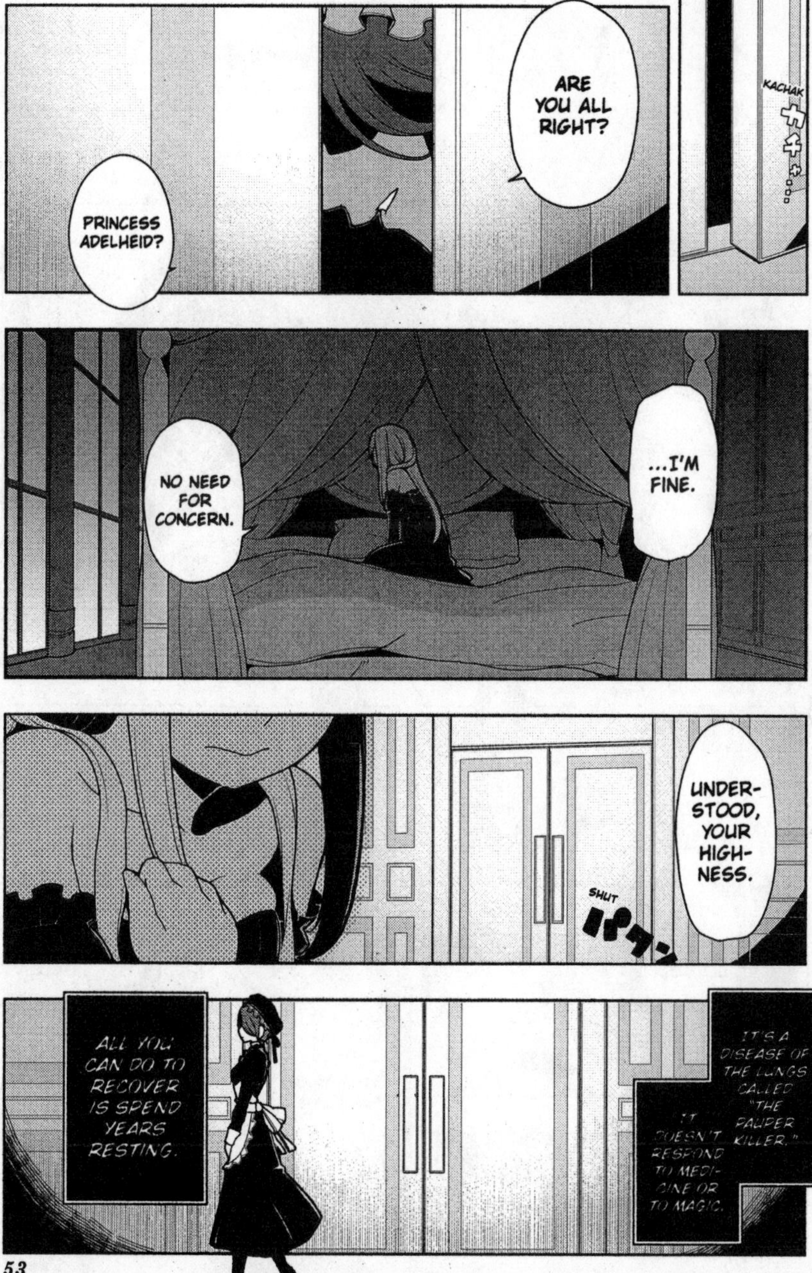
KACHAK
ARE YOU ALL RIGHT?
PRINCESS ADELHEID?
...I'M FINE.
NO NEED FOR CONCERN.
UNDERSTOOD, YOUR HIGHNESS.
SHUT
IT'S A DISEASE OF THE LUNGS CALLED "THE PAUPER KILLER."
IT DOESN'T RESPOND TO MEDICINE OR TO MAGIC.
ALL YOU CAN DO TO RECOVER IS SPEND YEARS RESTING.

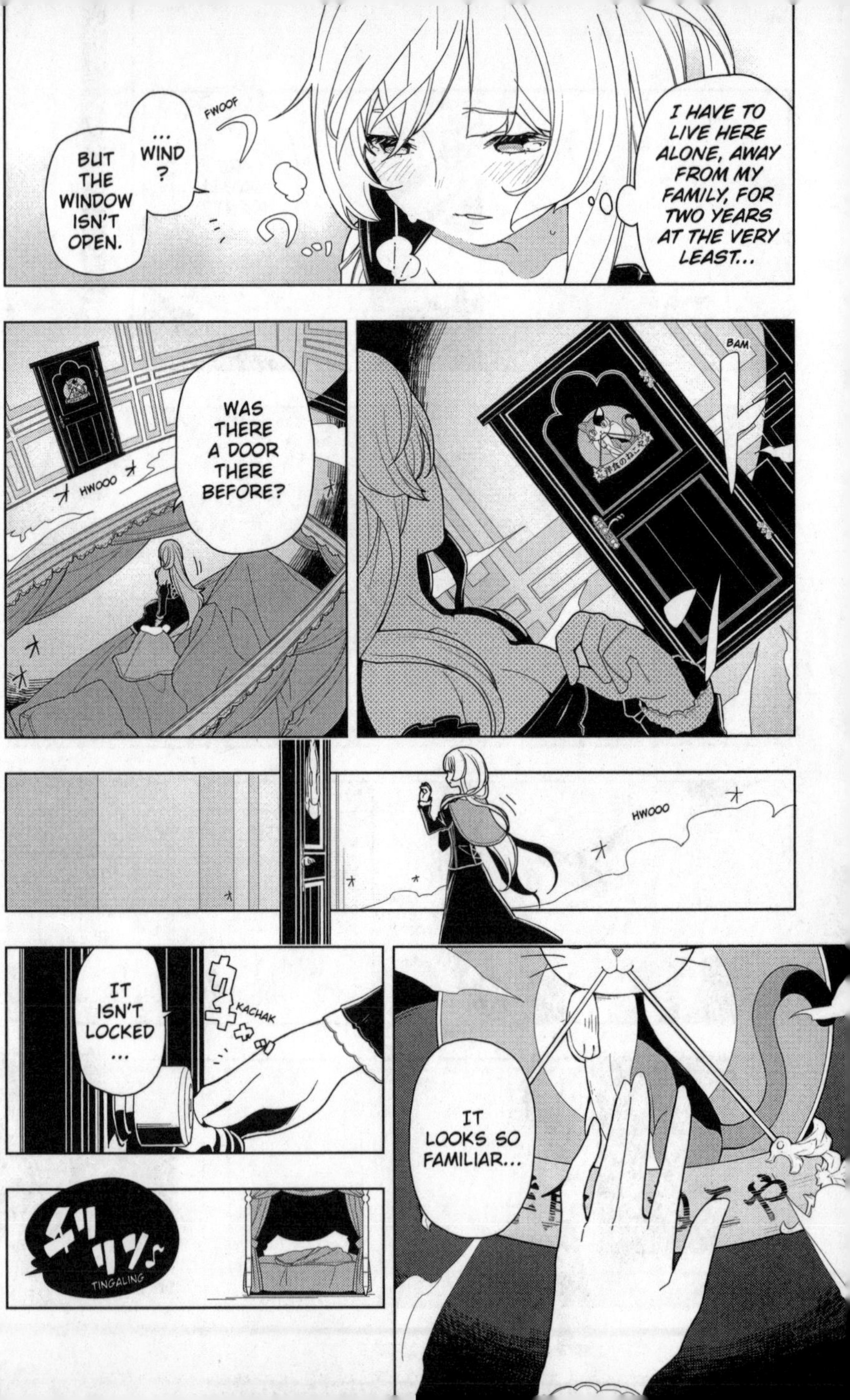
I HAVE TO LIVE HERE ALONE, AWAY FROM MY FAMILY, FOR TWO YEARS AT THE VERY LEAST...
FWOOF
... WIND ?
BUT THE WINDOW ISN'T OPEN.
BAM
WAS THERE A DOOR THERE BEFORE?
HWOOO
HWOOO
IT LOOKS SO FAMILIAR...
IT ISN'T LOCKED ...
KACHAK
TINGALING

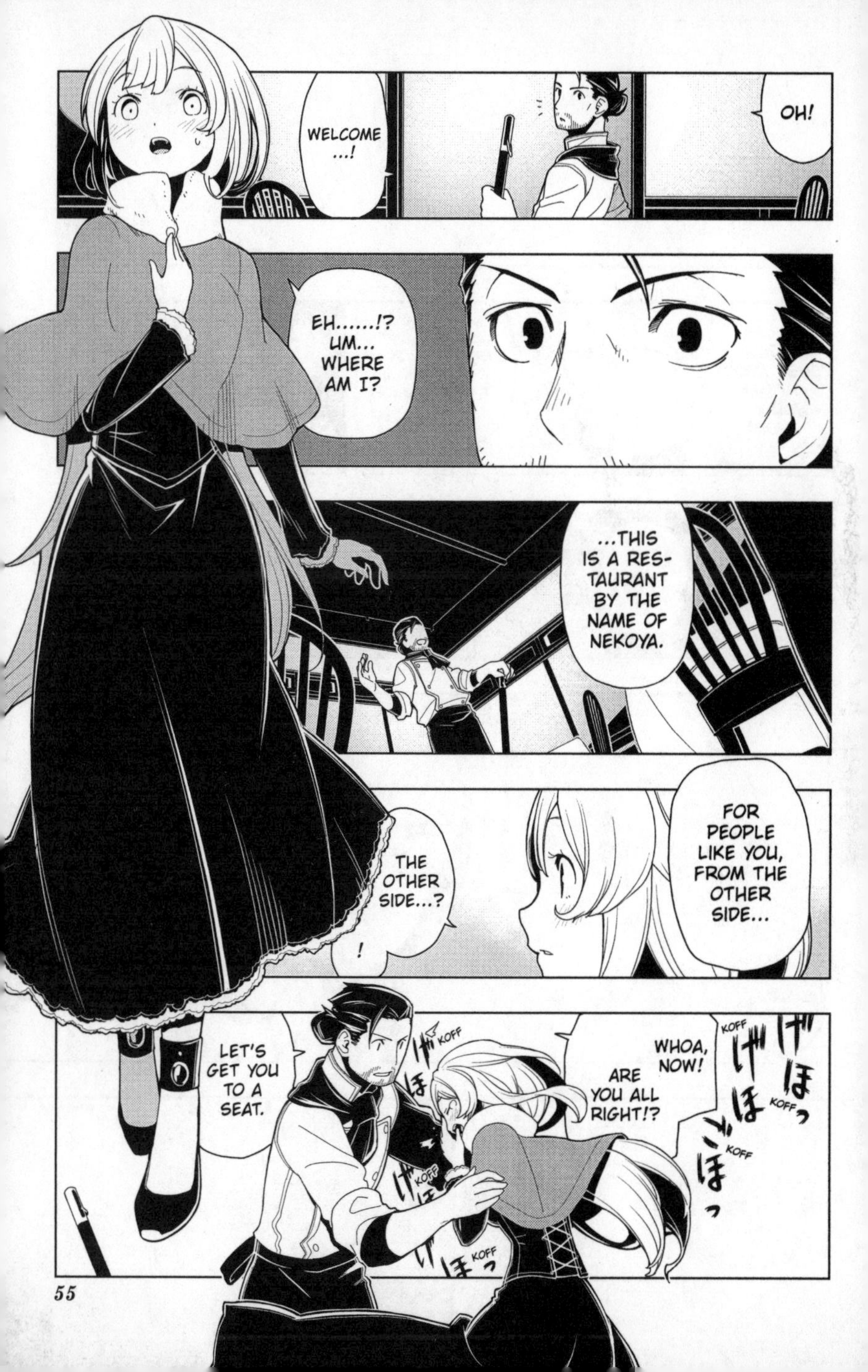
OH!
WELCOME ...!
EH......!? UM... WHERE AM I?
...THIS IS A RES-TAURANT BY THE NAME OF NEKOYA.
FOR PEOPLE LIKE YOU, FROM THE OTHER SIDE...
THE OTHER SIDE...?
!
KOFF
KOFF
KOFF
WHOA, NOW!
ARE YOU ALL RIGHT!?
LET'S GET YOU TO A SEAT.
KOFF
KOFF
KOFF

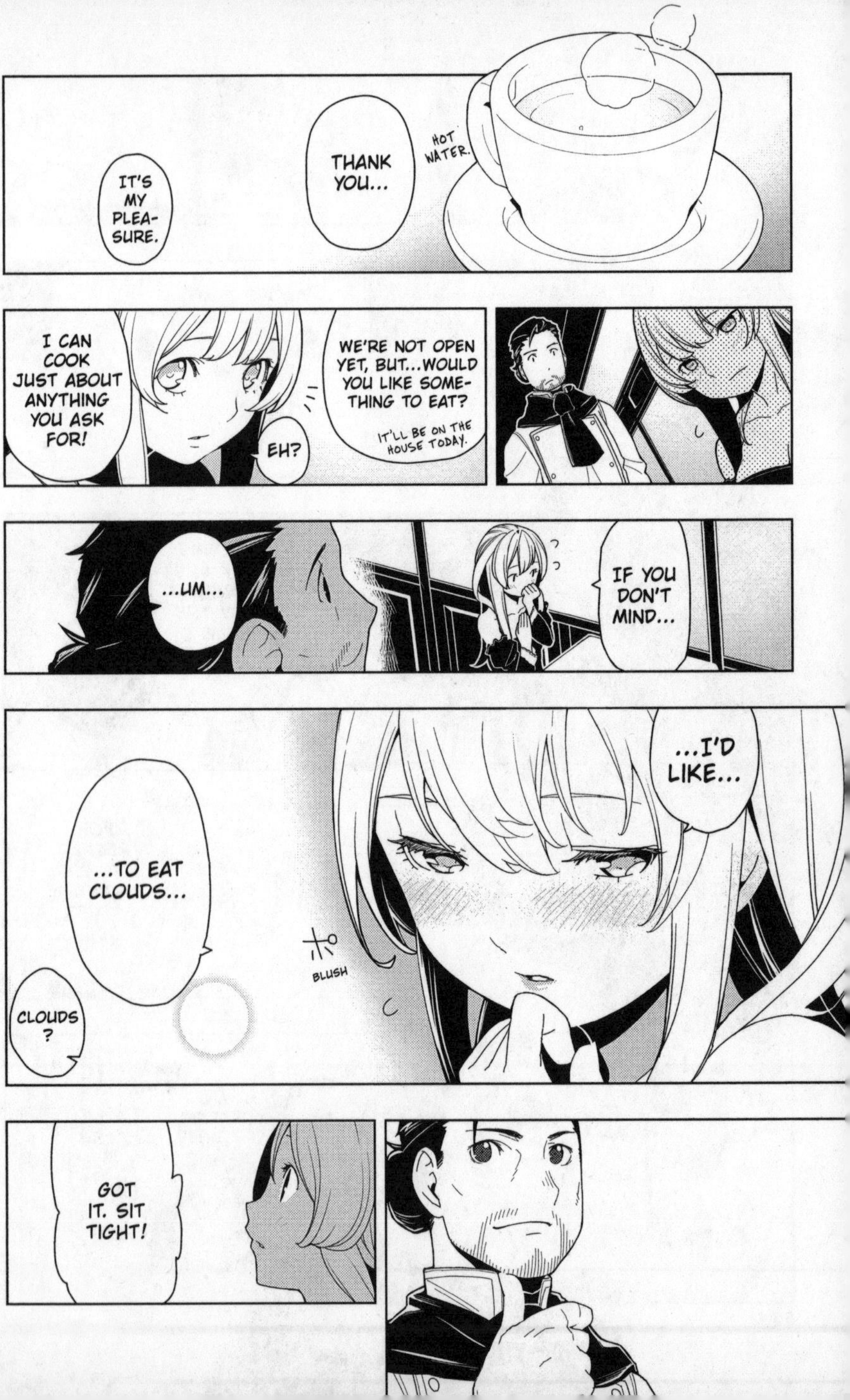
HOT WATER.
THANK YOU...
IT'S MY PLEASURE.
WE'RE NOT OPEN YET, BUT...WOULD YOU LIKE SOMETHING TO EAT?
IT'LL BE ON THE HOUSE TODAY.
EH?
I CAN COOK JUST ABOUT ANYTHING YOU ASK FOR!
IF YOU DON'T MIND...
...UM...
...I'D LIKE...
BLUSH
...TO EAT CLOUDS...
CLOUDS?
GOT IT. SIT TIGHT!

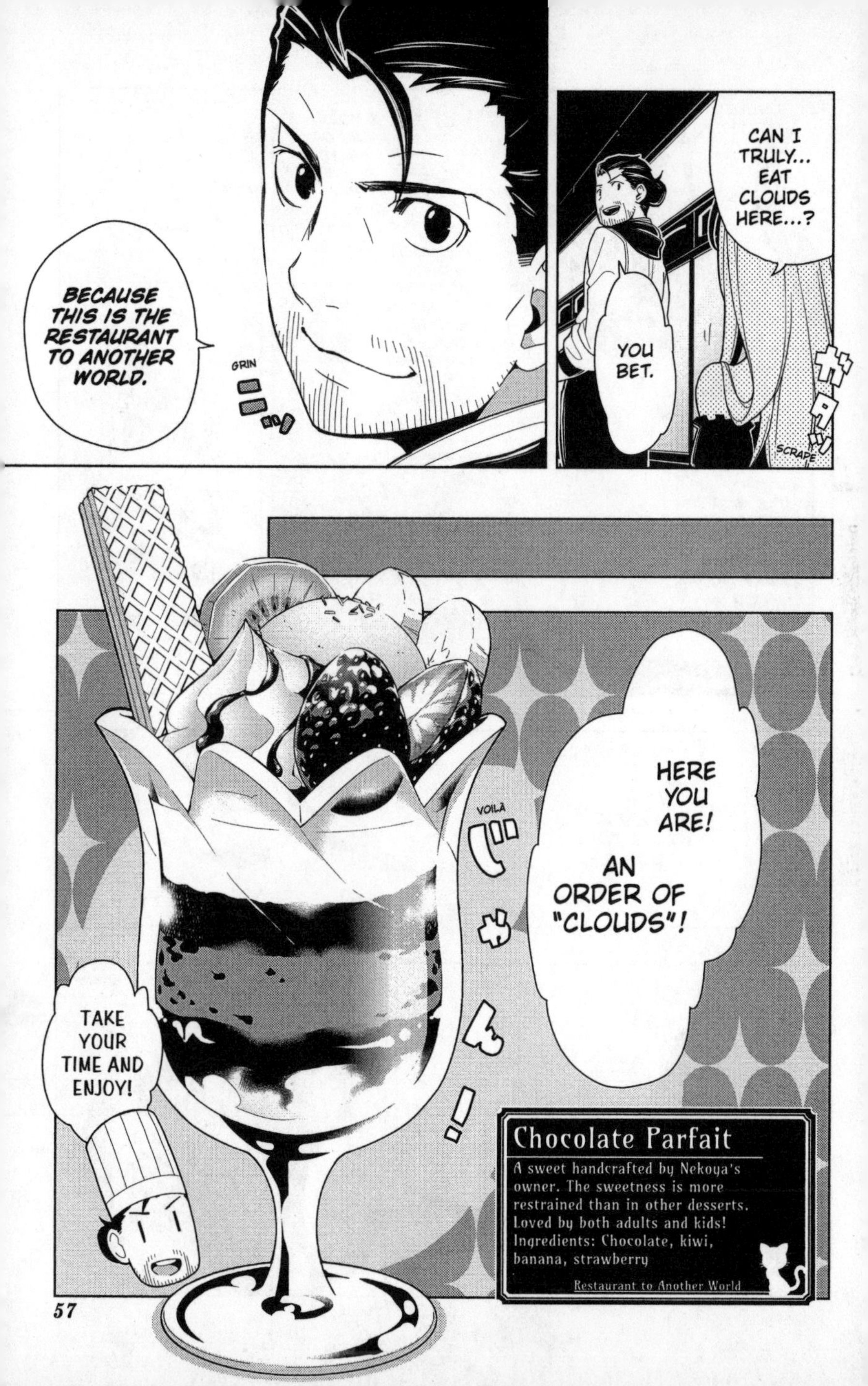
CAN I TRULY... EAT CLOUDS HERE...?
YOU BET.
SCRAPE
BECAUSE THIS IS THE RESTAURANT TO ANOTHER WORLD.
GRIN
HERE YOU ARE!
AN ORDER OF "CLOUDS"!
VOILÀ
TAKE YOUR TIME AND ENJOY!
Chocolate Parfait
A sweet handcrafted by Nekoya's owner. The sweetness is more restrained than in other desserts. Loved by both adults and kids!
Ingredients: Chocolate, kiwi, banana, strawberry
Restaurant to Another World

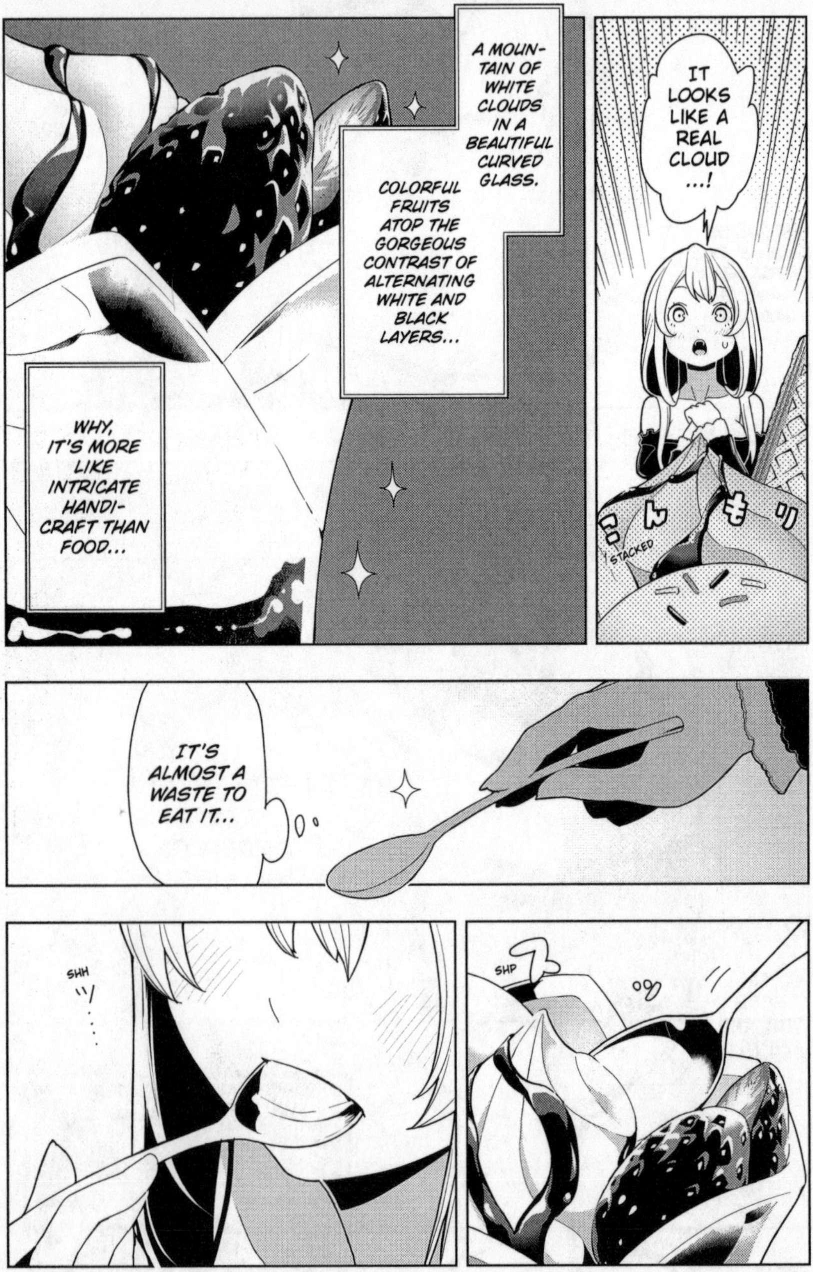
IT LOOKS LIKE A REAL CLOUD ...!
STACKED
A MOUN-TAIN OF WHITE CLOUDS IN A BEAUTIFUL CURVED GLASS.
COLORFUL FRUITS ATOP THE GORGEOUS CONTRAST OF ALTERNATING WHITE AND BLACK LAYERS...
WHY, IT'S MORE LIKE INTRICATE HANDI-CRAFT THAN FOOD...
IT'S ALMOST A WASTE TO EAT IT...
SHP
SHH

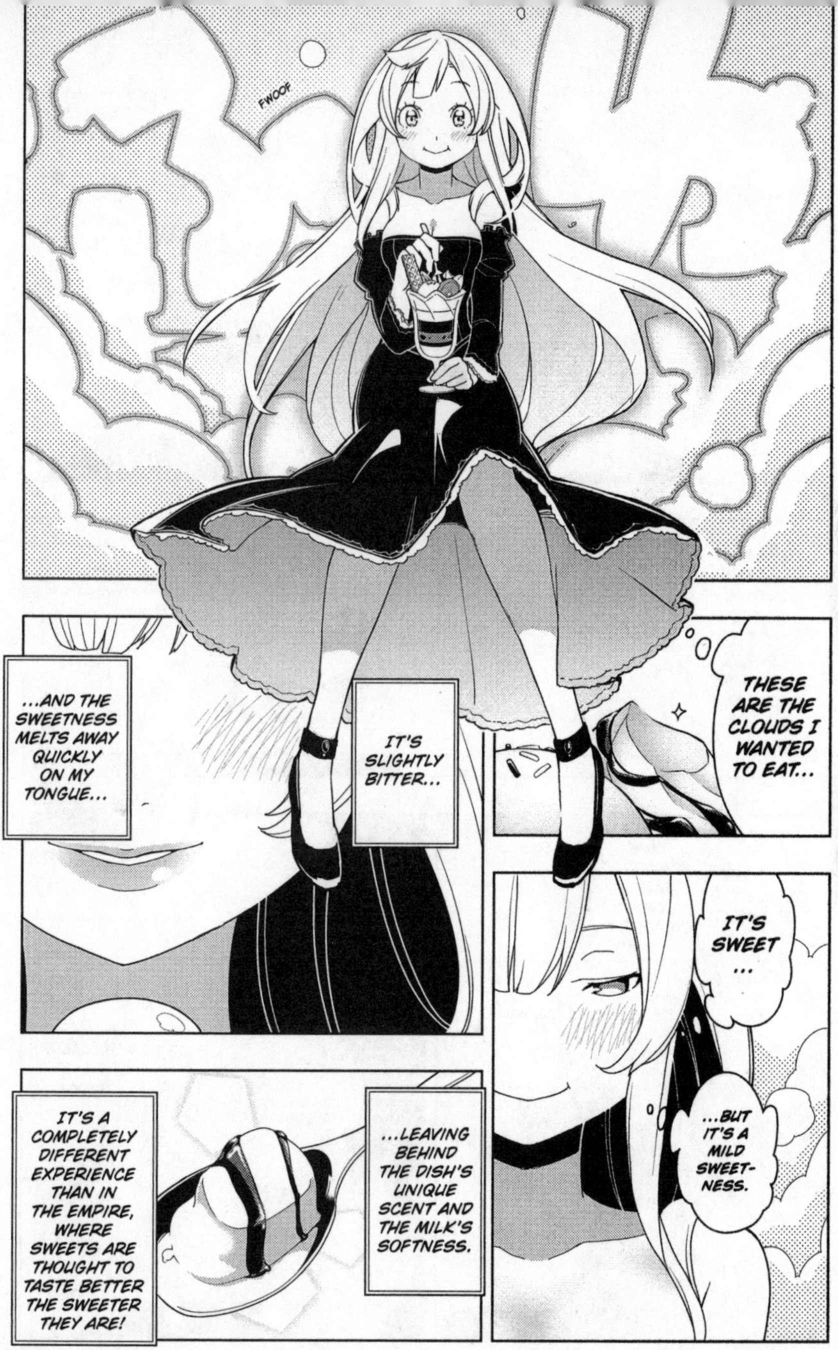
FWOOF
THESE ARE THE CLOUDS I WANTED TO EAT...
IT'S SLIGHTLY BITTER...
...AND THE SWEETNESS MELTS AWAY QUICKLY ON MY TONGUE...
IT'S SWEET...
...BUT IT'S A MILD SWEETNESS.
...LEAVING BEHIND THE DISH'S UNIQUE SCENT AND THE MILK'S SOFTNESS.
IT'S A COMPLETELY DIFFERENT EXPERIENCE THAN IN THE EMPIRE, WHERE SWEETS ARE THOUGHT TO TASTE BETTER THE SWEETER THEY ARE!

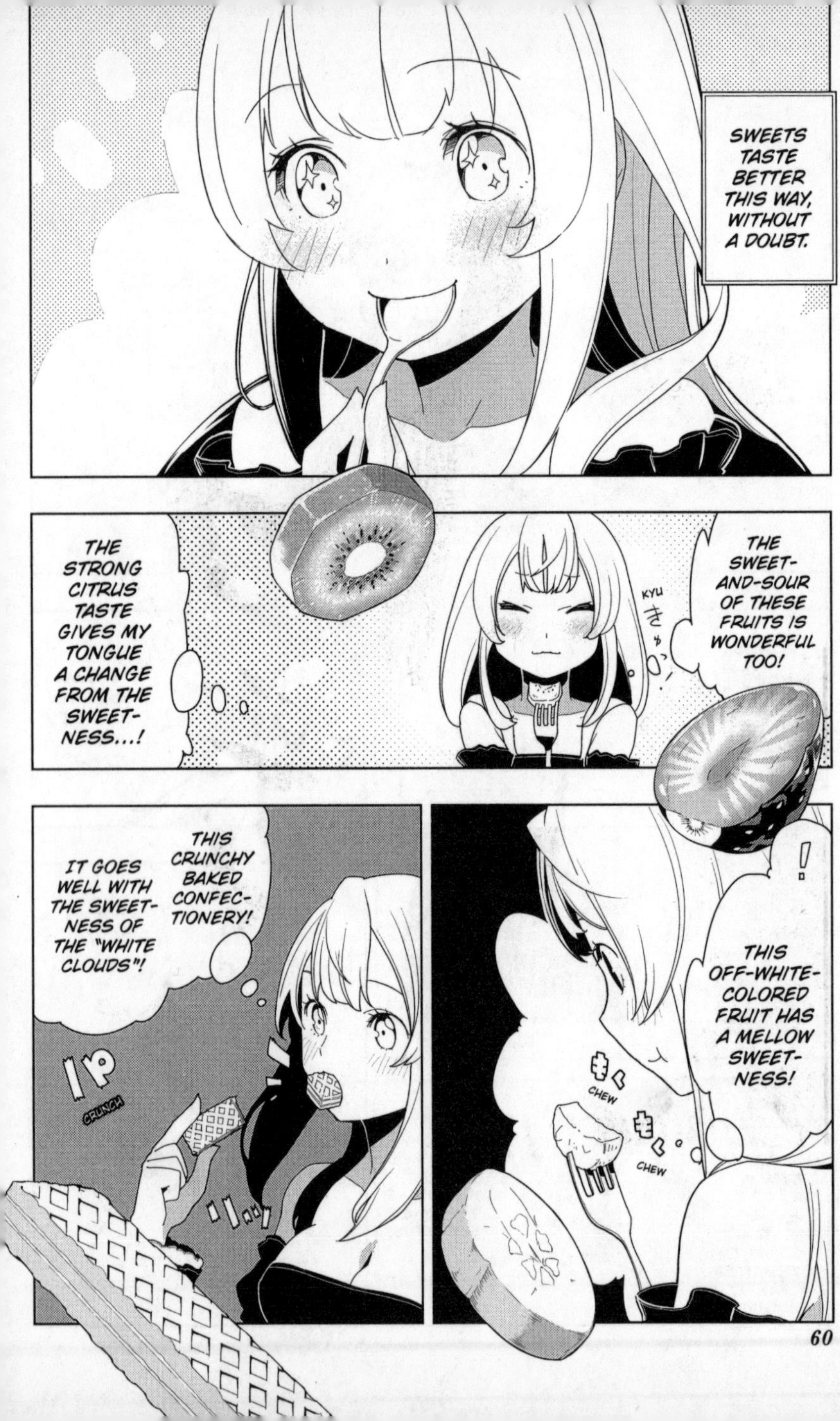
SWEETS TASTE BETTER THIS WAY, WITHOUT A DOUBT.
THE SWEET-AND-SOUR OF THESE FRUITS IS WONDERFUL TOO!
KYU
THE STRONG CITRUS TASTE GIVES MY TONGUE A CHANGE FROM THE SWEETNESS...!
!
THIS OFF-WHITE-COLORED FRUIT HAS A MELLOW SWEETNESS!
CHEW
CHEW
THIS CRUNCHY BAKED CONFECTIONERY!
IT GOES WELL WITH THE SWEETNESS OF THE "WHITE CLOUDS"!
CRUNCH

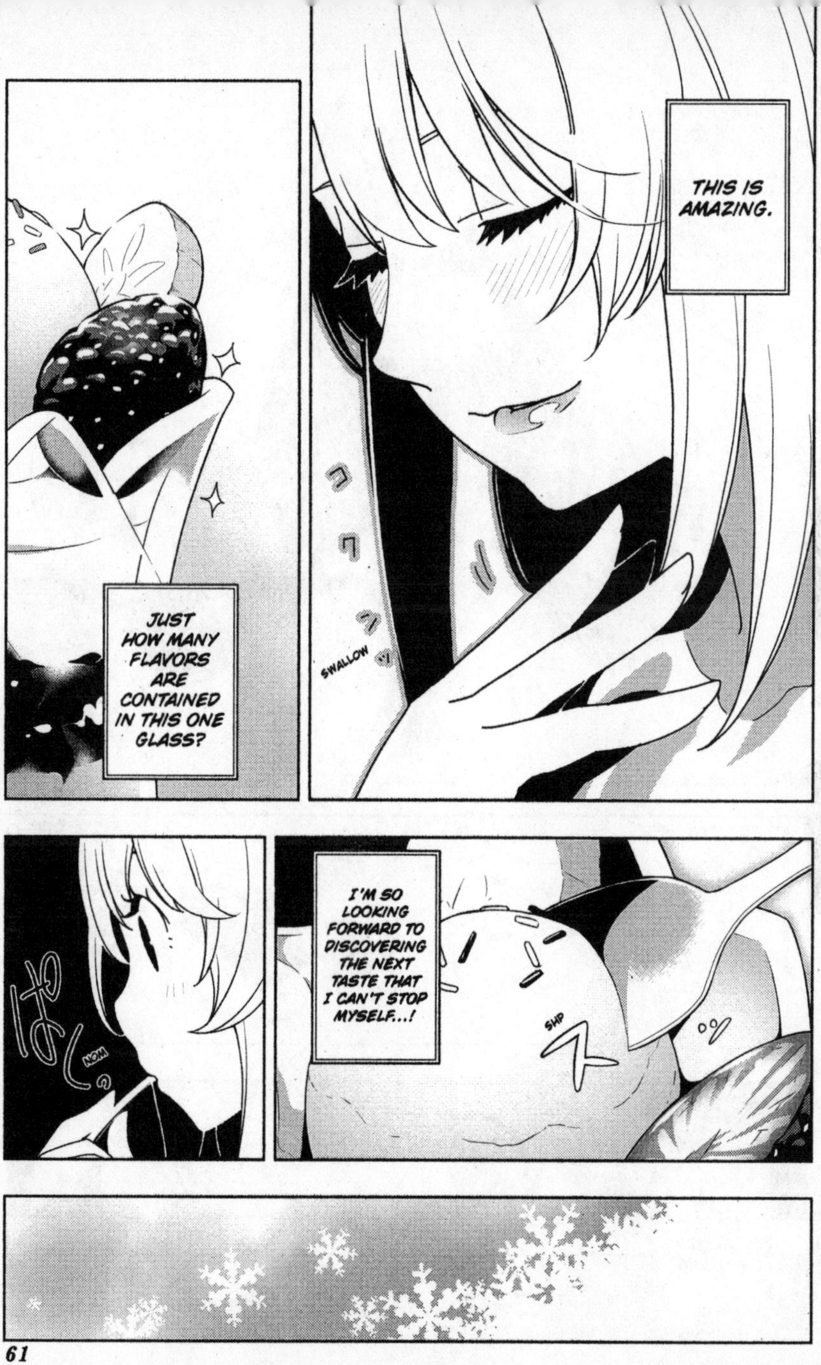
THIS IS AMAZING.
SWALLOW
JUST HOW MANY FLAVORS ARE CONTAINED IN THIS ONE GLASS?
I'M SO LOOKING FORWARD TO DISCOVERING THE NEXT TASTE THAT I CAN'T STOP MYSELF...!
SHP
NOM

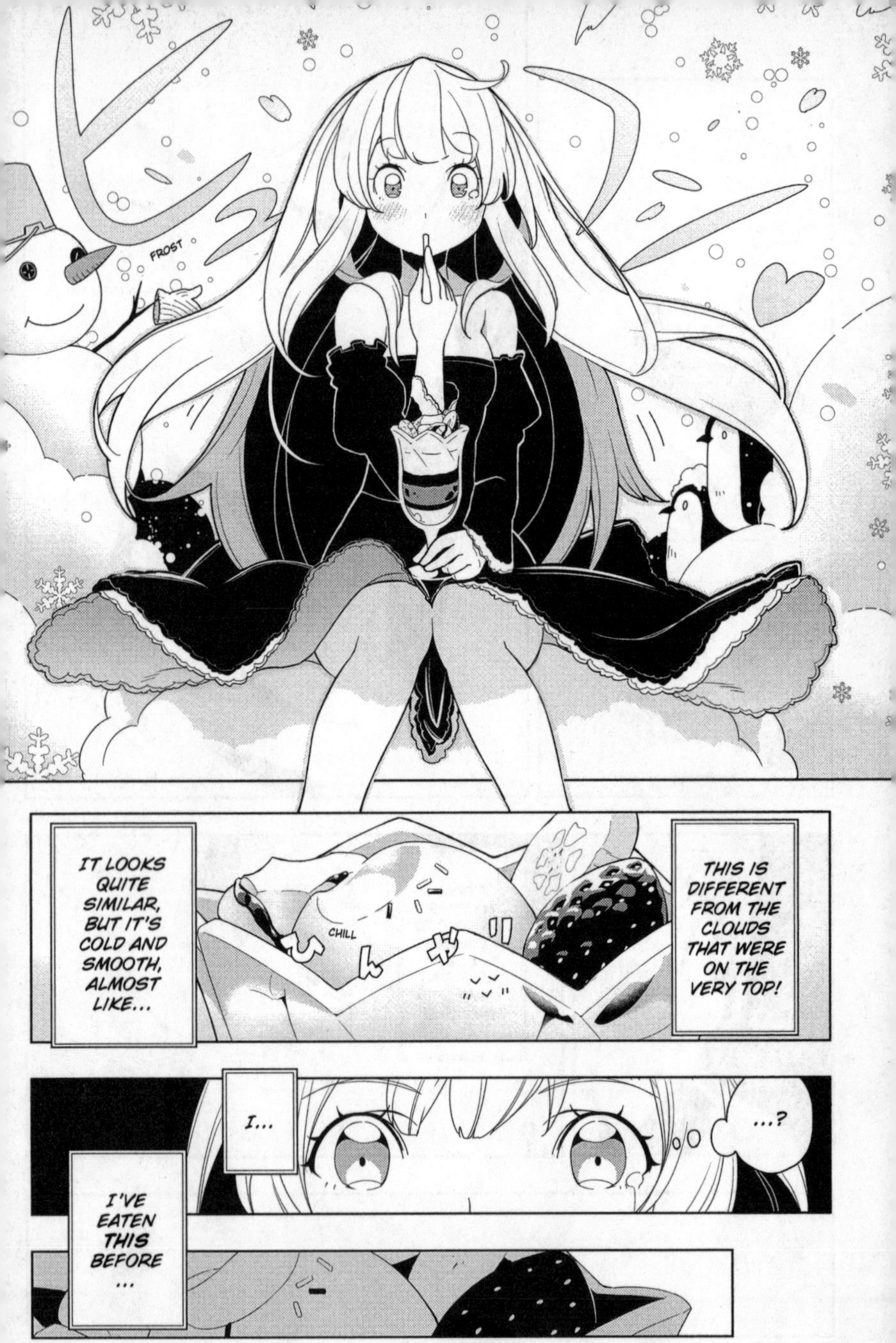
FROST
THIS IS DIFFERENT FROM THE CLOUDS THAT WERE ON THE VERY TOP!
IT LOOKS QUITE SIMILAR, BUT IT'S COLD AND SMOOTH, ALMOST LIKE...
CHILL
...?
I...
I'VE EATEN THIS BEFORE...

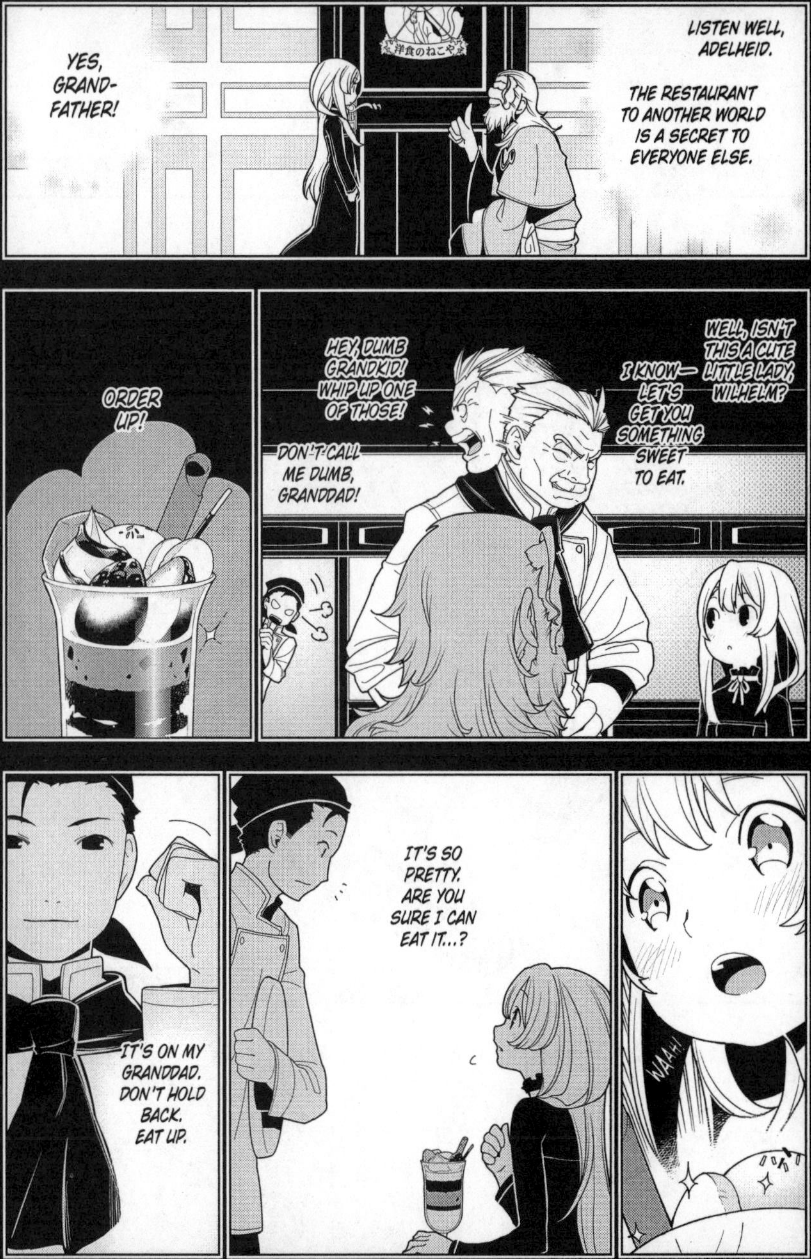
洋食のねこや
LISTEN WELL, ADELHEID.
THE RESTAURANT TO ANOTHER WORLD IS A SECRET TO EVERYONE ELSE.
YES, GRAND-FATHER!
WELL, ISN'T THIS A CUTE LITTLE LADY, WILHELM?
I KNOW— LET'S GET YOU SOMETHING SWEET TO EAT.
HEY, DUMB GRANDKID! WHIP UP ONE OF THOSE!
DON'T CALL ME DUMB, GRANDDAD!
ORDER UP!
WAAH!
IT'S SO PRETTY. ARE YOU SURE I CAN EAT IT...?
IT'S ON MY GRANDDAD. DON'T HOLD BACK. EAT UP.

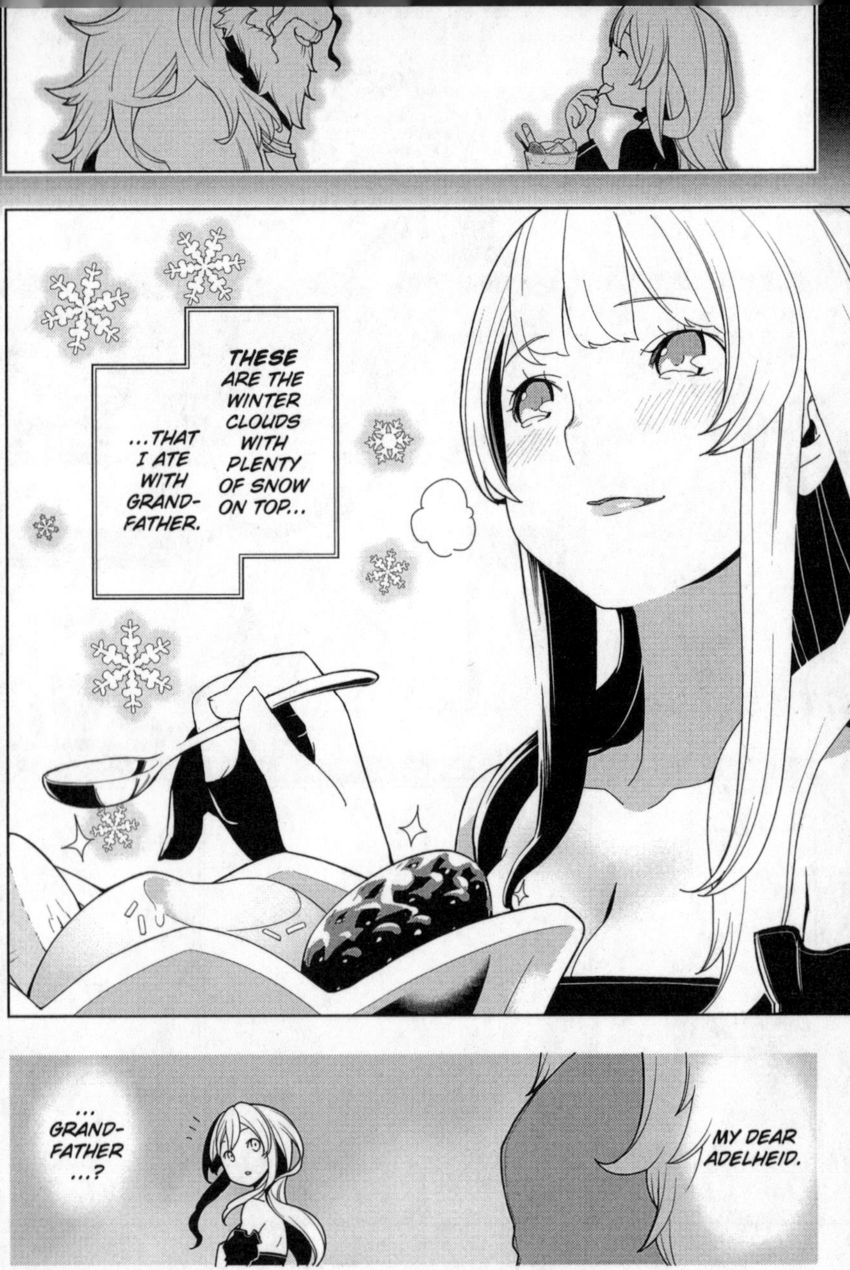
THESE ARE THE WINTER CLOUDS WITH PLENTY OF SNOW ON TOP...
...THAT I ATE WITH GRAND-FATHER.
MY DEAR ADELHEID.
...GRAND-FATHER...?

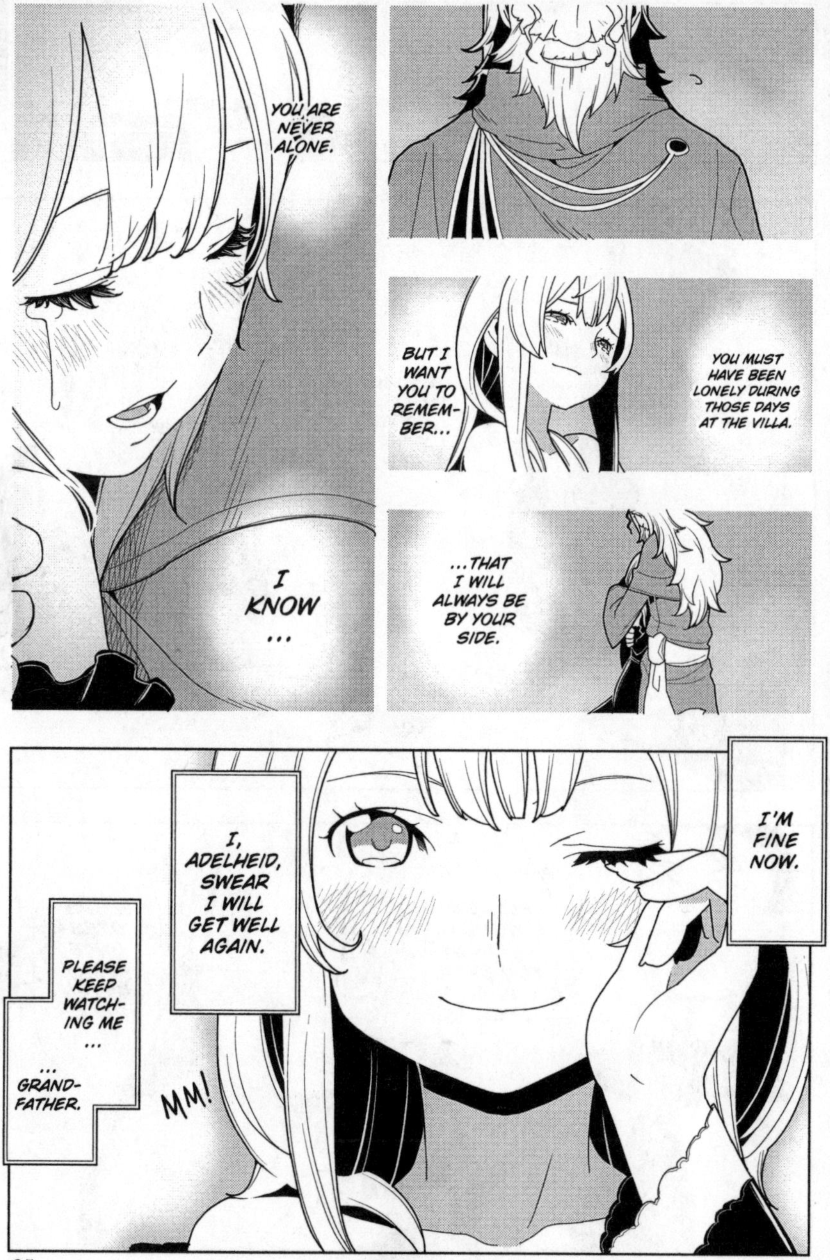
YOU MUST HAVE BEEN LONELY DURING THOSE DAYS AT THE VILLA.
BUT I WANT YOU TO REMEMBER...
...THAT I WILL ALWAYS BE BY YOUR SIDE.
YOU ARE NEVER ALONE.
I KNOW ...
I'M FINE NOW.
I, ADELHEID, SWEAR I WILL GET WELL AGAIN.
MM!
PLEASE KEEP WATCHING ME ...
... GRANDFATHER.

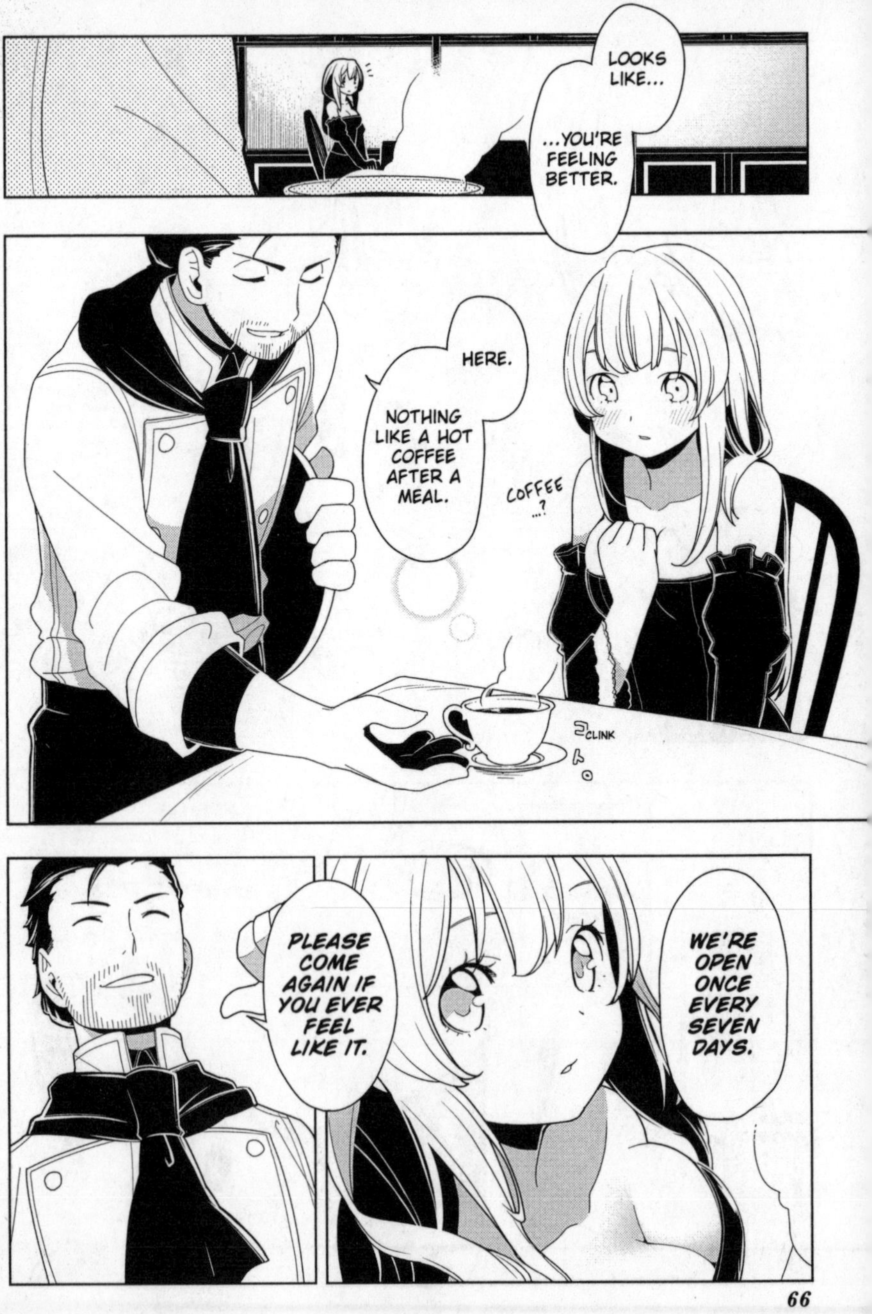
LOOKS LIKE...
...YOU'RE FEELING BETTER.
HERE.
NOTHING LIKE A HOT COFFEE AFTER A MEAL.
COFFEE ...?
CLINK
WE'RE OPEN ONCE EVERY SEVEN DAYS.
PLEASE COME AGAIN IF YOU EVER FEEL LIKE IT.

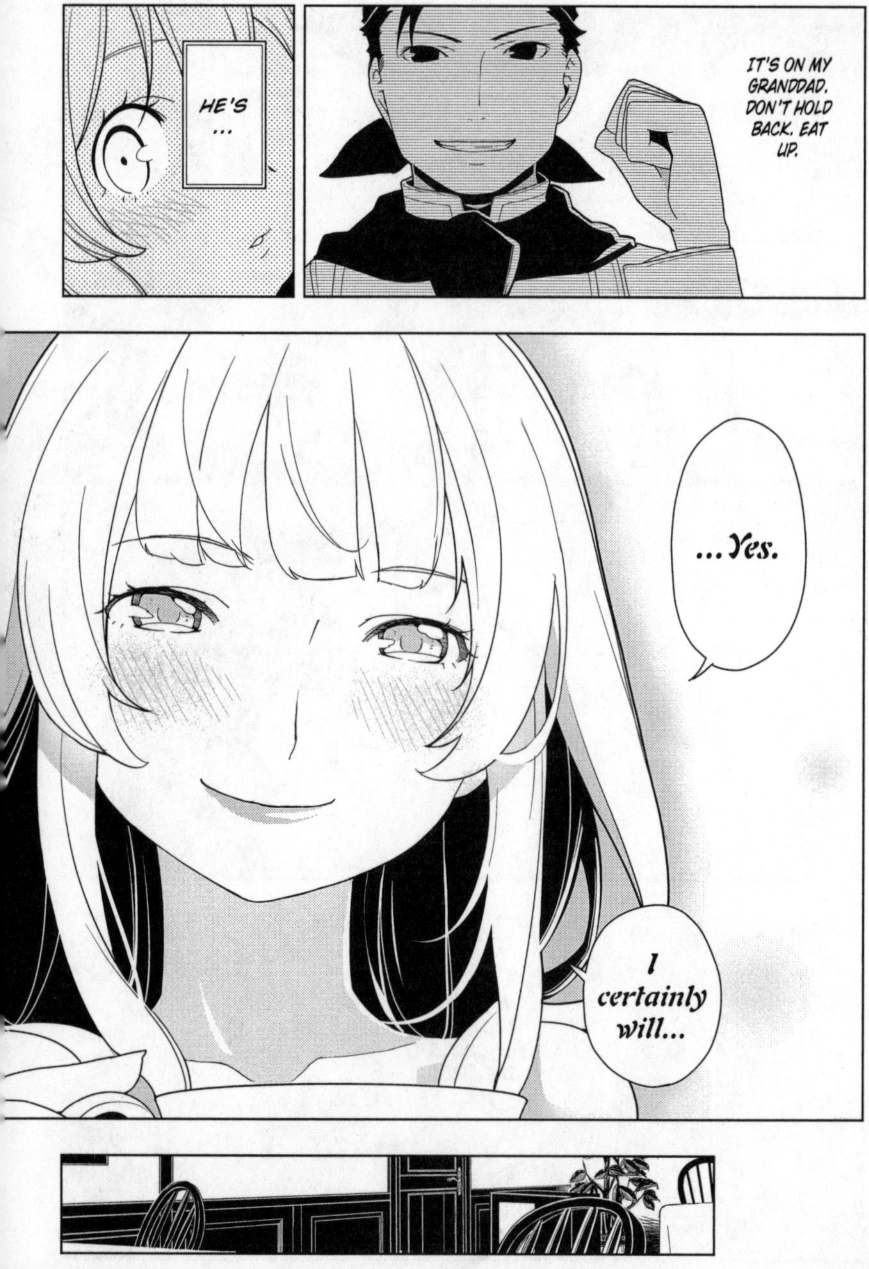
IT'S ON MY GRANDDAD. DON'T HOLD BACK. EAT UP.
HE'S ...
...Yes.
I certainly will...

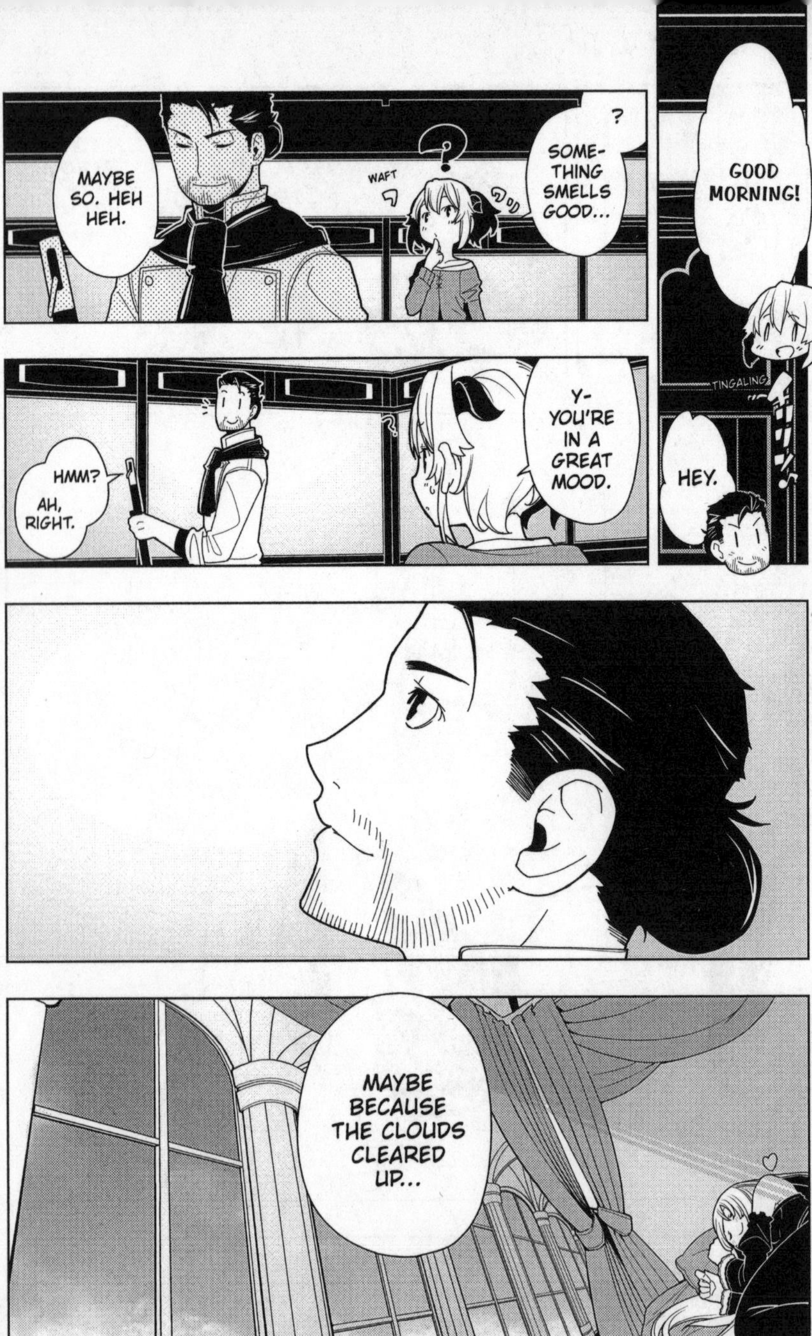
GOOD MORNING!
TINGALING
HEY.
?
SOME-THING SMELLS GOOD...
WAFT
MAYBE SO. HEH HEH.
Y-YOU'RE IN A GREAT MOOD.
HMM? AH, RIGHT.
MAYBE BECAUSE THE CLOUDS CLEARED UP...

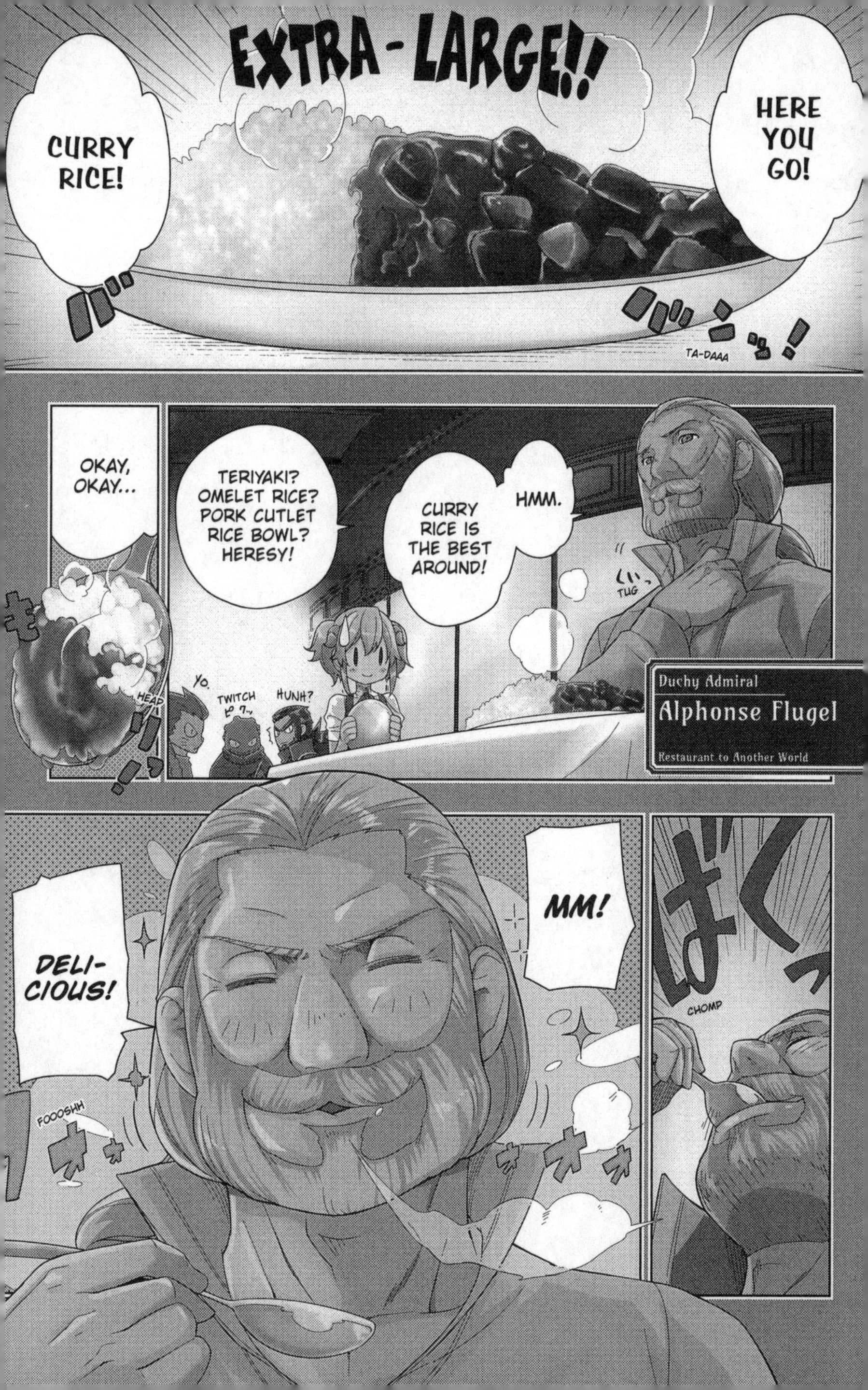
HERE YOU GO!
EXTRA-LARGE!!
CURRY RICE!
TA-DAAA
HMM.
CURRY RICE IS THE BEST AROUND!
TERIYAKI? OMELET RICE? PORK CUTLET RICE BOWL? HERESY!
TUG
Duchy Admiral
Alphonse Flugel
Restaurant to Another World
HUNH?
TWITCH
YO.
OKAY, OKAY...
HEAP
CHOMP
MM!
DELI-CIOUS!
FOOOSHH

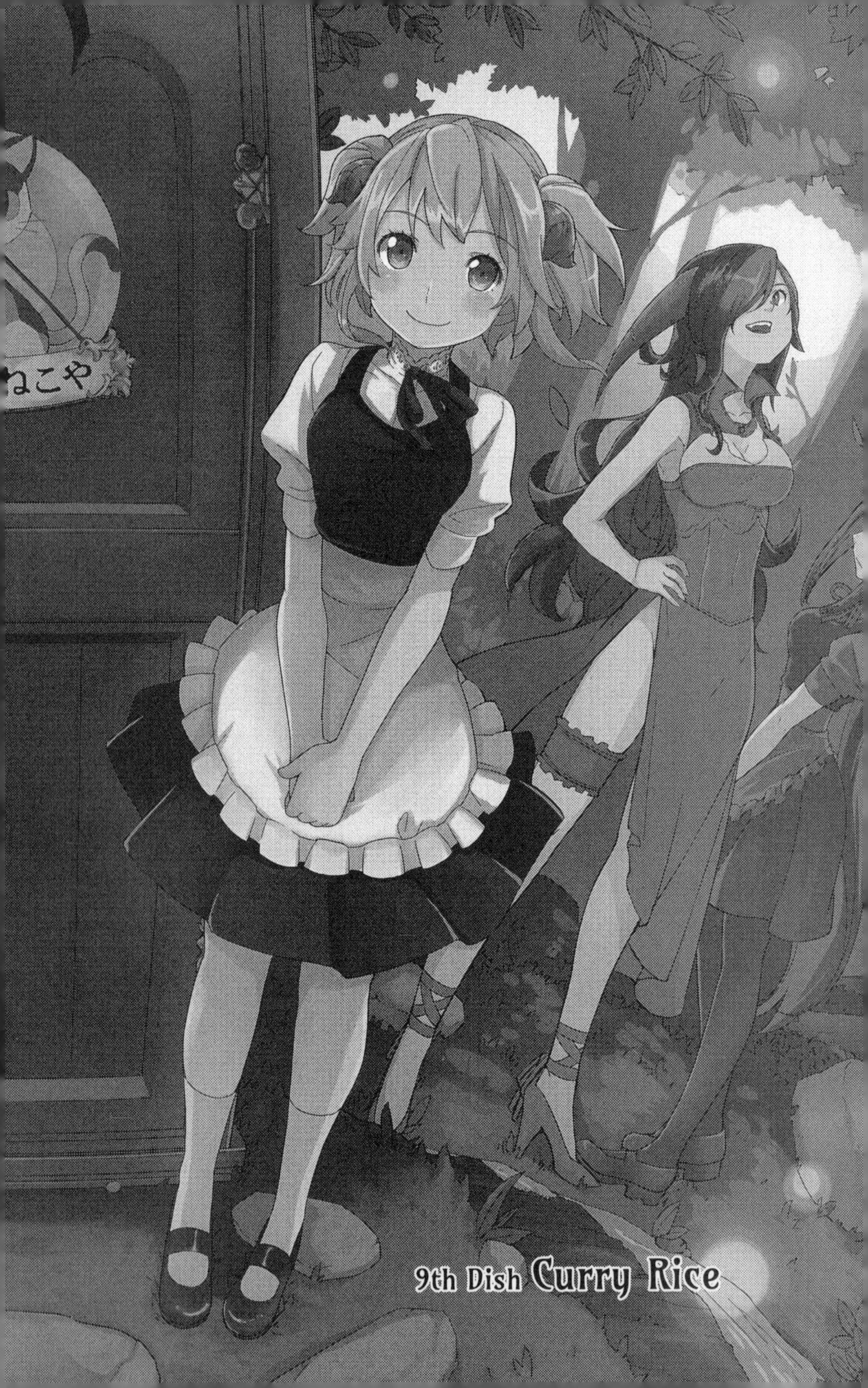
ねこや
9th Dish Curry Rice

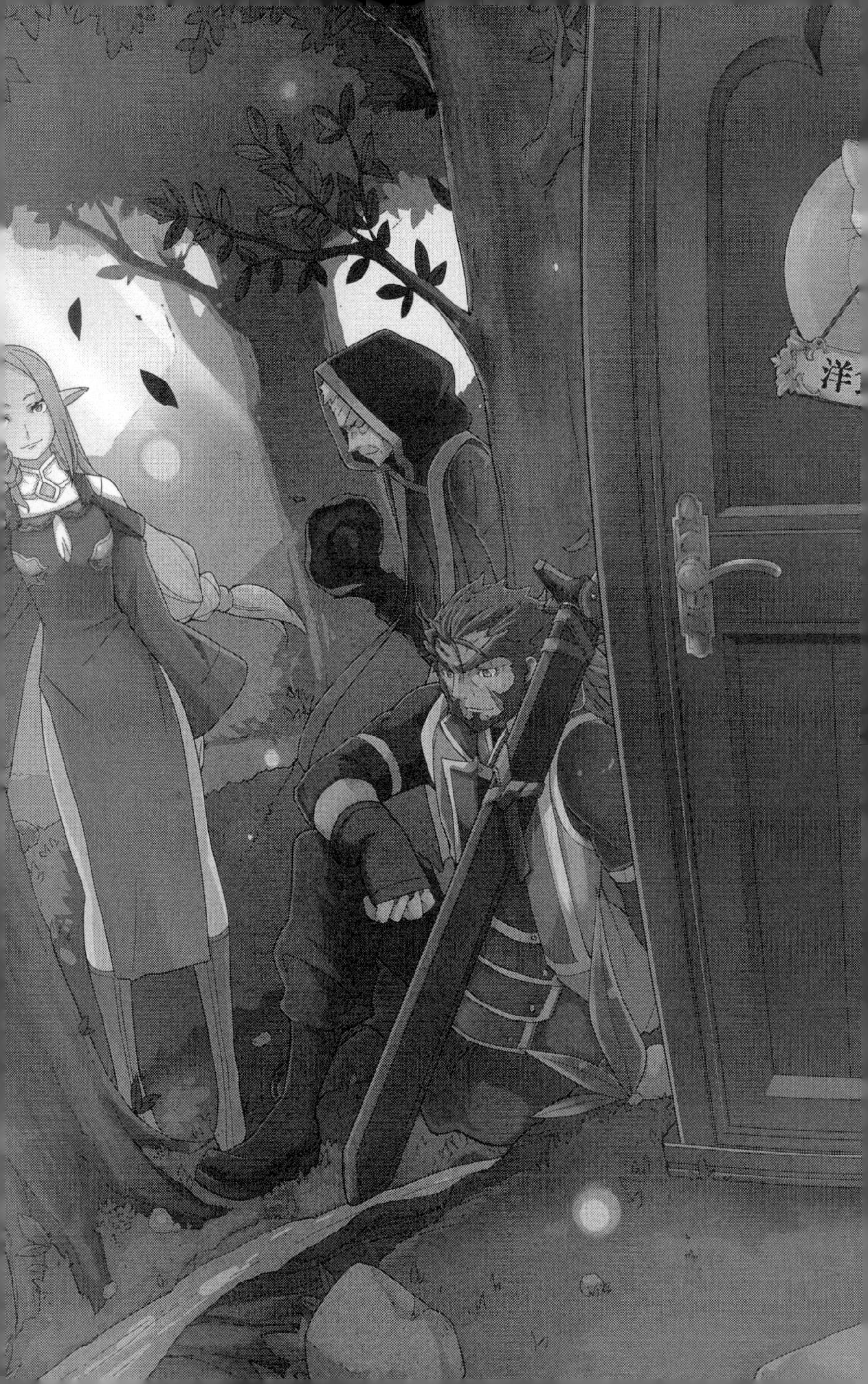

洋

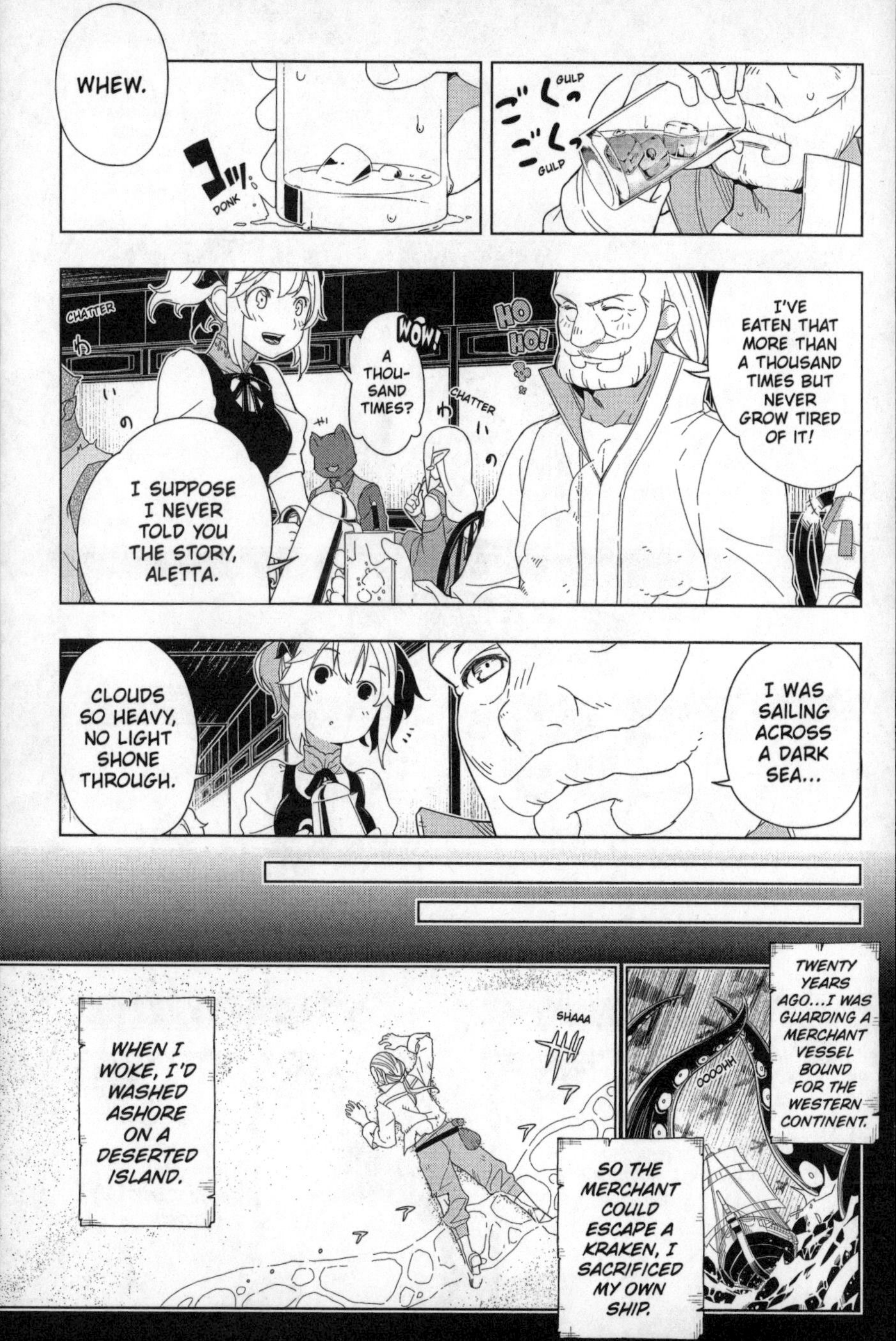
GULP
ごくっ
ごくっ
GULP
DONK
WHEW.
I'VE EATEN THAT MORE THAN A THOUSAND TIMES BUT NEVER GROW TIRED OF IT!
HO HO!
WOW!
A THOUSAND TIMES?
CHATTER
CHATTER
I SUPPOSE I NEVER TOLD YOU THE STORY, ALETTA.
I WAS SAILING ACROSS A DARK SEA...
CLOUDS SO HEAVY, NO LIGHT SHONE THROUGH.
TWENTY YEARS AGO...I WAS GUARDING A MERCHANT VESSEL BOUND FOR THE WESTERN CONTINENT.
OOOOHH
SO THE MERCHANT COULD ESCAPE A KRAKEN, I SACRIFICED MY OWN SHIP.
SHAAA
WHEN I WOKE, I'D WASHED ASHORE ON A DESERTED ISLAND.

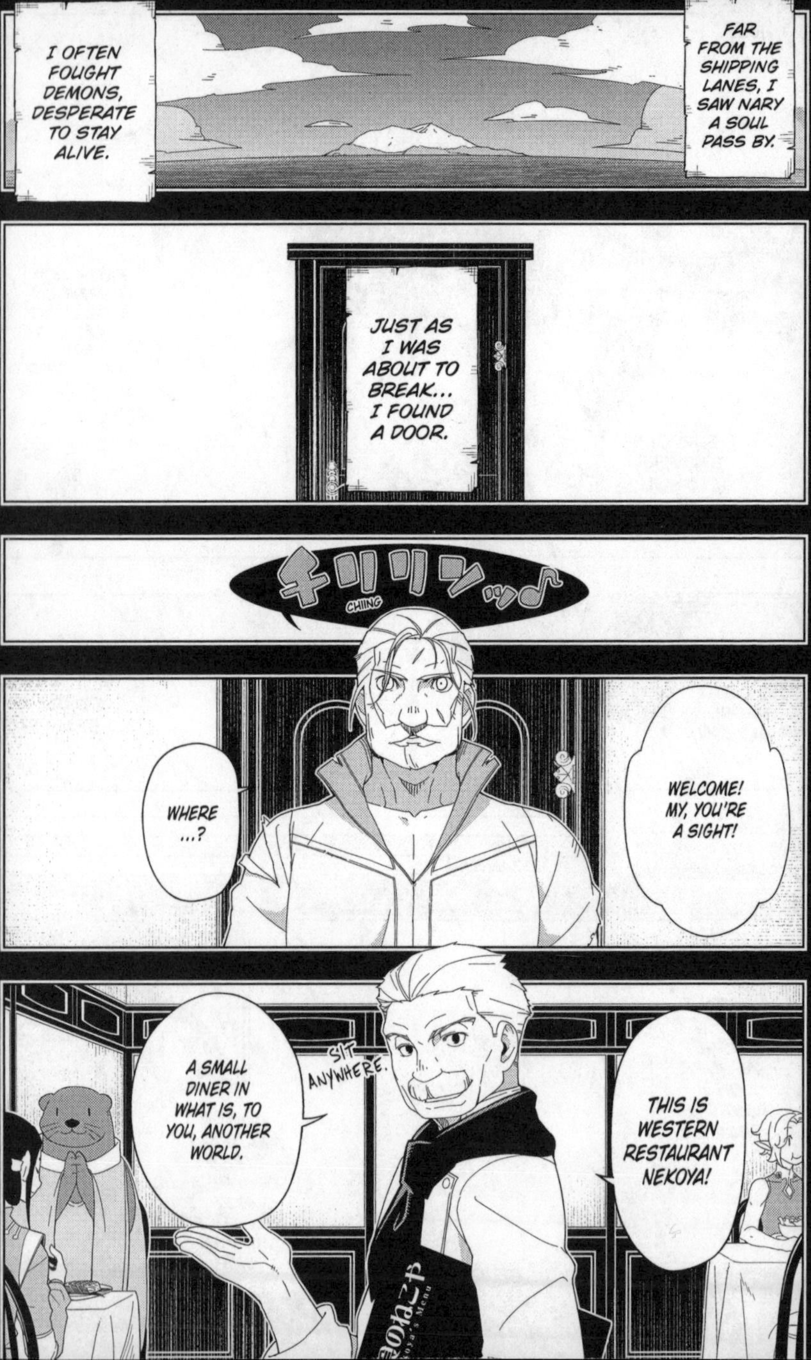
FAR FROM THE SHIPPING LANES, I SAW NARY A SOUL PASS BY.
I OFTEN FOUGHT DEMONS, DESPERATE TO STAY ALIVE.
JUST AS I WAS ABOUT TO BREAK... I FOUND A DOOR.
チリリンッ♪
CHIING
WELCOME! MY, YOU'RE A SIGHT!
WHERE ...?
THIS IS WESTERN RESTAURANT NEKOYA!
SIT ANYWHERE.
A SMALL DINER IN WHAT IS, TO YOU, ANOTHER WORLD.

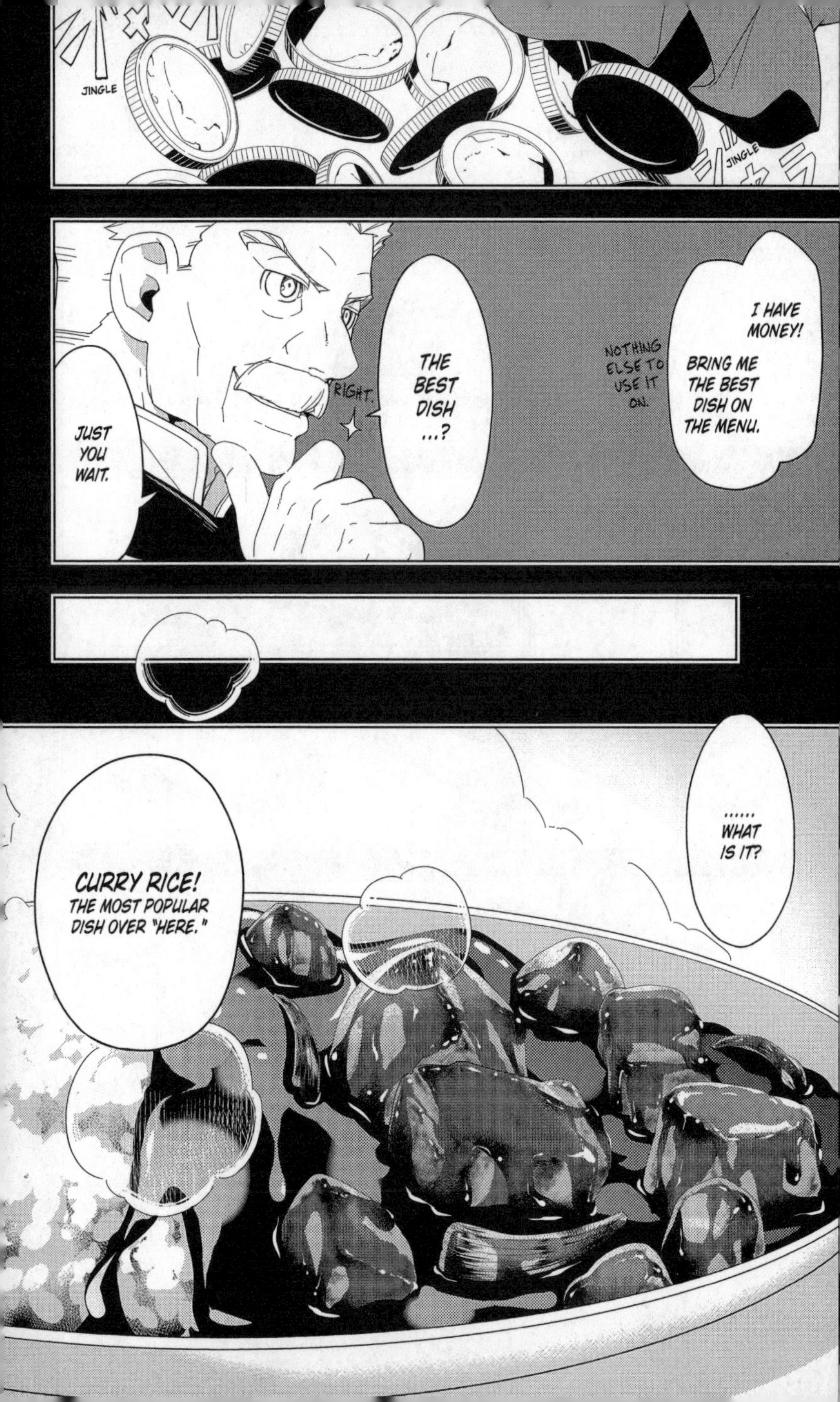
JINGLE
JINGLE
I HAVE MONEY! BRING ME THE BEST DISH ON THE MENU.
NOTHING ELSE TO USE IT ON.
THE BEST DISH ...?
RIGHT.
JUST YOU WAIT.
...... WHAT IS IT?
CURRY RICE! THE MOST POPULAR DISH OVER "HERE."

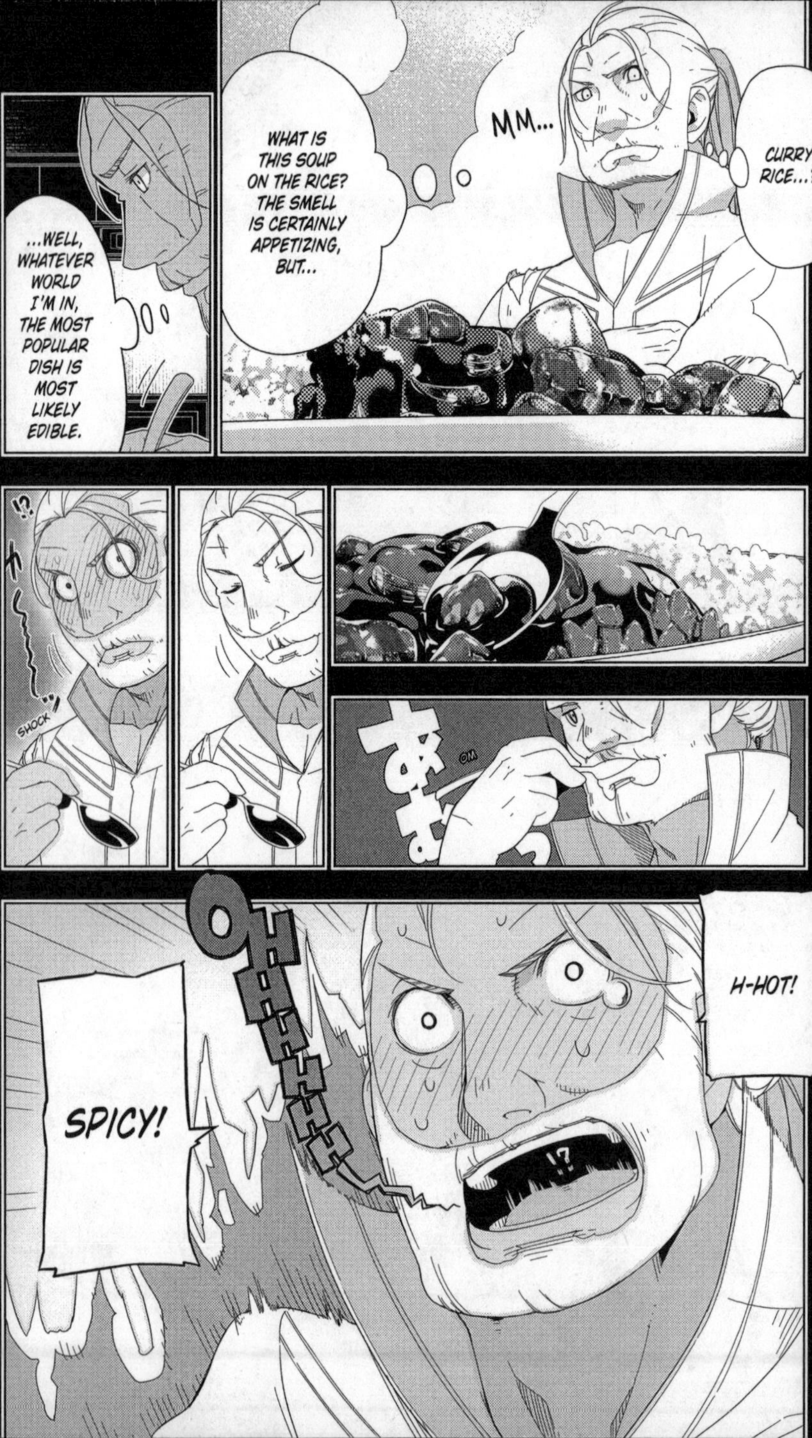
CURRY RICE...?
MM...
WHAT IS THIS SOUP ON THE RICE? THE SMELL IS CERTAINLY APPETIZING, BUT...
...WELL, WHATEVER WORLD I'M IN, THE MOST POPULAR DISH IS MOST LIKELY EDIBLE.
OM
!?
SHOCK
H-HOT!
SPICY!

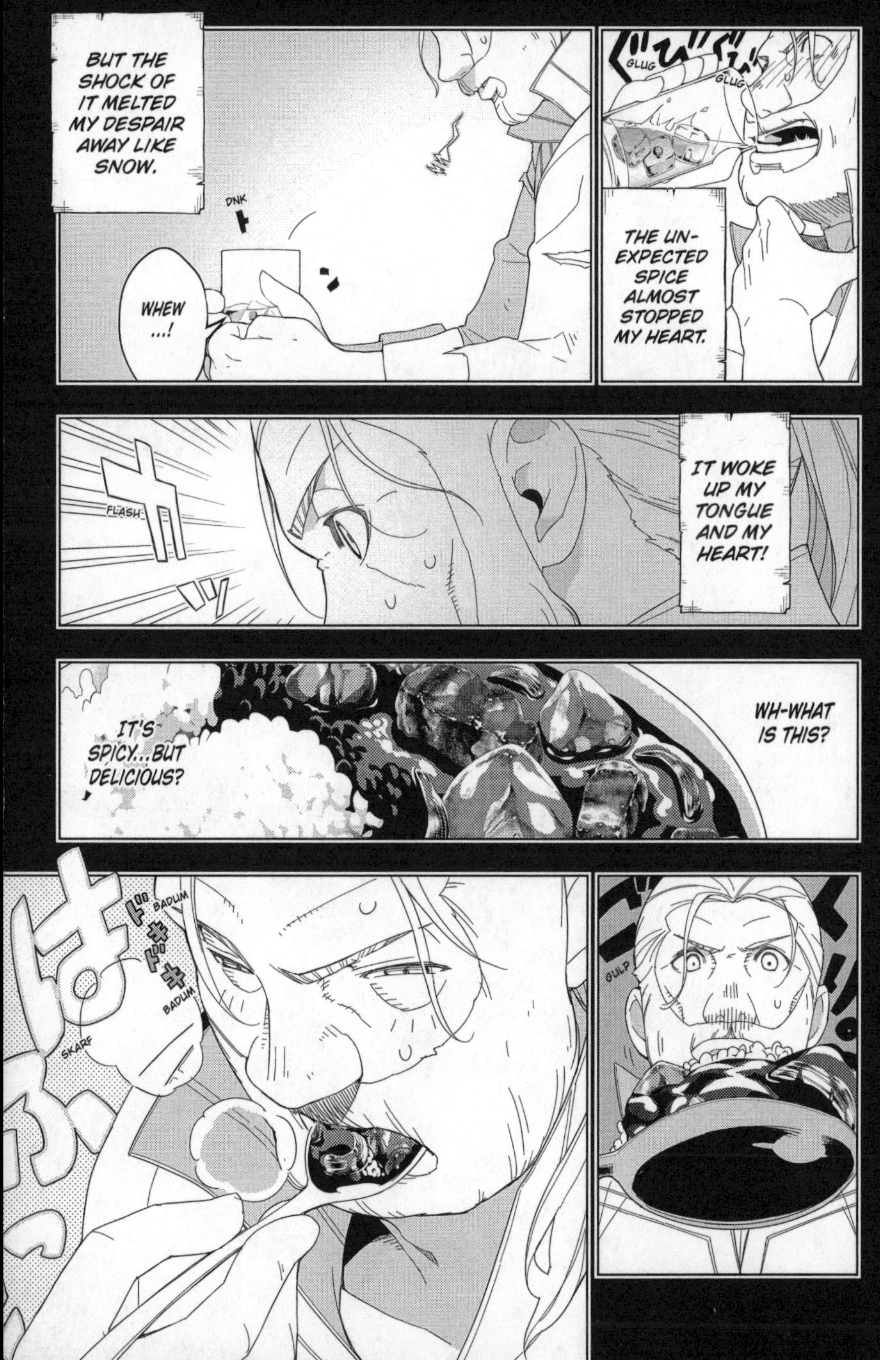
GLUG
GLUG
THE UN-EXPECTED SPICE ALMOST STOPPED MY HEART.
BUT THE SHOCK OF IT MELTED MY DESPAIR AWAY LIKE SNOW.
DNK
WHEW ...!
IT WOKE UP MY TONGUE AND MY HEART!
FLASH
WH-WHAT IS THIS?
IT'S SPICY...BUT DELICIOUS?
GULP
BADUM
BADUM
SKARF

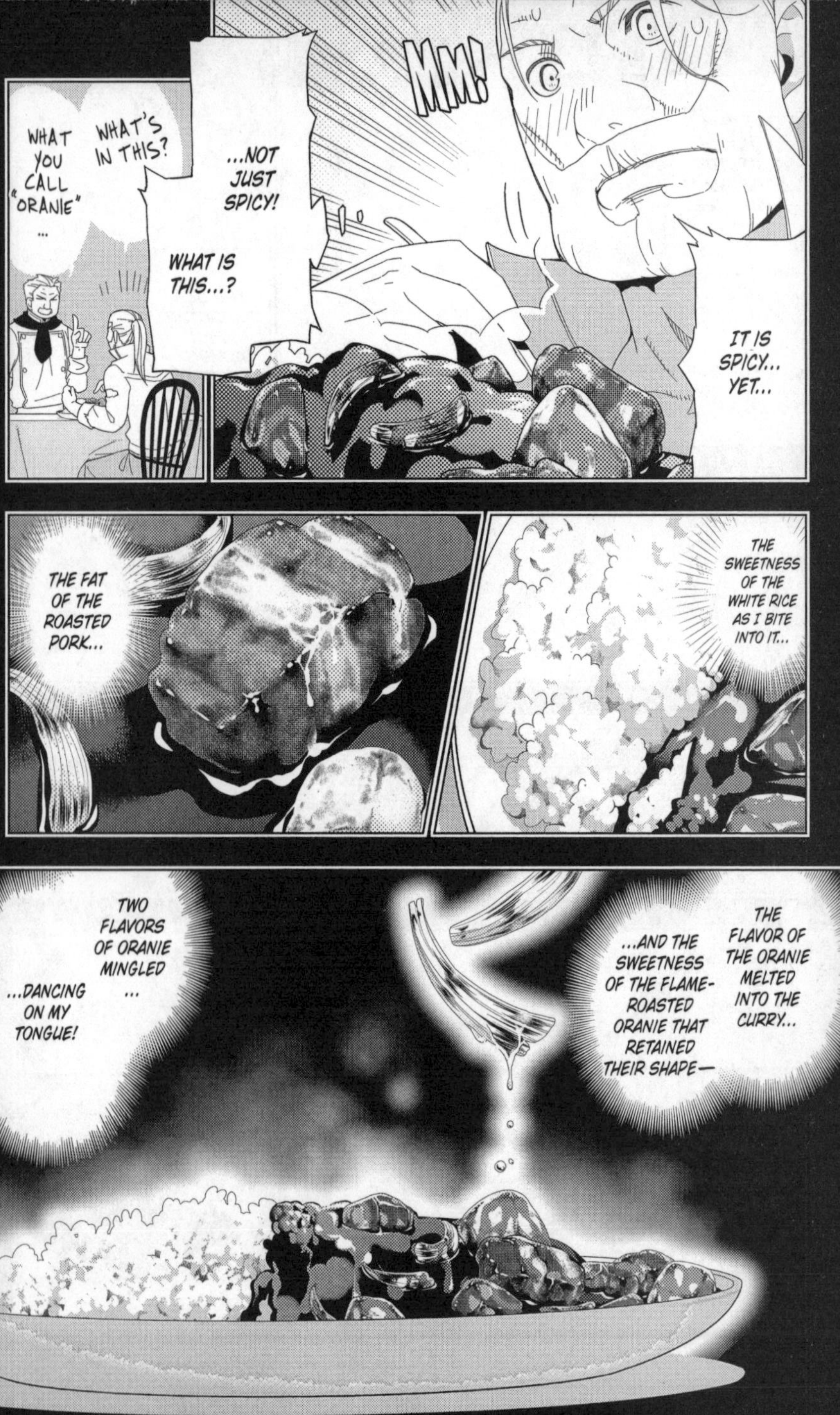
MM!
IT IS SPICY... YET...
...NOT JUST SPICY!
WHAT IS THIS...?
WHAT'S IN THIS?
WHAT YOU CALL "ORANIE"...
THE SWEETNESS OF THE WHITE RICE AS I BITE INTO IT...
THE FAT OF THE ROASTED PORK...
THE FLAVOR OF THE ORANIE MELTED INTO THE CURRY...
...AND THE SWEETNESS OF THE FLAME-ROASTED ORANIE THAT RETAINED THEIR SHAPE—
TWO FLAVORS OF ORANIE MINGLED...
...DANCING ON MY TONGUE!

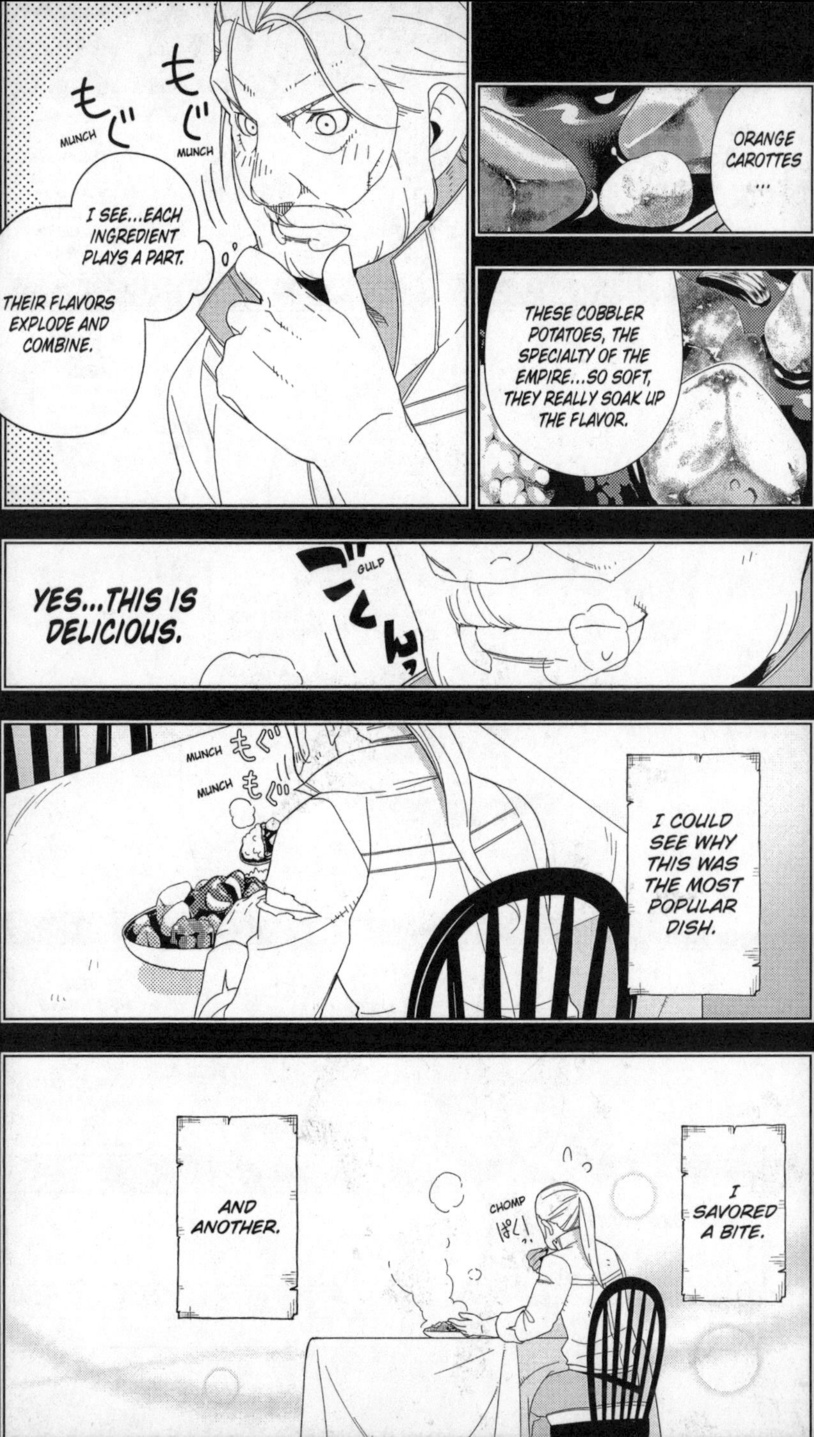
ORANGE CAROTTES ...
THESE COBBLER POTATOES, THE SPECIALTY OF THE EMPIRE...SO SOFT, THEY REALLY SOAK UP THE FLAVOR.
MUNCH
MUNCH
I SEE...EACH INGREDIENT PLAYS A PART.
THEIR FLAVORS EXPLODE AND COMBINE.
GULP
YES...THIS IS DELICIOUS.
MUNCH
MUNCH
I COULD SEE WHY THIS WAS THE MOST POPULAR DISH.
I SAVORED A BITE.
CHOMP
AND ANOTHER.

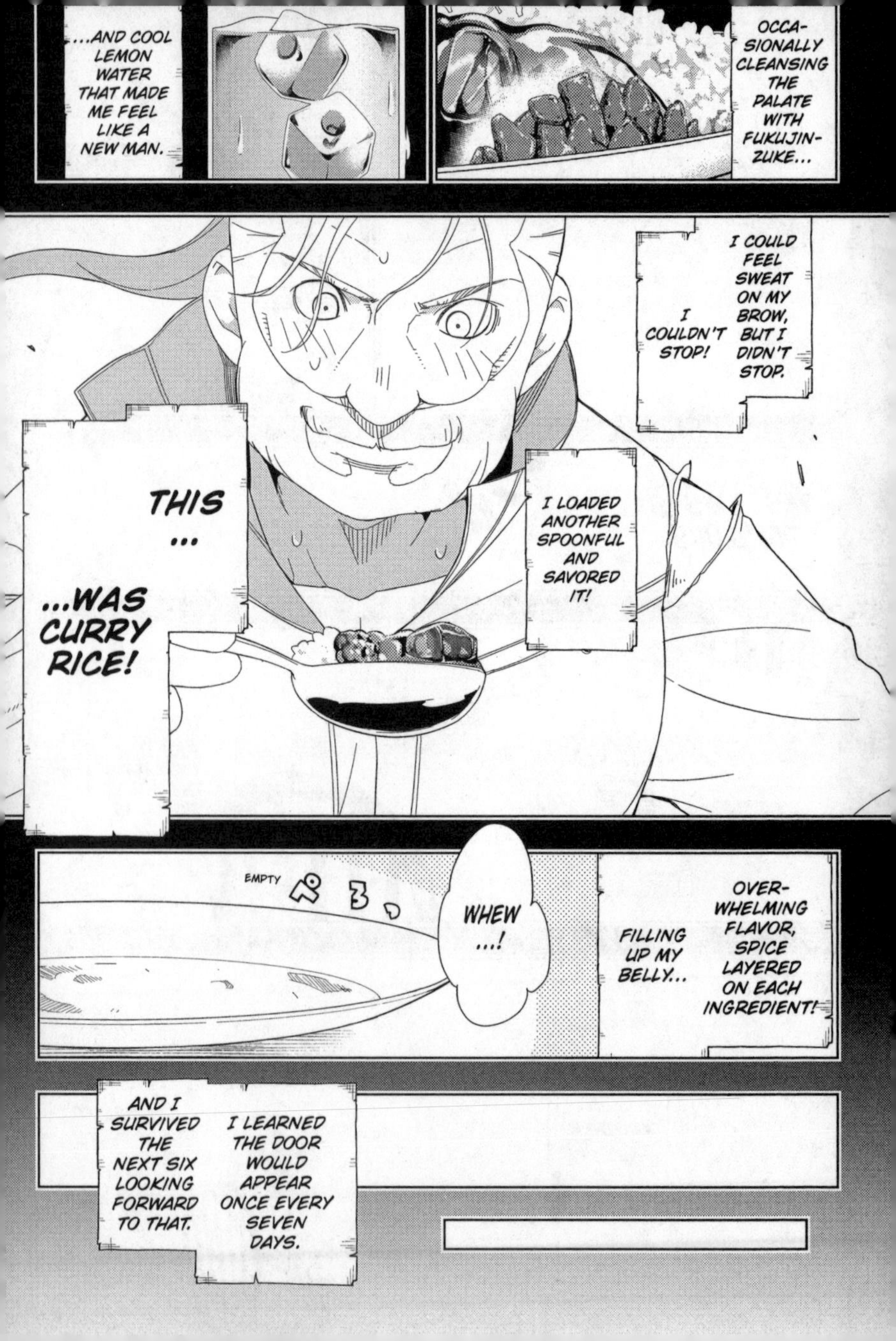
OCCASIONALLY CLEANSING THE PALATE WITH FUKUJIN-ZUKE...
...AND COOL LEMON WATER THAT MADE ME FEEL LIKE A NEW MAN.
I COULD FEEL SWEAT ON MY BROW, BUT I DIDN'T STOP.
I COULDN'T STOP!
I LOADED ANOTHER SPOONFUL AND SAVORED IT!
THIS...
...WAS CURRY RICE!
OVER-WHELMING FLAVOR, SPICE LAYERED ON EACH INGREDIENT!
FILLING UP MY BELLY...
WHEW...!
EMPTY
I LEARNED THE DOOR WOULD APPEAR ONCE EVERY SEVEN DAYS.
AND I SURVIVED THE NEXT SIX LOOKING FORWARD TO THAT.

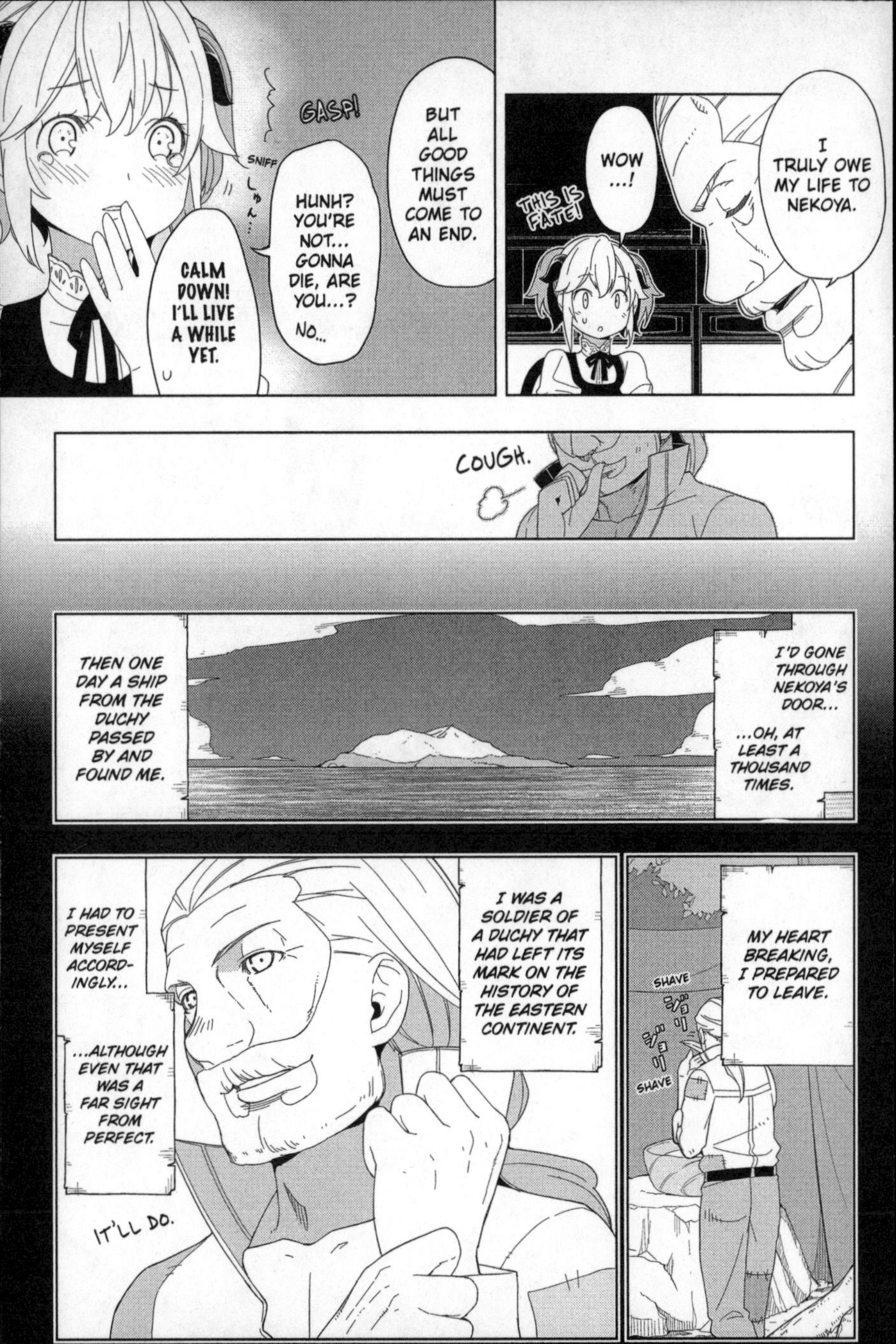
I TRULY OWE MY LIFE TO NEKOYA.
WOW ...!
THIS IS FATE!
BUT ALL GOOD THINGS MUST COME TO AN END.
GASP!
SNIFF
しゅん…
HUNH? YOU'RE NOT... GONNA DIE, ARE YOU...?
NO...
CALM DOWN! I'LL LIVE A WHILE YET.
COUGH.
I'D GONE THROUGH NEKOYA'S DOOR...
...OH, AT LEAST A THOUSAND TIMES.
THEN ONE DAY A SHIP FROM THE DUCHY PASSED BY AND FOUND ME.
MY HEART BREAKING, I PREPARED TO LEAVE.
SHAVE
ジョリ
ジョリ
SHAVE
I WAS A SOLDIER OF A DUCHY THAT HAD LEFT ITS MARK ON THE HISTORY OF THE EASTERN CONTINENT.
I HAD TO PRESENT MYSELF ACCORDINGLY...
...ALTHOUGH EVEN THAT WAS A FAR SIGHT FROM PERFECT.
IT'LL DO.

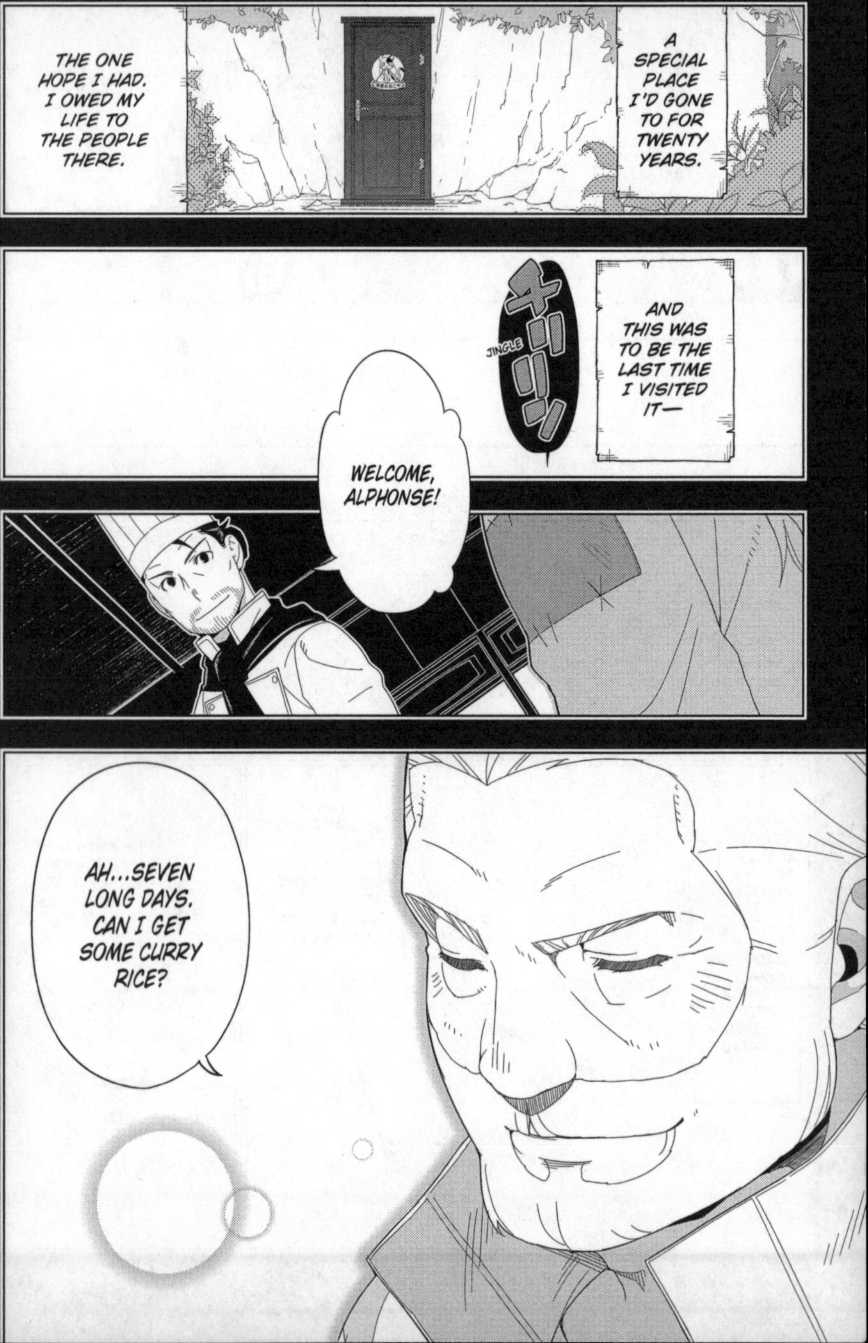
A SPECIAL PLACE I'D GONE TO FOR TWENTY YEARS.
THE ONE HOPE I HAD. I OWED MY LIFE TO THE PEOPLE THERE.
AND THIS WAS TO BE THE LAST TIME I VISITED IT—
チリリン
JINGLE
WELCOME, ALPHONSE!
AH...SEVEN LONG DAYS. CAN I GET SOME CURRY RICE?

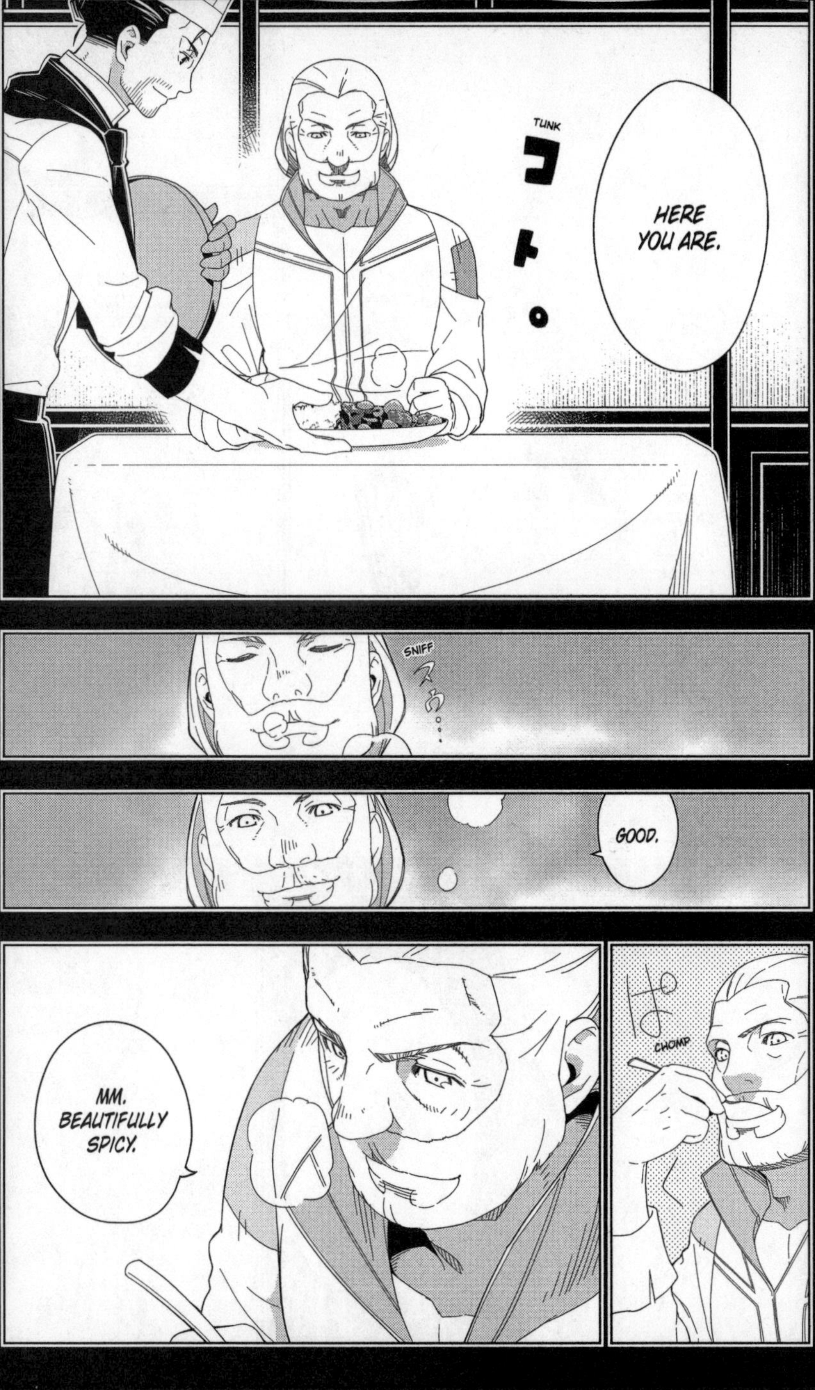
TUNK
HERE YOU ARE.
SNIFF
GOOD.
CHOMP
MM. BEAUTIFULLY SPICY.

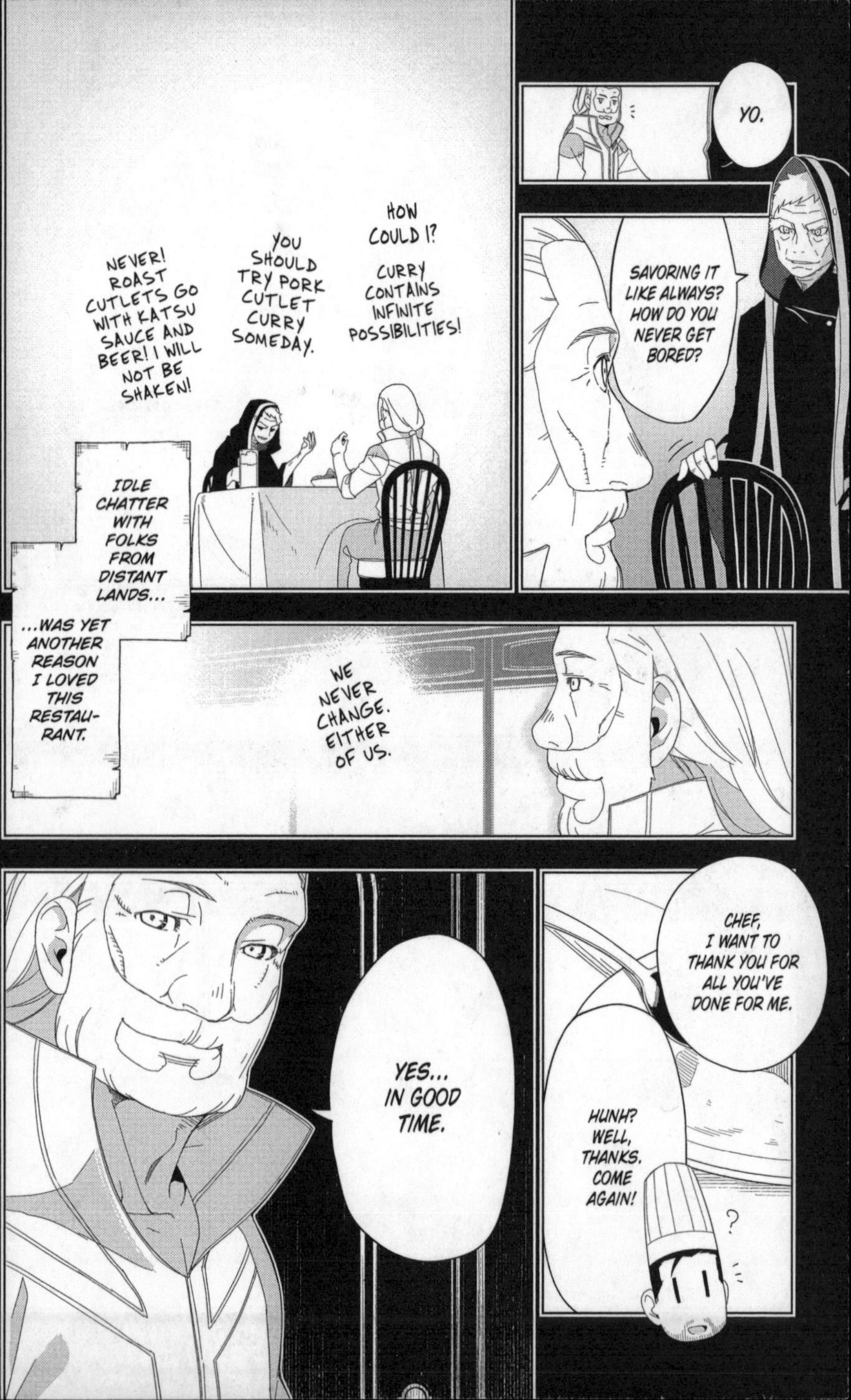

YO.
SAVORING IT LIKE ALWAYS? HOW DO YOU NEVER GET BORED?
HOW COULD I? CURRY CONTAINS INFINITE POSSIBILITIES!
YOU SHOULD TRY PORK CUTLET CURRY SOMEDAY.
NEVER! ROAST CUTLETS GO WITH KATSU SAUCE AND BEER! I WILL NOT BE SHAKEN!
IDLE CHATTER WITH FOLKS FROM DISTANT LANDS...
...WAS YET ANOTHER REASON I LOVED THIS RESTAU-RANT.
WE NEVER CHANGE. EITHER OF US.
CHEF, I WANT TO THANK YOU FOR ALL YOU'VE DONE FOR ME.
HUNH? WELL, THANKS. COME AGAIN!
?
YES... IN GOOD TIME.

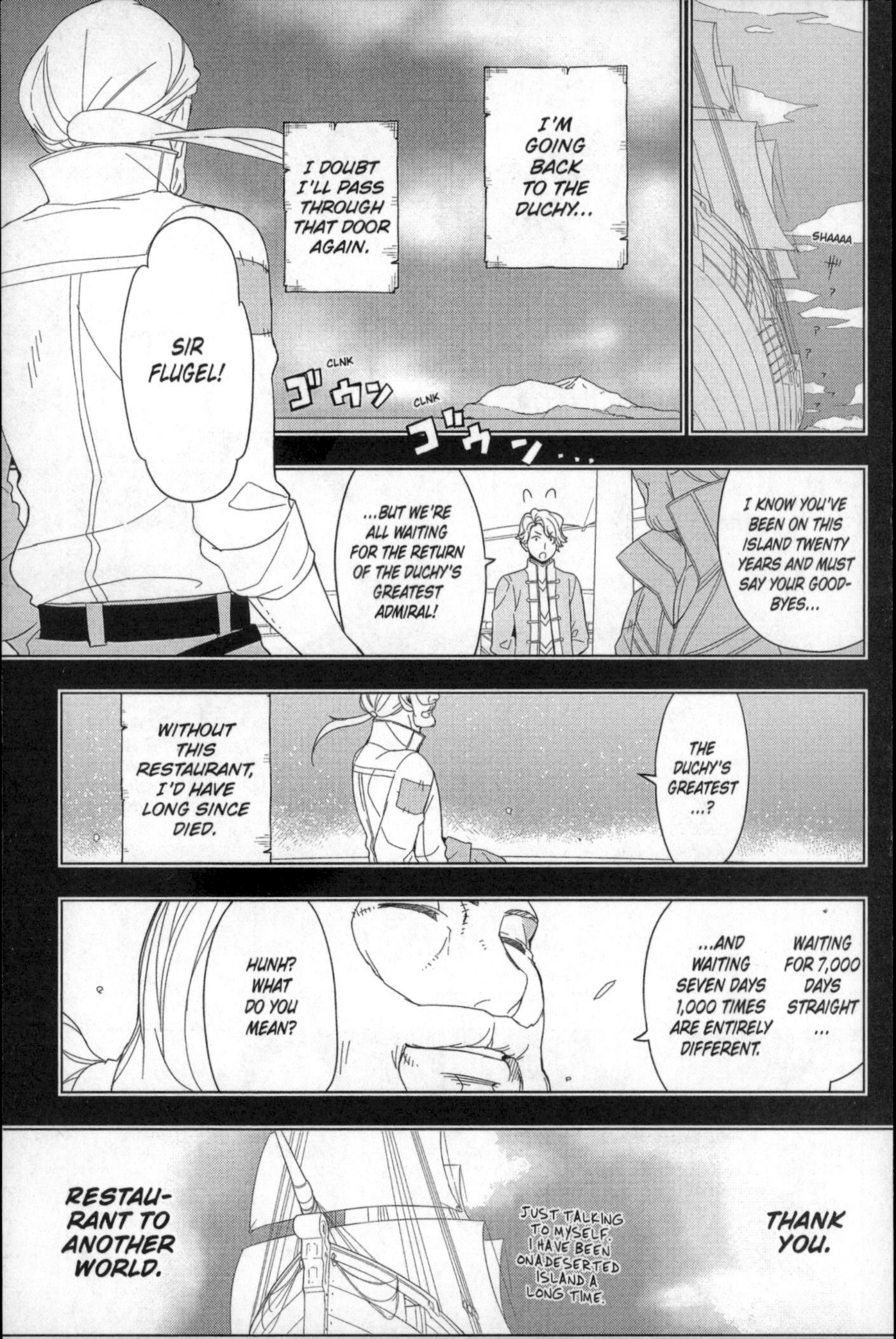
SHAAAA
I'M GOING BACK TO THE DUCHY...
I DOUBT I'LL PASS THROUGH THAT DOOR AGAIN.
SIR FLUGEL!
CLNK
ゴウン
CLNK
ゴウン...
I KNOW YOU'VE BEEN ON THIS ISLAND TWENTY YEARS AND MUST SAY YOUR GOOD-BYES...
...BUT WE'RE ALL WAITING FOR THE RETURN OF THE DUCHY'S GREATEST ADMIRAL!
THE DUCHY'S GREATEST ...?
WITHOUT THIS RESTAURANT, I'D HAVE LONG SINCE DIED.
WAITING FOR 7,000 DAYS STRAIGHT ...
...AND WAITING SEVEN DAYS 1,000 TIMES ARE ENTIRELY DIFFERENT.
HUNH? WHAT DO YOU MEAN?
THANK YOU.
JUST TALKING TO MYSELF. I HAVE BEEN ON A DESERTED ISLAND A LONG TIME.
RESTAURANT TO ANOTHER WORLD.

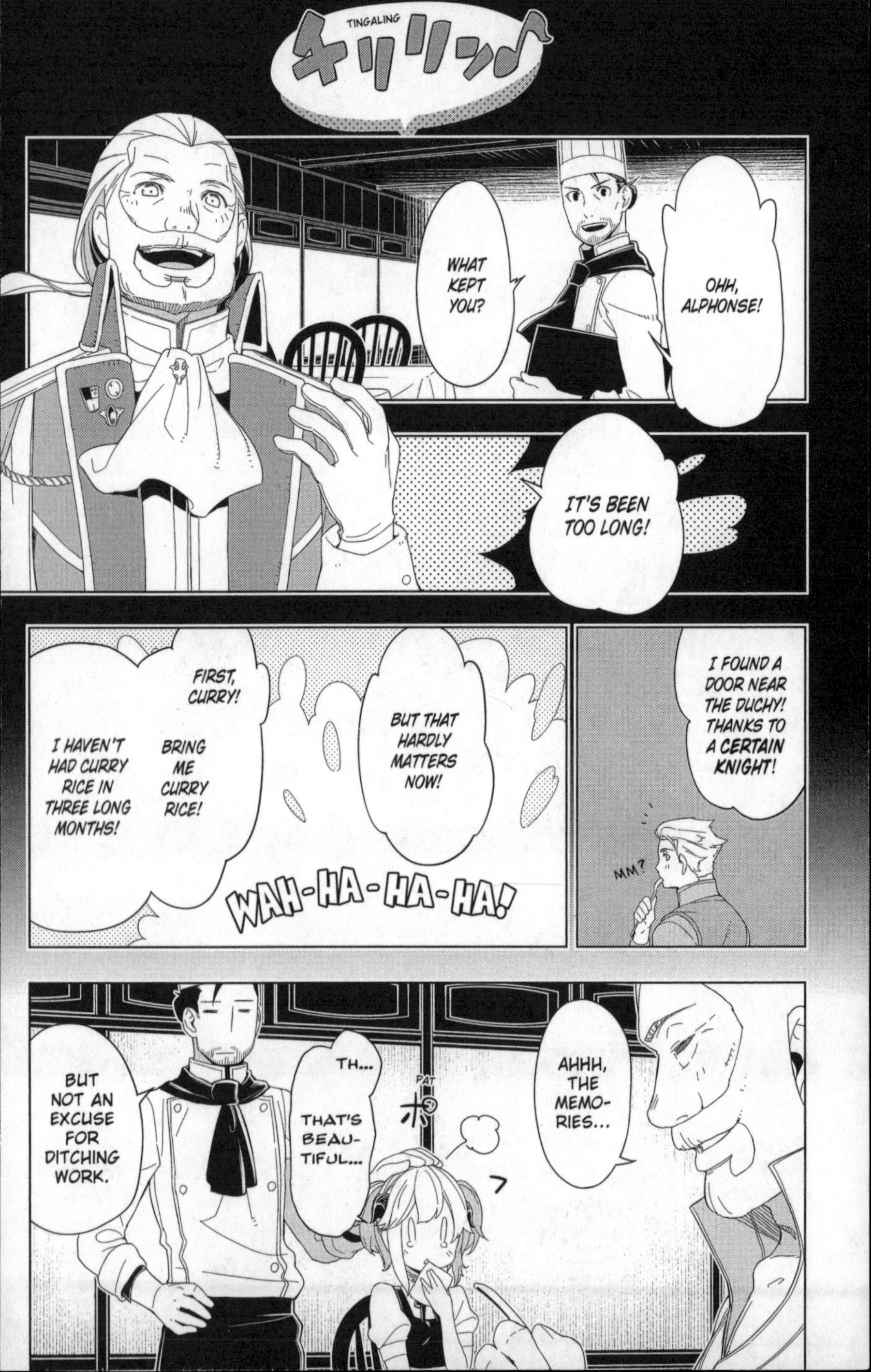
TINGALING
チリリッ♪
OHH, ALPHONSE!
WHAT KEPT YOU?
IT'S BEEN TOO LONG!
I FOUND A DOOR NEAR THE DUCHY! THANKS TO A CERTAIN KNIGHT!
MM?
BUT THAT HARDLY MATTERS NOW!
FIRST, CURRY!
BRING ME CURRY RICE!
I HAVEN'T HAD CURRY RICE IN THREE LONG MONTHS!
WAH-HA-HA-HA!
AHHH, THE MEMO-RIES...
PAT
ポ
TH...
THAT'S BEAU-TIFUL...
BUT NOT AN EXCUSE FOR DITCHING WORK.

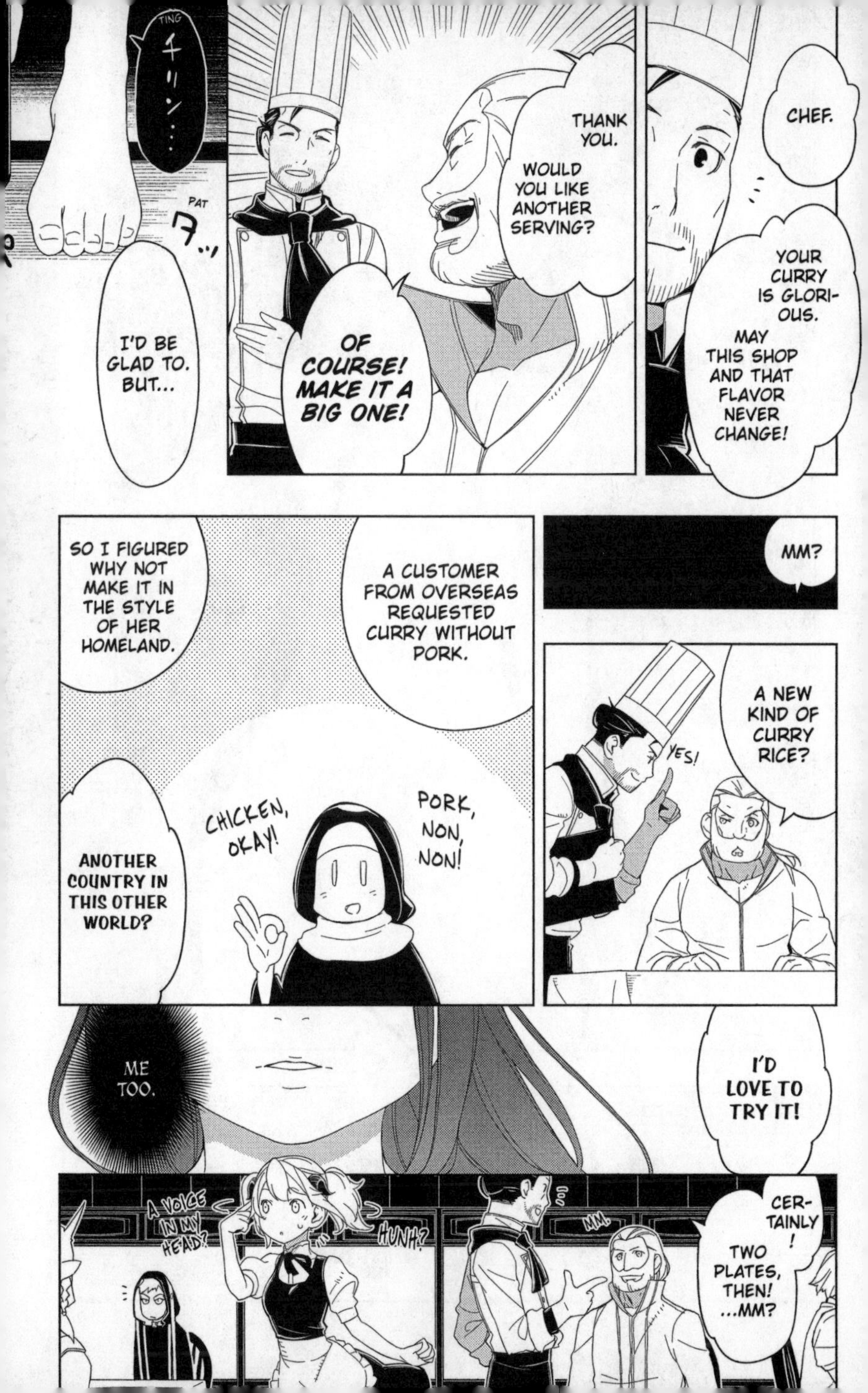
CHEF.
YOUR CURRY IS GLORIOUS.
MAY THIS SHOP AND THAT FLAVOR NEVER CHANGE!
THANK YOU.
WOULD YOU LIKE ANOTHER SERVING?
OF COURSE! MAKE IT A BIG ONE!
TING
チリン…
PAT
I'D BE GLAD TO. BUT...
MM?
A NEW KIND OF CURRY RICE?
YES!
A CUSTOMER FROM OVERSEAS REQUESTED CURRY WITHOUT PORK.
SO I FIGURED WHY NOT MAKE IT IN THE STYLE OF HER HOMELAND.
PORK, NON, NON!
CHICKEN, OKAY!
ANOTHER COUNTRY IN THIS OTHER WORLD?
I'D LOVE TO TRY IT!
ME TOO.
CERTAINLY! TWO PLATES, THEN! ...MM?
MM.
HUNH?
A VOICE IN MY HEAD?

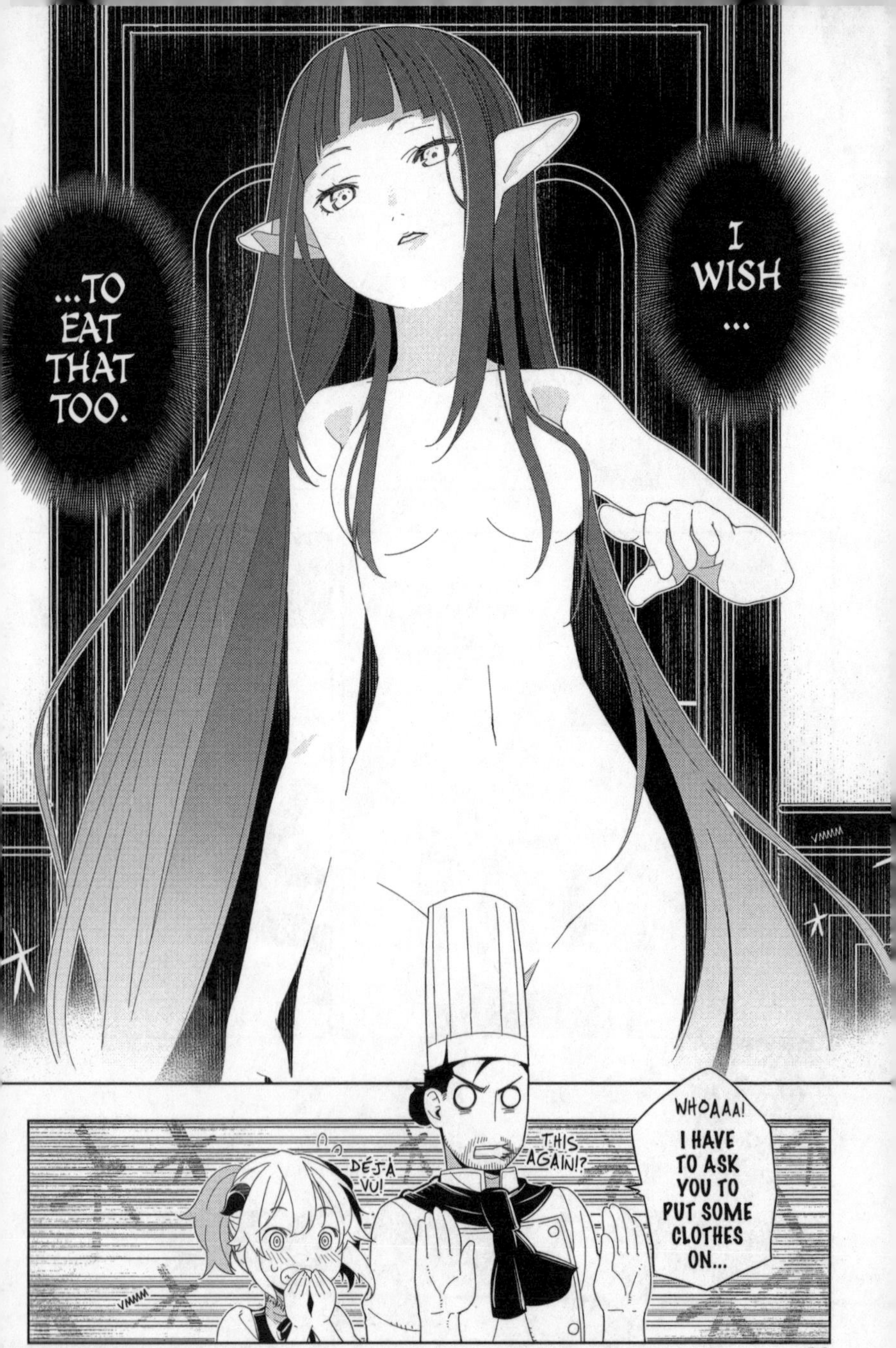
I WISH ...
...TO EAT THAT TOO.
VMMMM
WHOAAA! I HAVE TO ASK YOU TO PUT SOME CLOTHES ON...
THIS AGAIN!?
DÉJÀ VU!
VMMMM

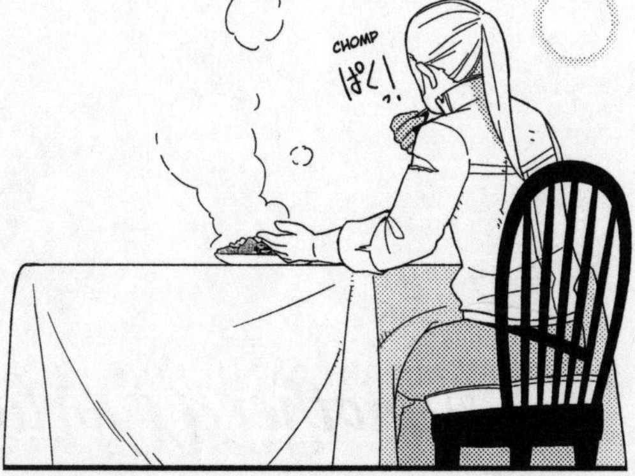
CHOMP
ぱく!

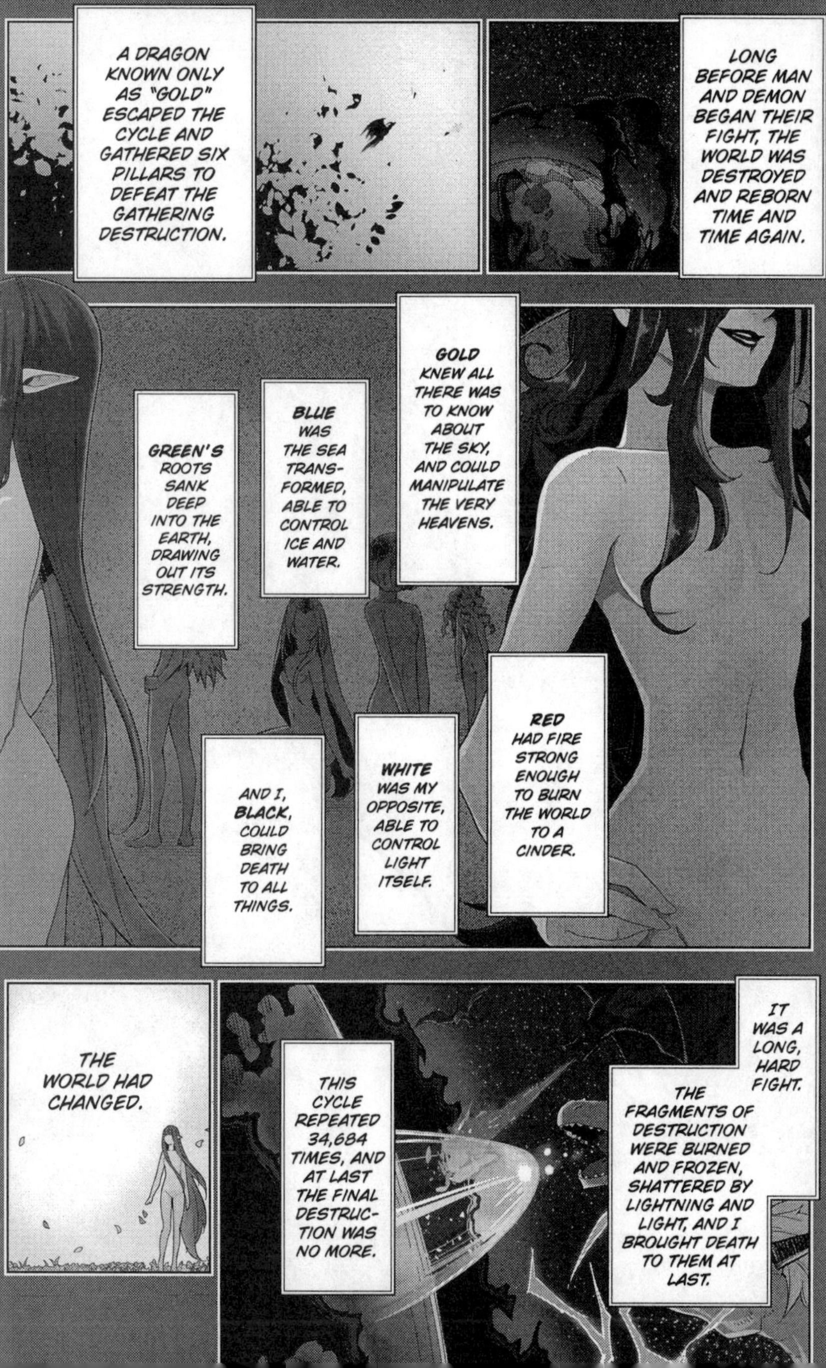
LONG BEFORE MAN AND DEMON BEGAN THEIR FIGHT, THE WORLD WAS DESTROYED AND REBORN TIME AND TIME AGAIN.
A DRAGON KNOWN ONLY AS "GOLD" ESCAPED THE CYCLE AND GATHERED SIX PILLARS TO DEFEAT THE GATHERING DESTRUCTION.
GOLD KNEW ALL THERE WAS TO KNOW ABOUT THE SKY, AND COULD MANIPULATE THE VERY HEAVENS.
BLUE WAS THE SEA TRANS-FORMED, ABLE TO CONTROL ICE AND WATER.
GREEN'S ROOTS SANK DEEP INTO THE EARTH, DRAWING OUT ITS STRENGTH.
RED HAD FIRE STRONG ENOUGH TO BURN THE WORLD TO A CINDER.
WHITE WAS MY OPPOSITE, ABLE TO CONTROL LIGHT ITSELF.
AND I, BLACK, COULD BRING DEATH TO ALL THINGS.
IT WAS A LONG, HARD FIGHT.
THE FRAGMENTS OF DESTRUCTION WERE BURNED AND FROZEN, SHATTERED BY LIGHTNING AND LIGHT, AND I BROUGHT DEATH TO THEM AT LAST.
THIS CYCLE REPEATED 34,684 TIMES, AND AT LAST THE FINAL DESTRUC-TION WAS NO MORE.
THE WORLD HAD CHANGED.

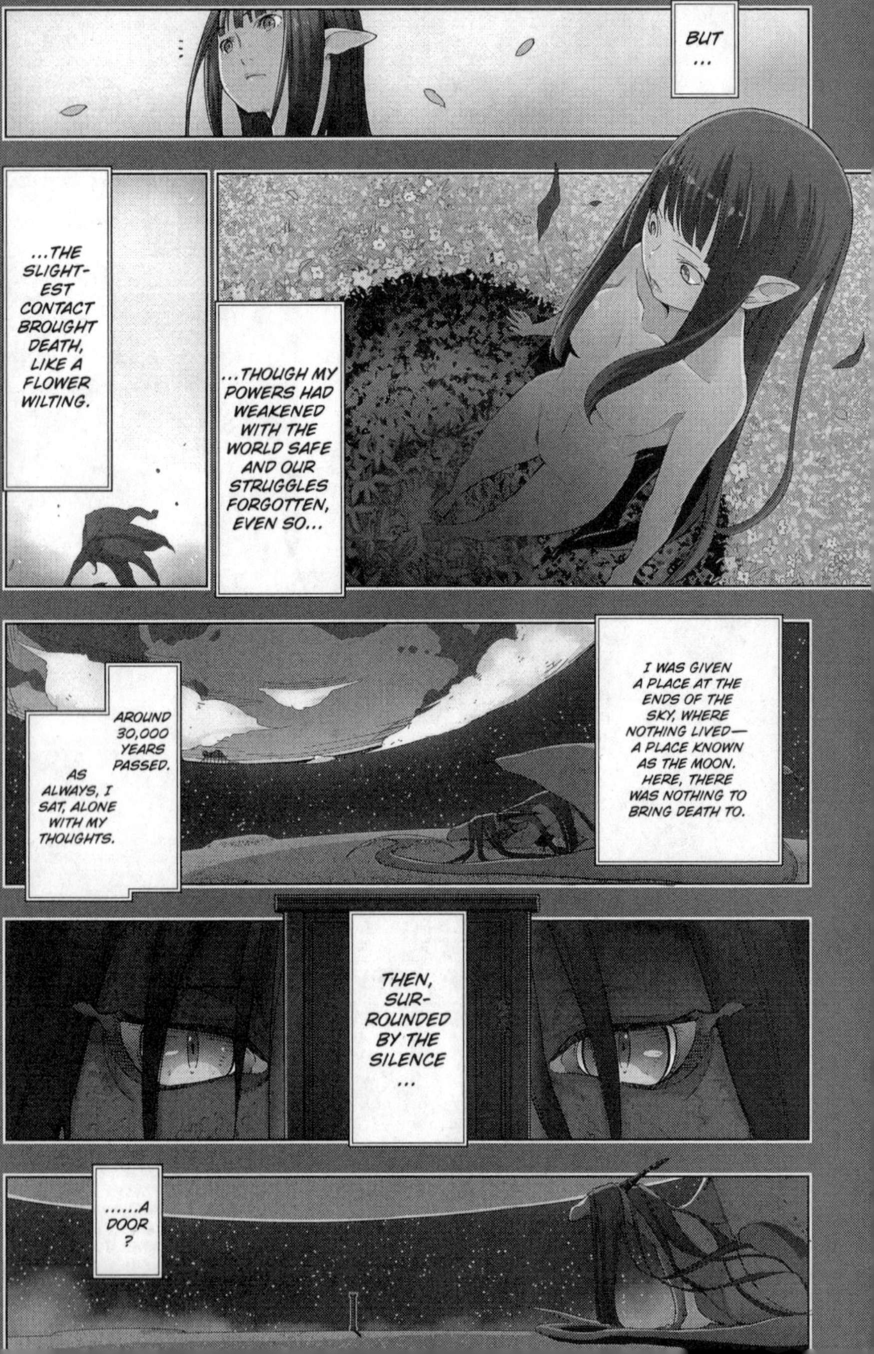
BUT ...
...THOUGH MY POWERS HAD WEAKENED WITH THE WORLD SAFE AND OUR STRUGGLES FORGOTTEN, EVEN SO...
...THE SLIGHT-EST CONTACT BROUGHT DEATH, LIKE A FLOWER WILTING.
I WAS GIVEN A PLACE AT THE ENDS OF THE SKY, WHERE NOTHING LIVED— A PLACE KNOWN AS THE MOON. HERE, THERE WAS NOTHING TO BRING DEATH TO.
AROUND 30,000 YEARS PASSED.
AS ALWAYS, I SAT, ALONE WITH MY THOUGHTS.
THEN, SUR-ROUNDED BY THE SILENCE ...
......A DOOR ?

10th Dish Curry Rice Again

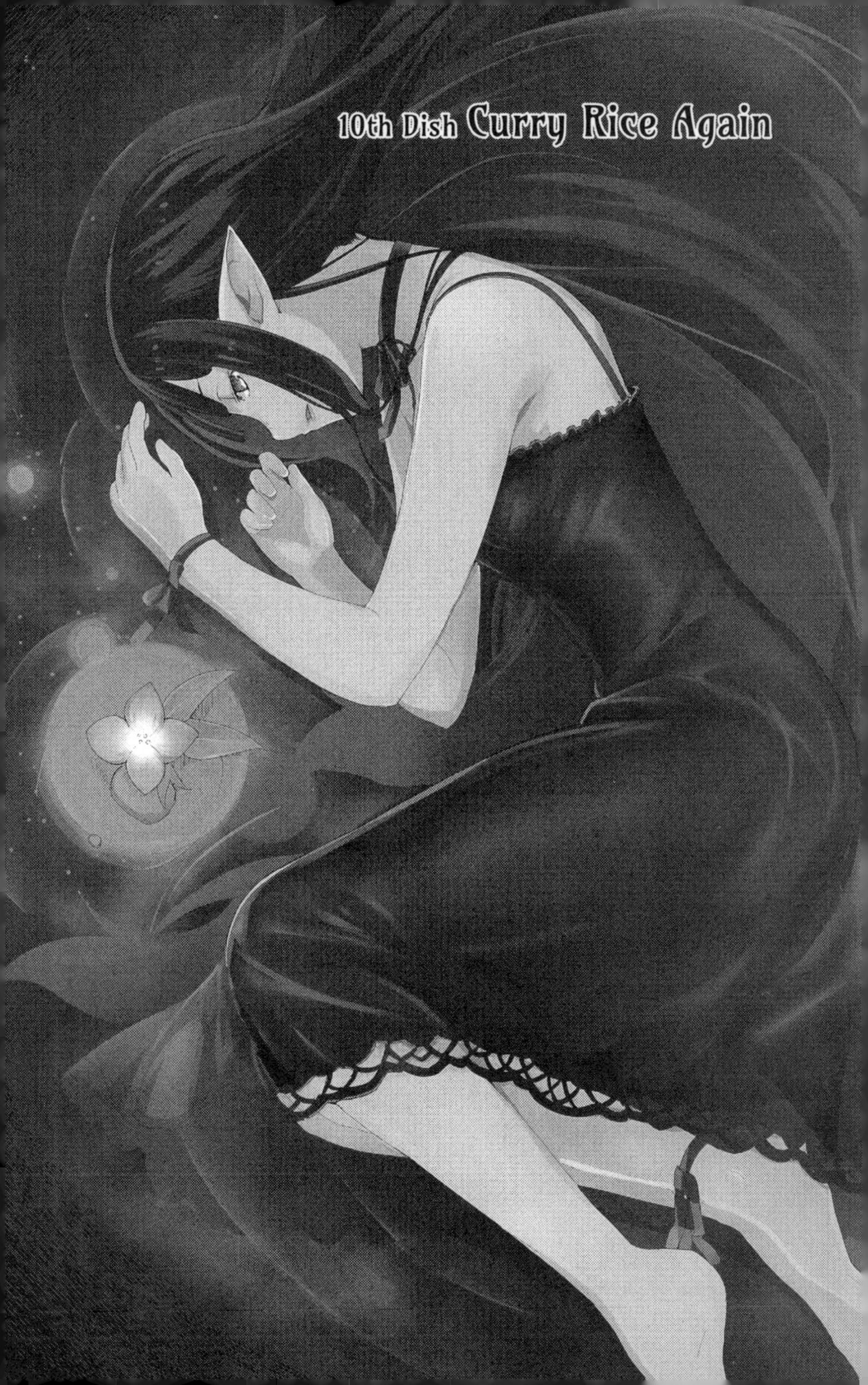

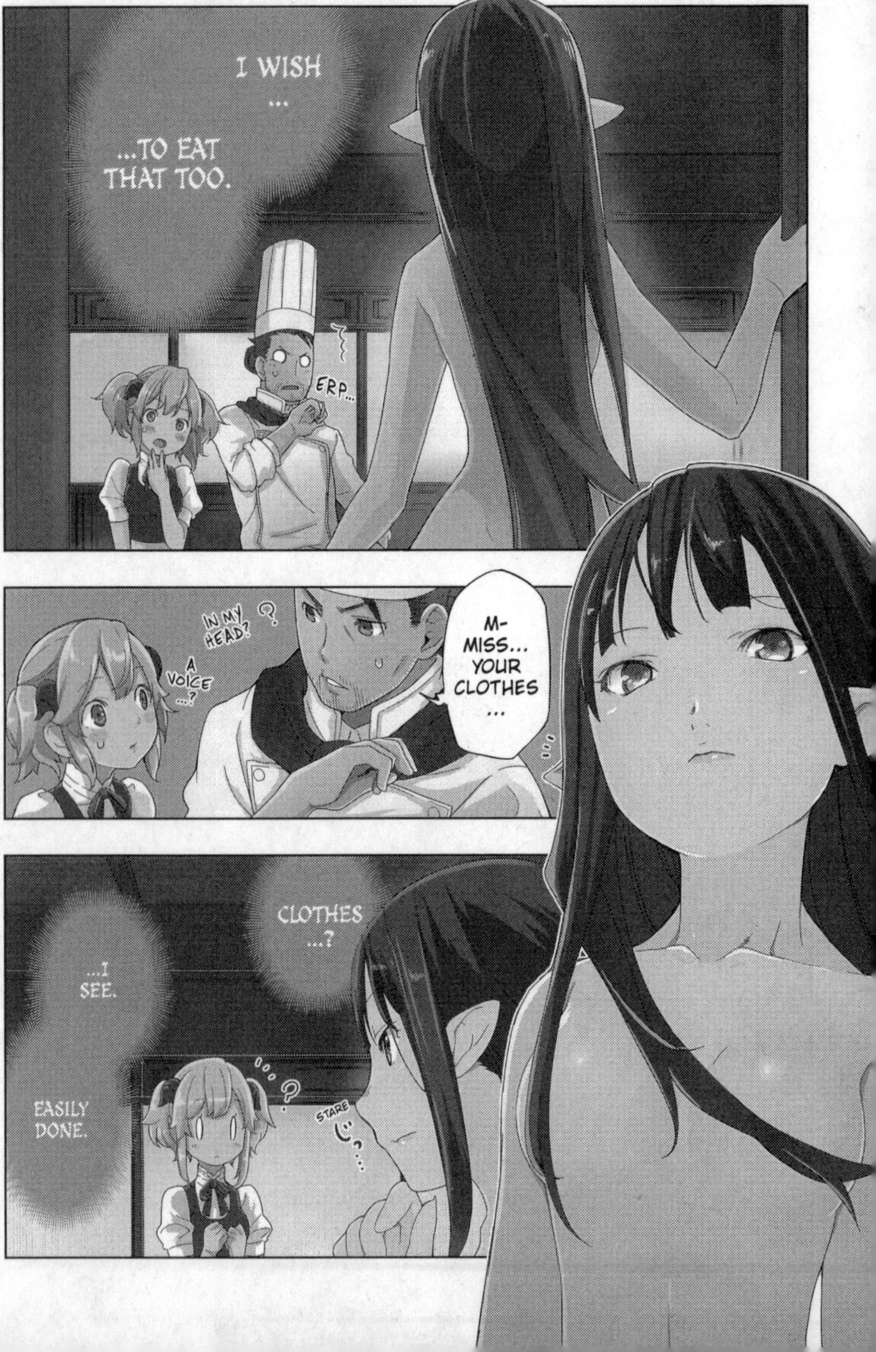
I WISH ...
...TO EAT THAT TOO.
ERP...
M-MISS... YOUR CLOTHES...
IN MY HEAD?
A VOICE...?
CLOTHES...?
...I SEE.
EASILY DONE.
STARE

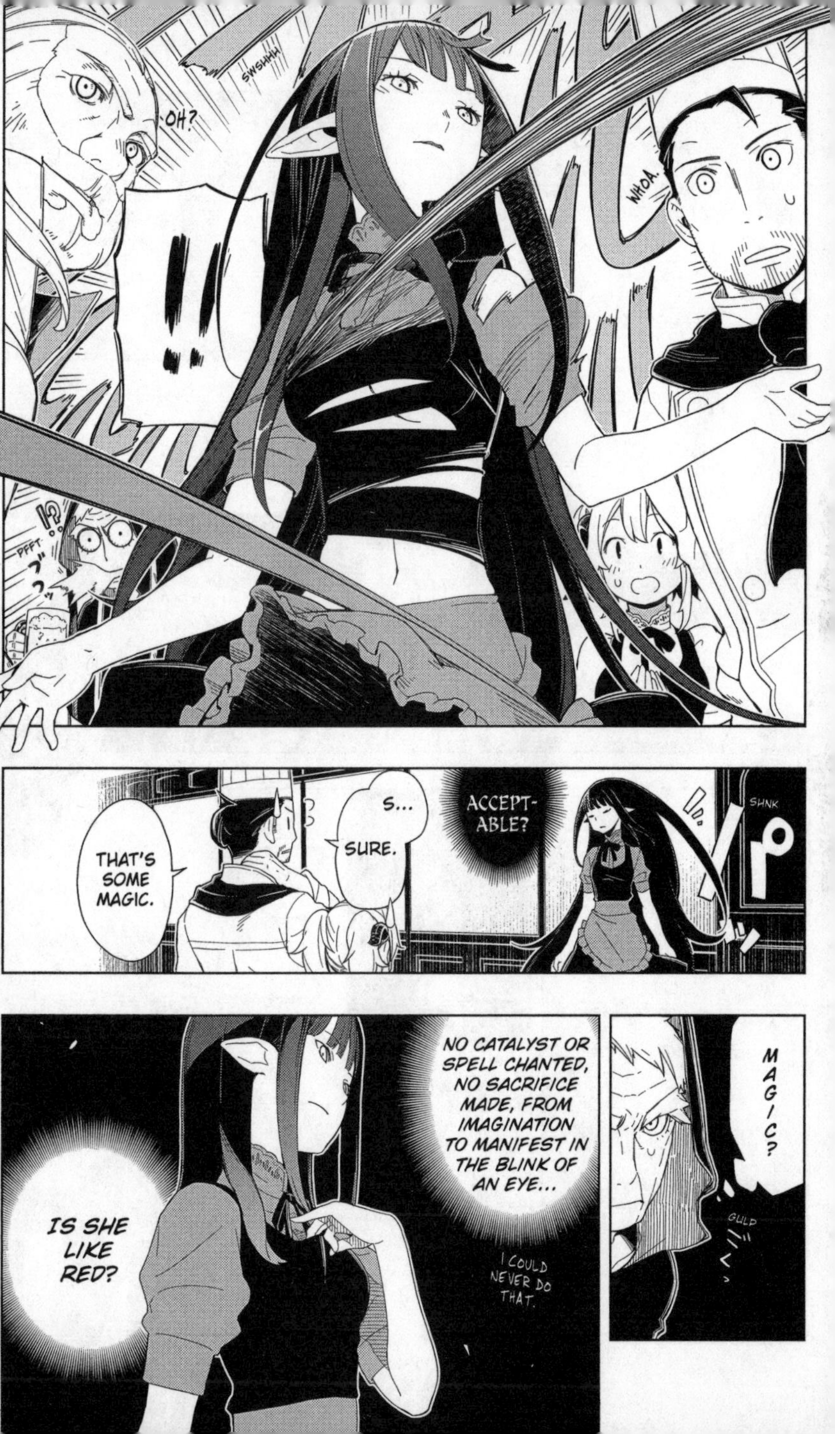
WHOA.
SWSHHH
OH?
!!
!?
PFFT
ブッ
!
SHNK
ACCEPT-ABLE?
S...
SURE.
THAT'S SOME MAGIC.
MAGIC?
GULP
NO CATALYST OR SPELL CHANTED, NO SACRIFICE MADE, FROM IMAGINATION TO MANIFEST IN THE BLINK OF AN EYE...
I COULD NEVER DO THAT.
IS SHE LIKE RED?

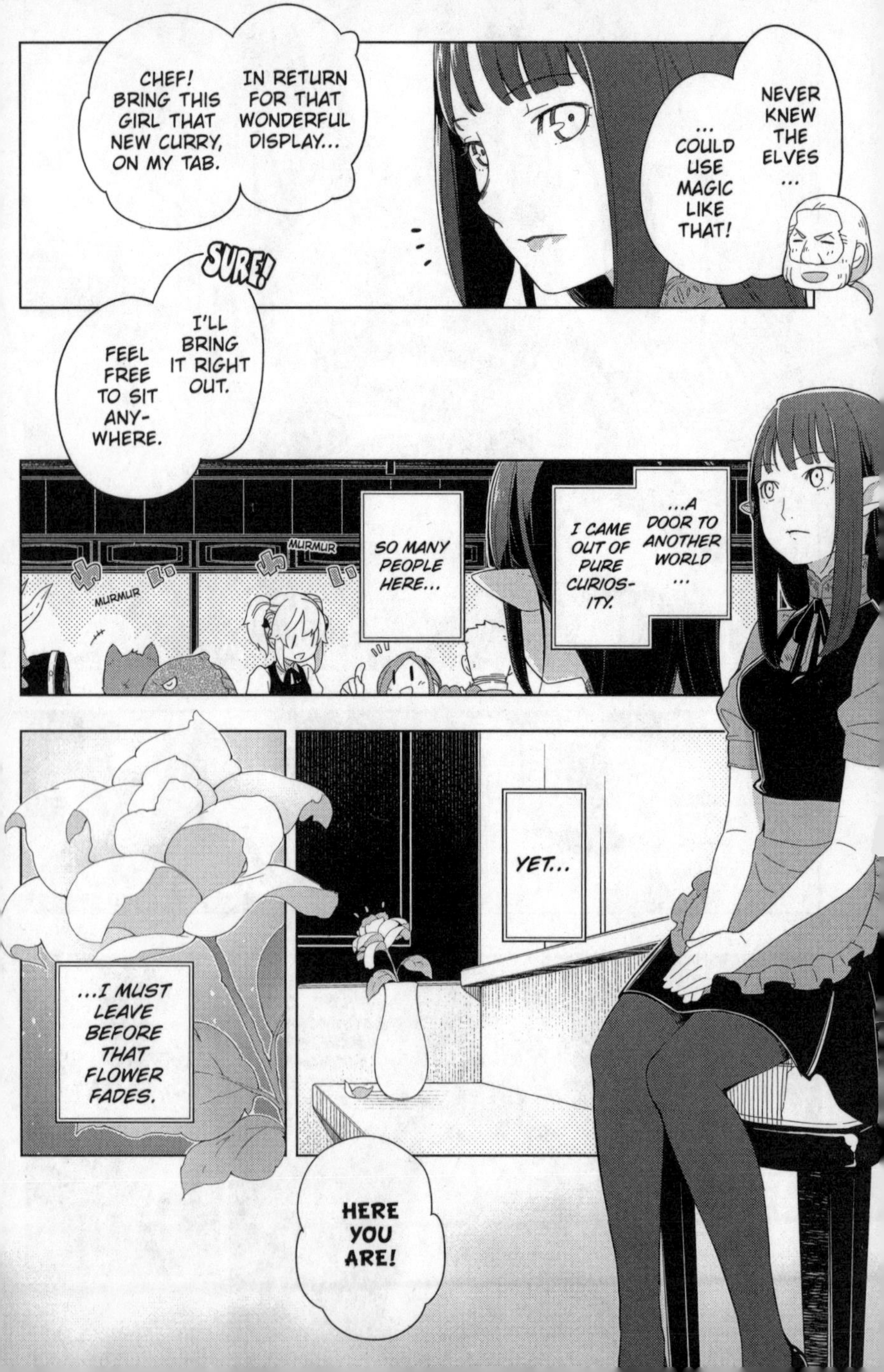
NEVER KNEW THE ELVES...
...COULD USE MAGIC LIKE THAT!
IN RETURN FOR THAT WONDERFUL DISPLAY...
CHEF! BRING THIS GIRL THAT NEW CURRY, ON MY TAB.
SURE!
I'LL BRING IT RIGHT OUT.
FEEL FREE TO SIT ANY-WHERE.
...A DOOR TO ANOTHER WORLD...
I CAME OUT OF PURE CURIOS-ITY.
SO MANY PEOPLE HERE...
MURMUR
MURMUR
YET...
...I MUST LEAVE BEFORE THAT FLOWER FADES.
HERE YOU ARE!

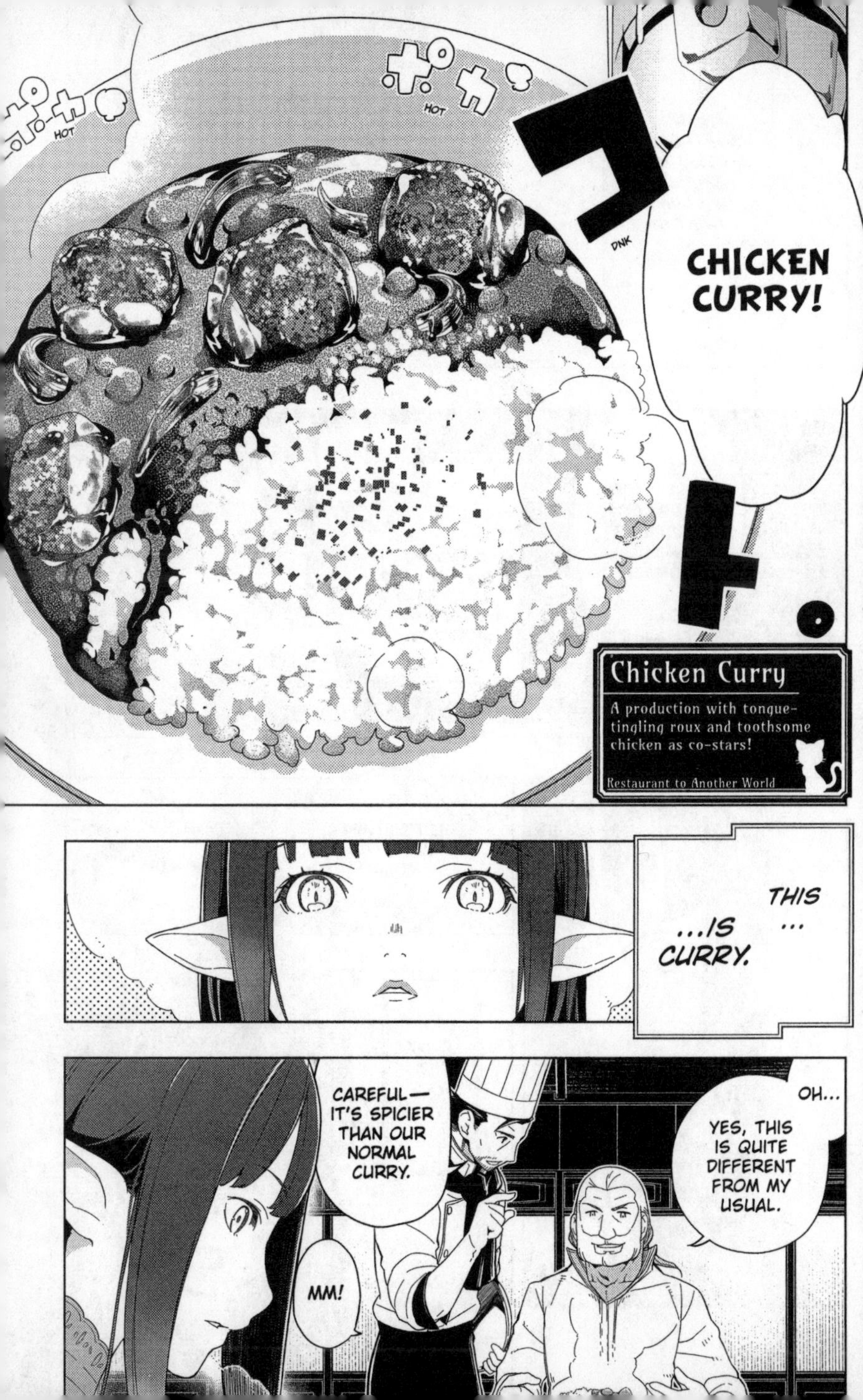
CHICKEN CURRY!
DNK
HOT
HOT
Chicken Curry
A production with tongue-tingling roux and toothsome chicken as co-stars!
Restaurant to Another World
THIS...
...IS CURRY.
OH...
YES, THIS IS QUITE DIFFERENT FROM MY USUAL.
CAREFUL— IT'S SPICIER THAN OUR NORMAL CURRY.
MM!

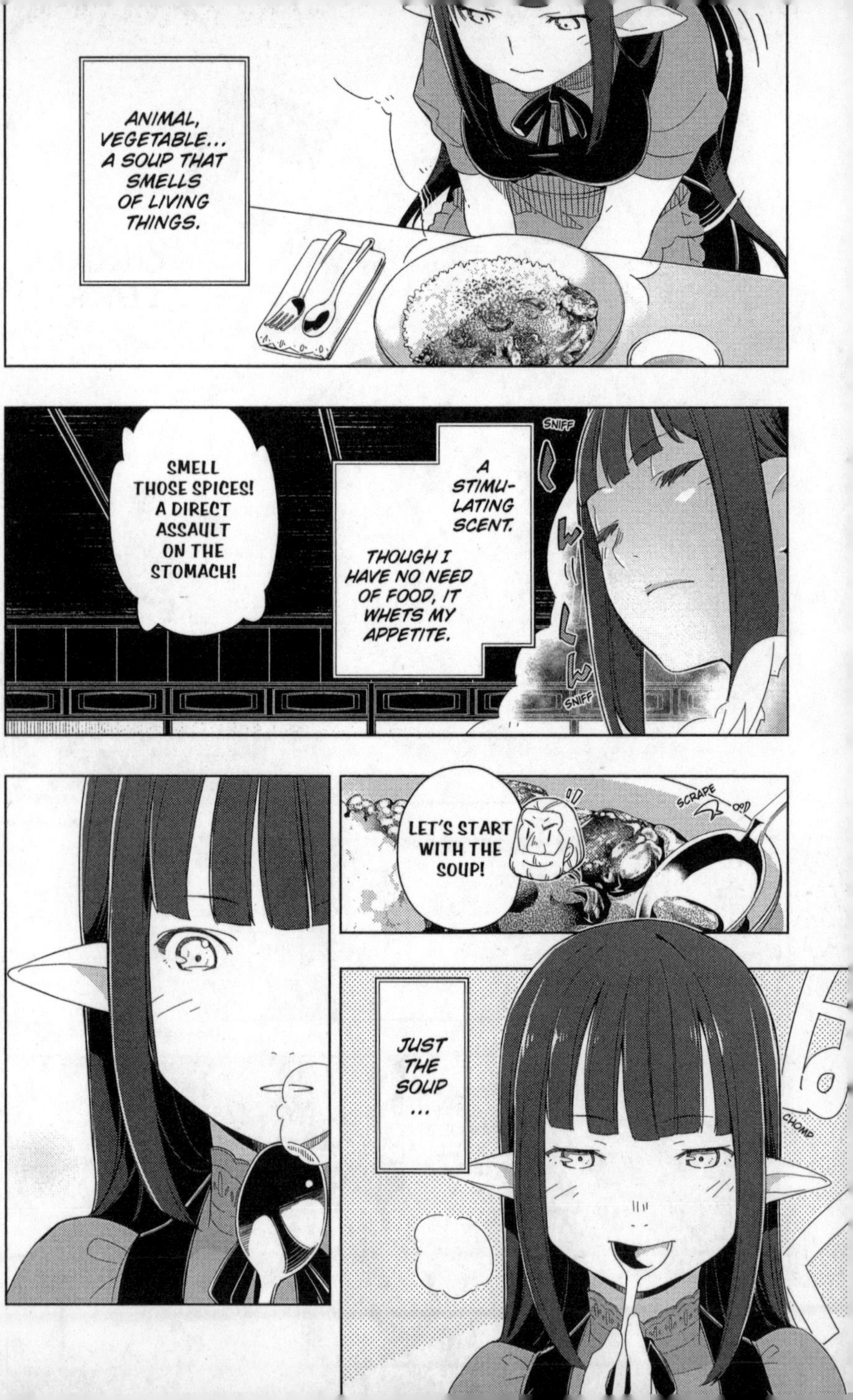
ANIMAL, VEGETABLE... A SOUP THAT SMELLS OF LIVING THINGS.
SNIFF
A STIMULATING SCENT.
THOUGH I HAVE NO NEED OF FOOD, IT WHETS MY APPETITE.
SMELL THOSE SPICES! A DIRECT ASSAULT ON THE STOMACH!
SNIFF
SCRAPE
LET'S START WITH THE SOUP!
JUST THE SOUP...
CHOMP

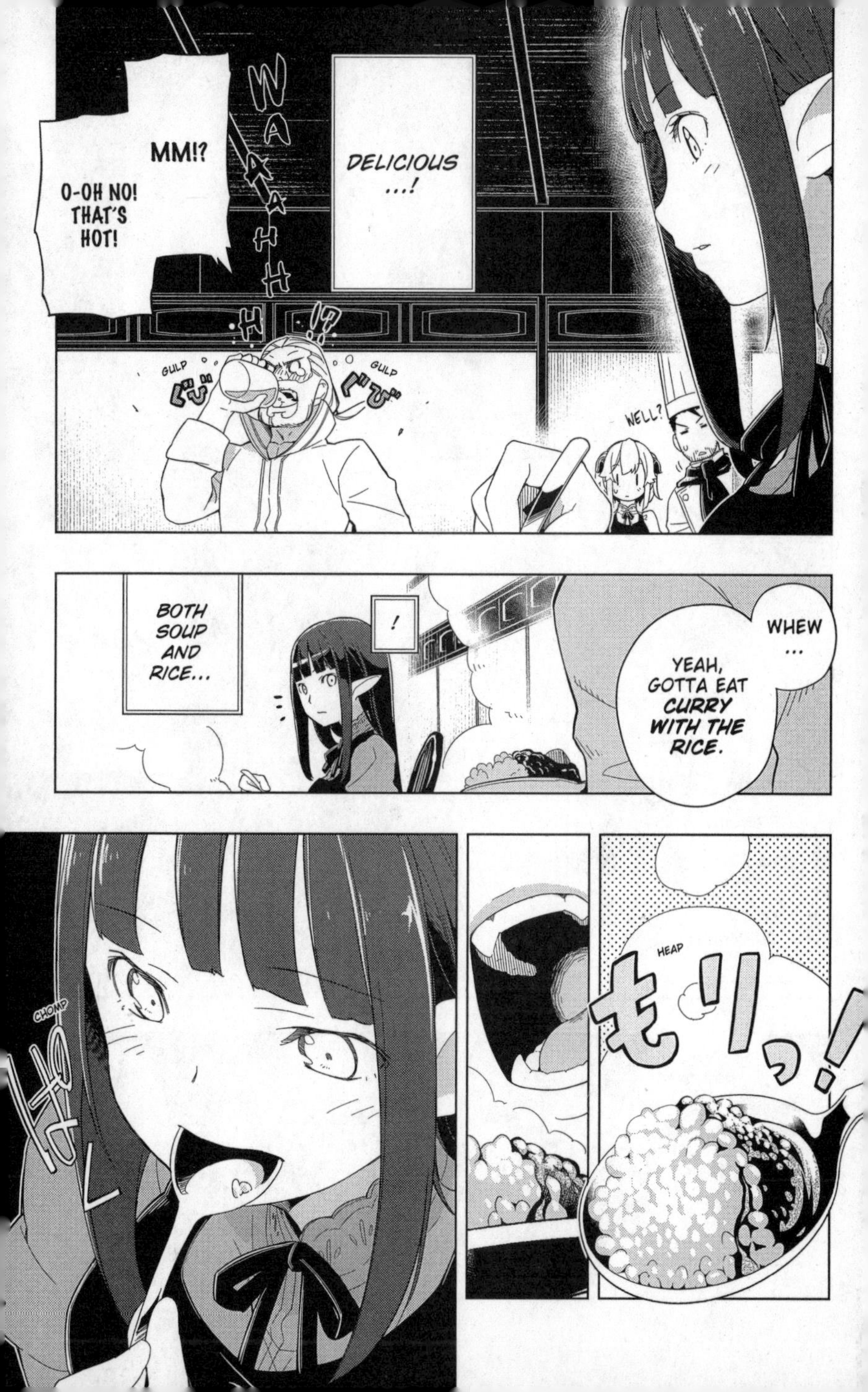
DELICIOUS ...!
MM!?
O-OH NO! THAT'S HOT!
WAAAHHH
!?
GULP
GULP
WELL?
WHEW ...
YEAH, GOTTA EAT CURRY WITH THE RICE.
!
BOTH SOUP AND RICE...
HEAP
もりっ!
CHOMP

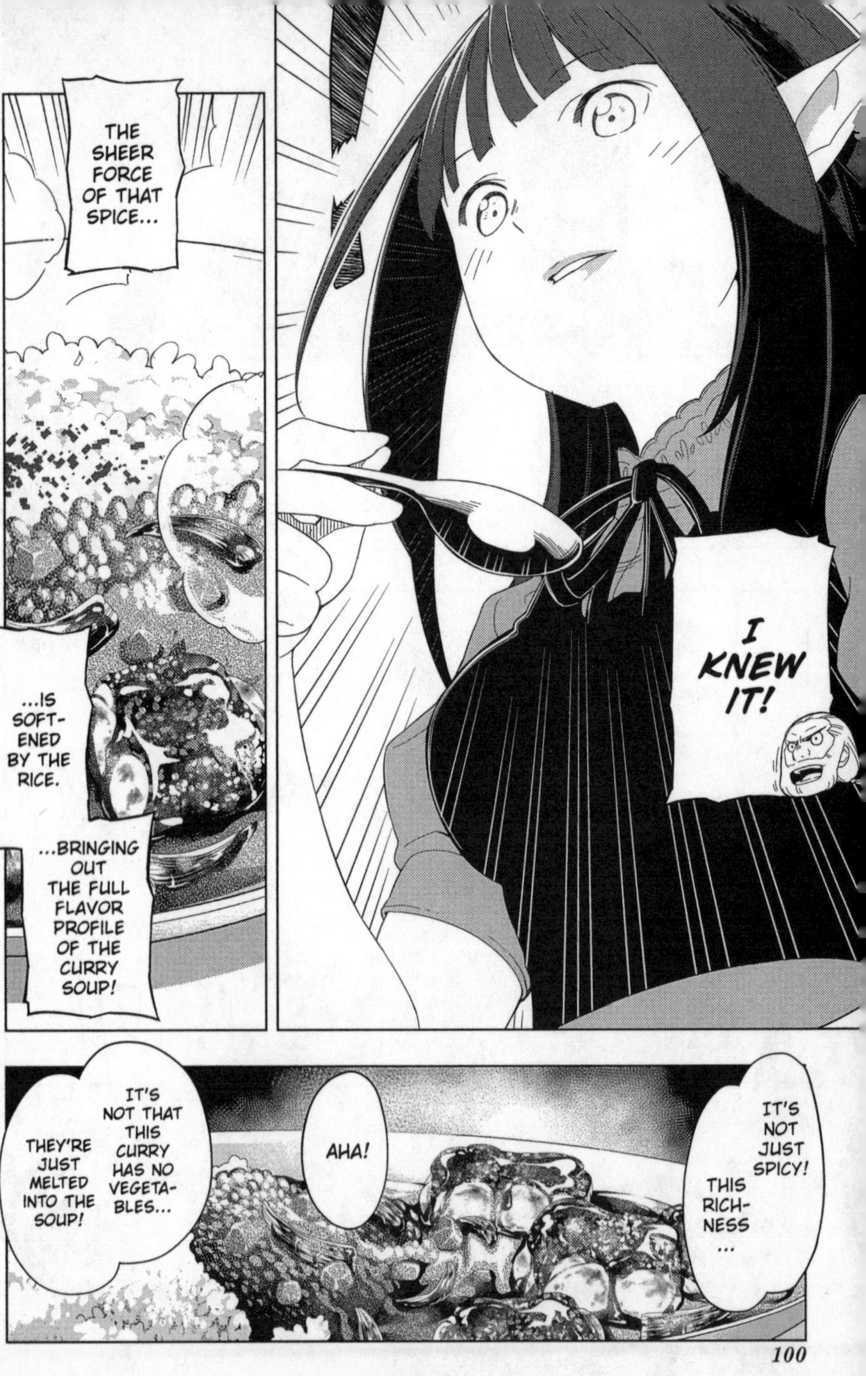
I KNEW IT!
THE SHEER FORCE OF THAT SPICE...
...IS SOFTENED BY THE RICE.
...BRINGING OUT THE FULL FLAVOR PROFILE OF THE CURRY SOUP!
IT'S NOT JUST SPICY!
THIS RICHNESS...
AHA!
IT'S NOT THAT THIS CURRY HAS NO VEGETABLES...
THEY'RE JUST MELTED INTO THE SOUP!

AND THIS CHICK- EN!

SO SOFT ...

IT FALLS APART IN MY MOUTH.

WHAT A SHOCK!

JUST AS THE SAVORINESS OF THE CHICKEN AND VEGETABLES SEEPS INTO THE CURRY...

...THE CHICKEN AND VEGETABLES ARE SEEPED IN THE SAVORI- NESS OF THE CURRY.

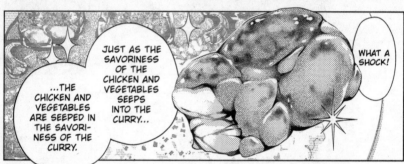

THE FLAVORS AREN'T JUST BROAD- ENED...

THE EXCESS GREASE IS WITHDRAWN AND FUSED WITH THE FLAVOR OF THE CURRY AND VEGETABLES ...!

I THINK I KNOW WHAT HE MEANS.

TRUE... THE DEPTH OF THIS MEAT...

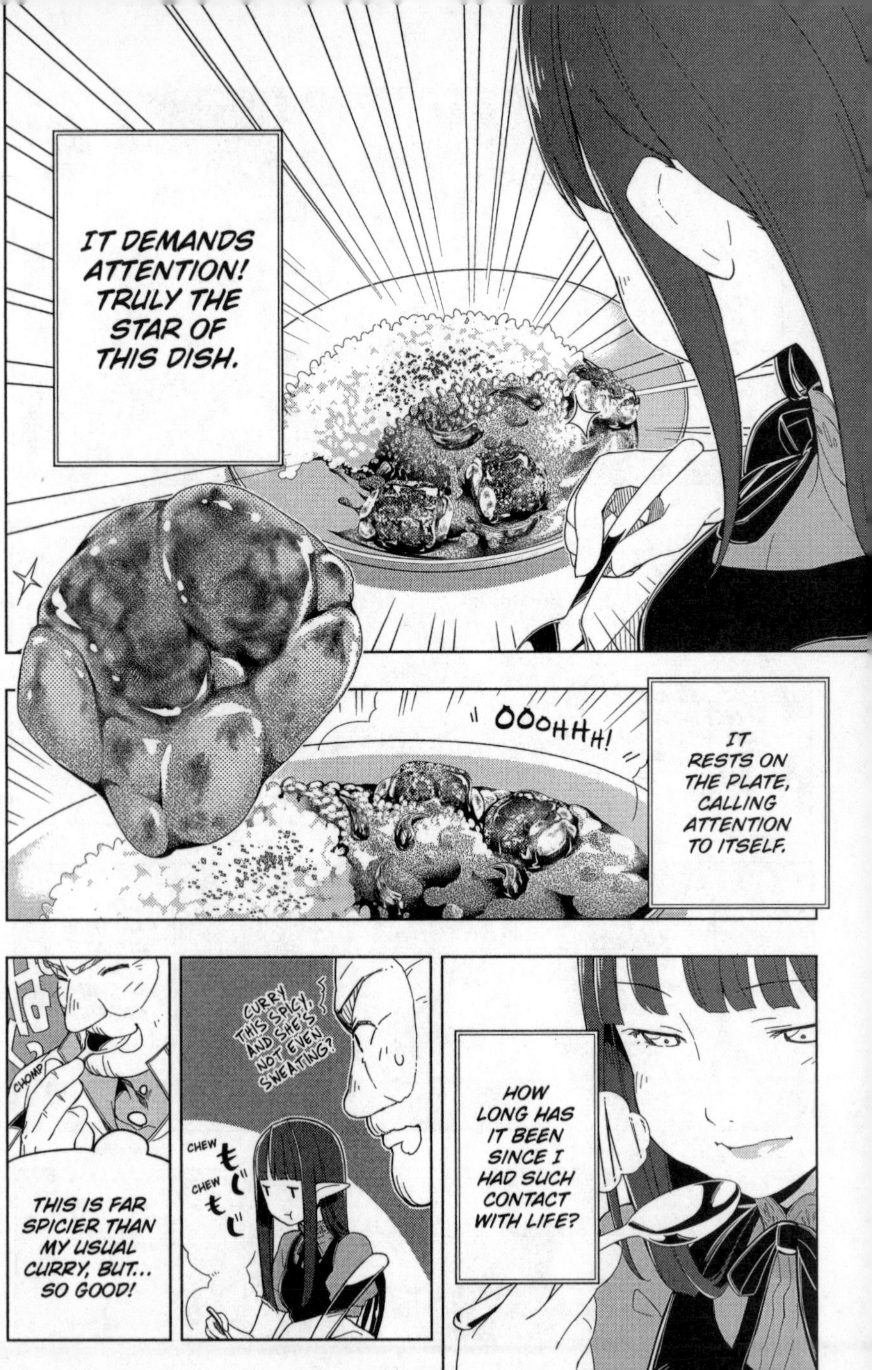
IT DEMANDS ATTENTION! TRULY THE STAR OF THIS DISH.
IT RESTS ON THE PLATE, CALLING ATTENTION TO ITSELF.
OOOHHH!
HOW LONG HAS IT BEEN SINCE I HAD SUCH CONTACT WITH LIFE?
CURRY THIS SPICY, AND SHE'S NOT EVEN SWEATING?
CHEW
CHEW
CHOMP
THIS IS FAR SPICIER THAN MY USUAL CURRY, BUT... SO GOOD!

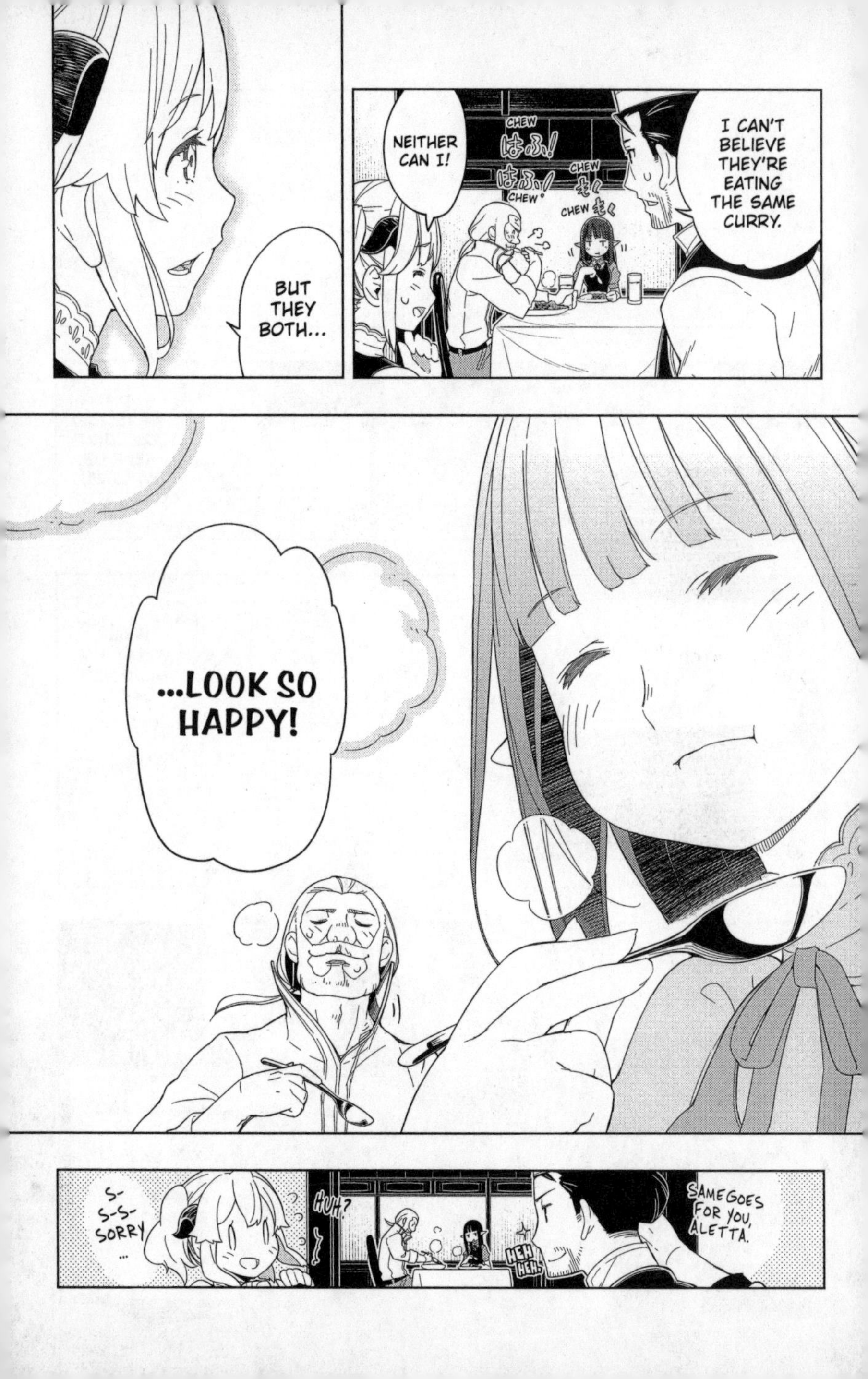
I CAN'T BELIEVE THEY'RE EATING THE SAME CURRY.
NEITHER CAN I!
CHEW はふ!
CHEW はふ!
CHEW もぐ
CHEW もぐ
BUT THEY BOTH...
...LOOK SO HAPPY!
SAME GOES FOR YOU, ALETTA.
HEH HEH
HUH?
S-S-S-SORRY...

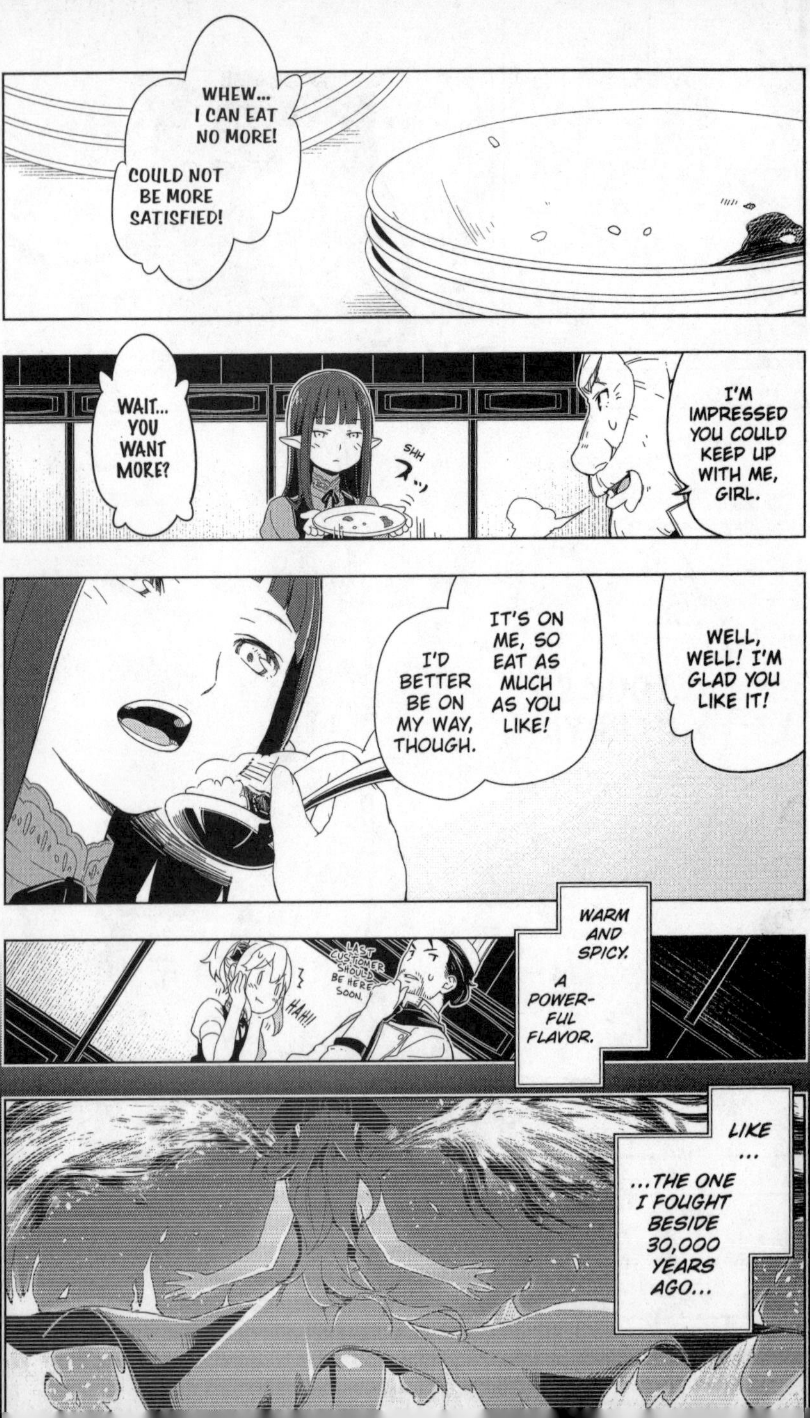
WHEW... I CAN EAT NO MORE!
COULD NOT BE MORE SATISFIED!
I'M IMPRESSED YOU COULD KEEP UP WITH ME, GIRL.
SHH
WAIT... YOU WANT MORE?
WELL, WELL! I'M GLAD YOU LIKE IT!
IT'S ON ME, SO EAT AS MUCH AS YOU LIKE!
I'D BETTER BE ON MY WAY, THOUGH.
WARM AND SPICY.
A POWER-FUL FLAVOR.
LAST CUSTOMER SHOULD BE HERE SOON.
HAH!!
LIKE...
...THE ONE I FOUGHT BESIDE 30,000 YEARS AGO...

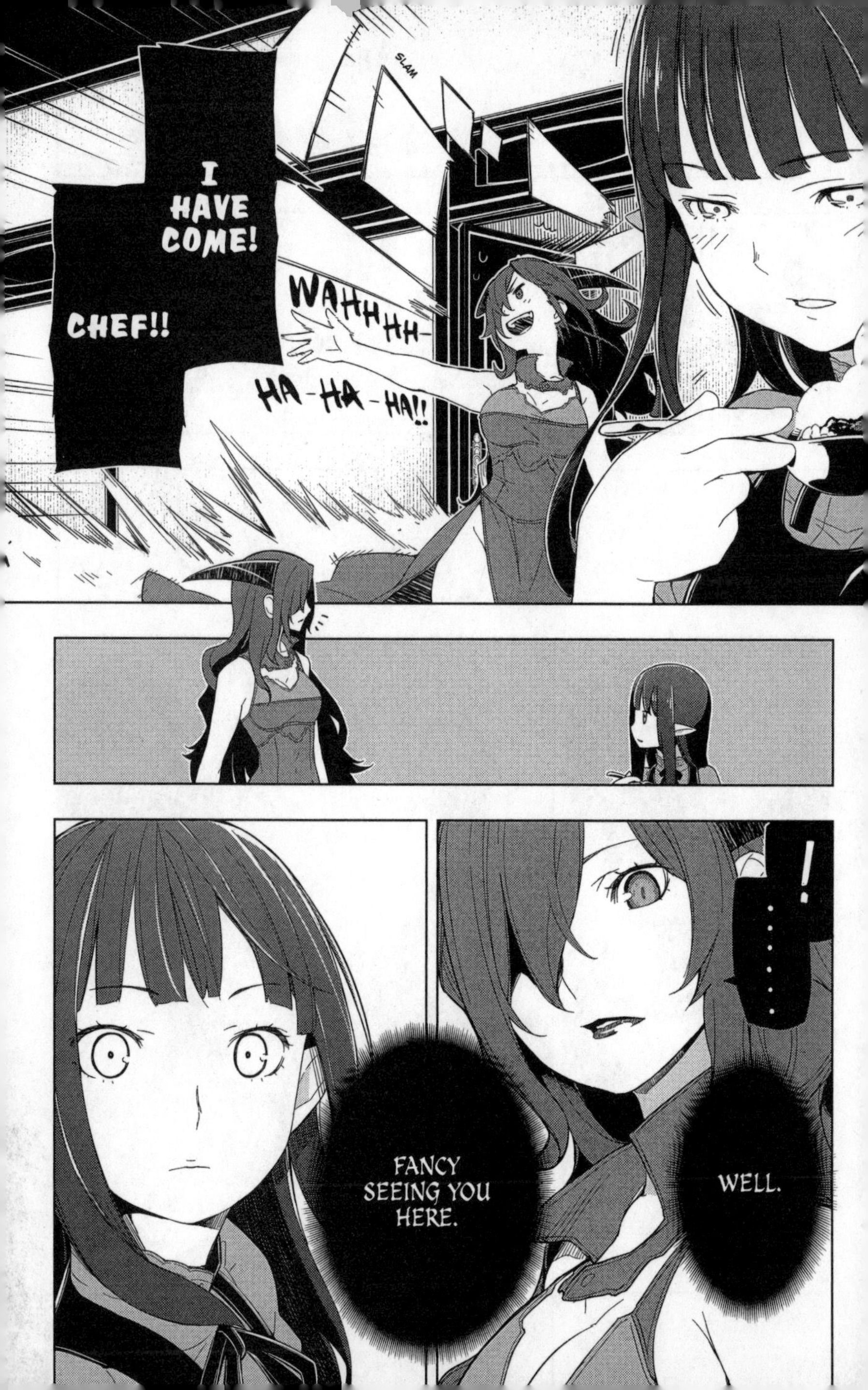
SLAM
I HAVE COME!
CHEF!!
WAHHHHH-
HA-HA-HA!!
!
......
WELL.
FANCY SEEING YOU HERE.

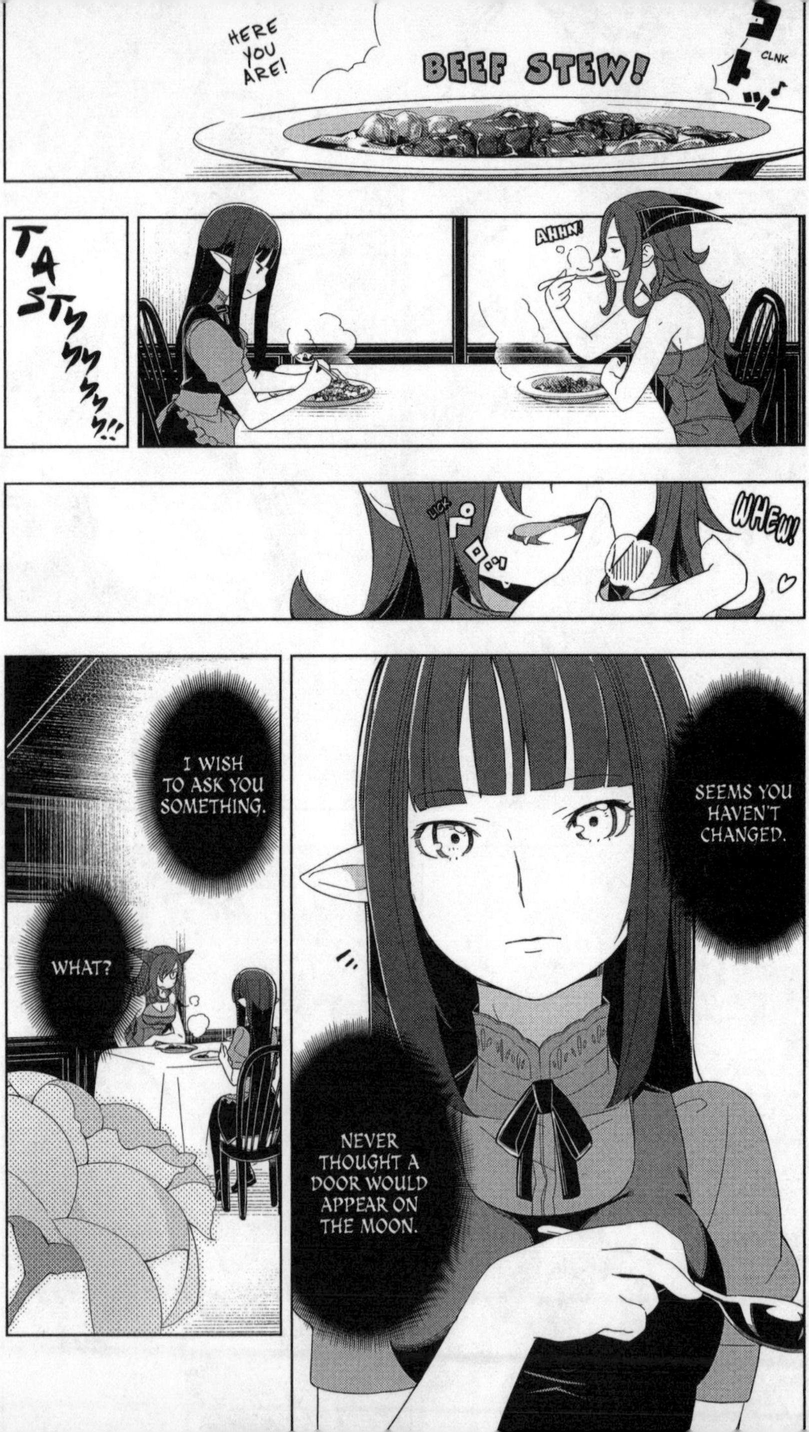
CLNK
BEEF STEW!
HERE YOU ARE!
AHHN!
TASTYYYYYY!!
WHEW!
LICK
SEEMS YOU HAVEN'T CHANGED.
NEVER THOUGHT A DOOR WOULD APPEAR ON THE MOON.
I WISH TO ASK YOU SOMETHING.
WHAT?

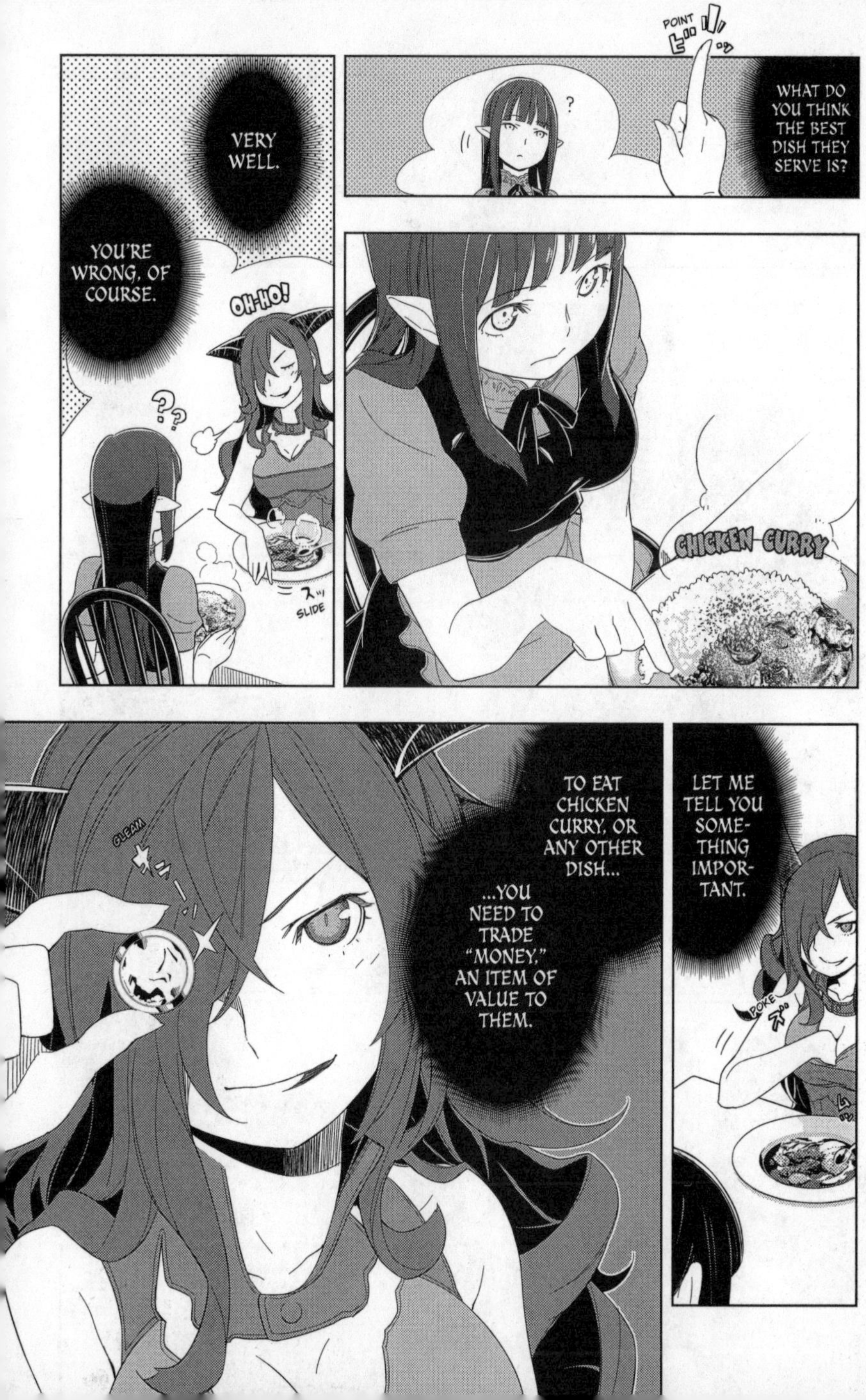
POINT
WHAT DO YOU THINK THE BEST DISH THEY SERVE IS?
CHICKEN CURRY
VERY WELL.
YOU'RE WRONG, OF COURSE.
OH-HO!
SLIDE
LET ME TELL YOU SOME-THING IMPOR-TANT.
POKE
TO EAT CHICKEN CURRY, OR ANY OTHER DISH...
...YOU NEED TO TRADE "MONEY," AN ITEM OF VALUE TO THEM.
GLEAM

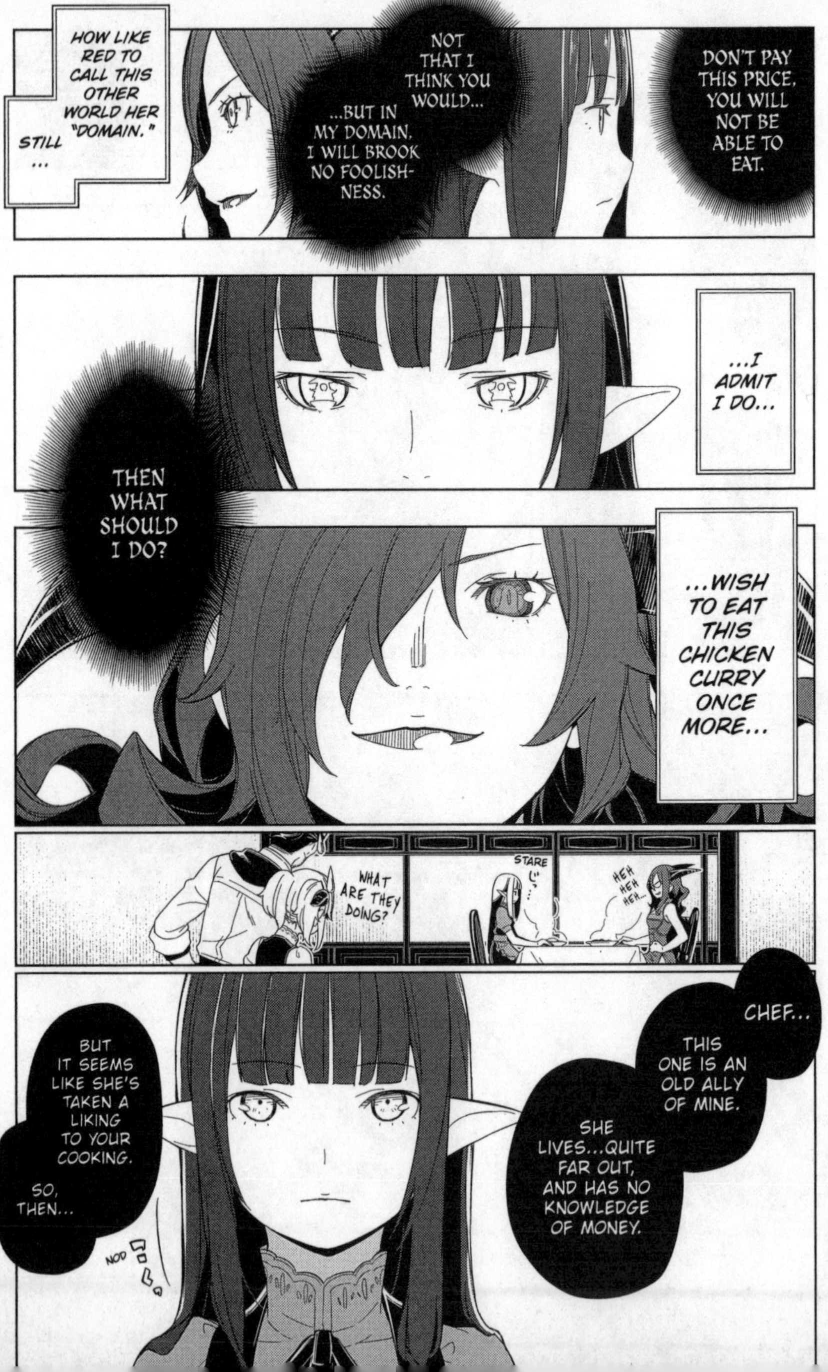
DON'T PAY THIS PRICE, YOU WILL NOT BE ABLE TO EAT.
NOT THAT I THINK YOU WOULD...
...BUT IN MY DOMAIN, I WILL BROOK NO FOOLISH-NESS.
HOW LIKE RED TO CALL THIS OTHER WORLD HER "DOMAIN."
STILL...
...I ADMIT I DO...
THEN WHAT SHOULD I DO?
...WISH TO EAT THIS CHICKEN CURRY ONCE MORE...
HEH HEH HEH...
STARE
WHAT ARE THEY DOING?
CHEF...
THIS ONE IS AN OLD ALLY OF MINE.
SHE LIVES...QUITE FAR OUT, AND HAS NO KNOWLEDGE OF MONEY.
BUT IT SEEMS LIKE SHE'S TAKEN A LIKING TO YOUR COOKING.
SO, THEN...
NOD

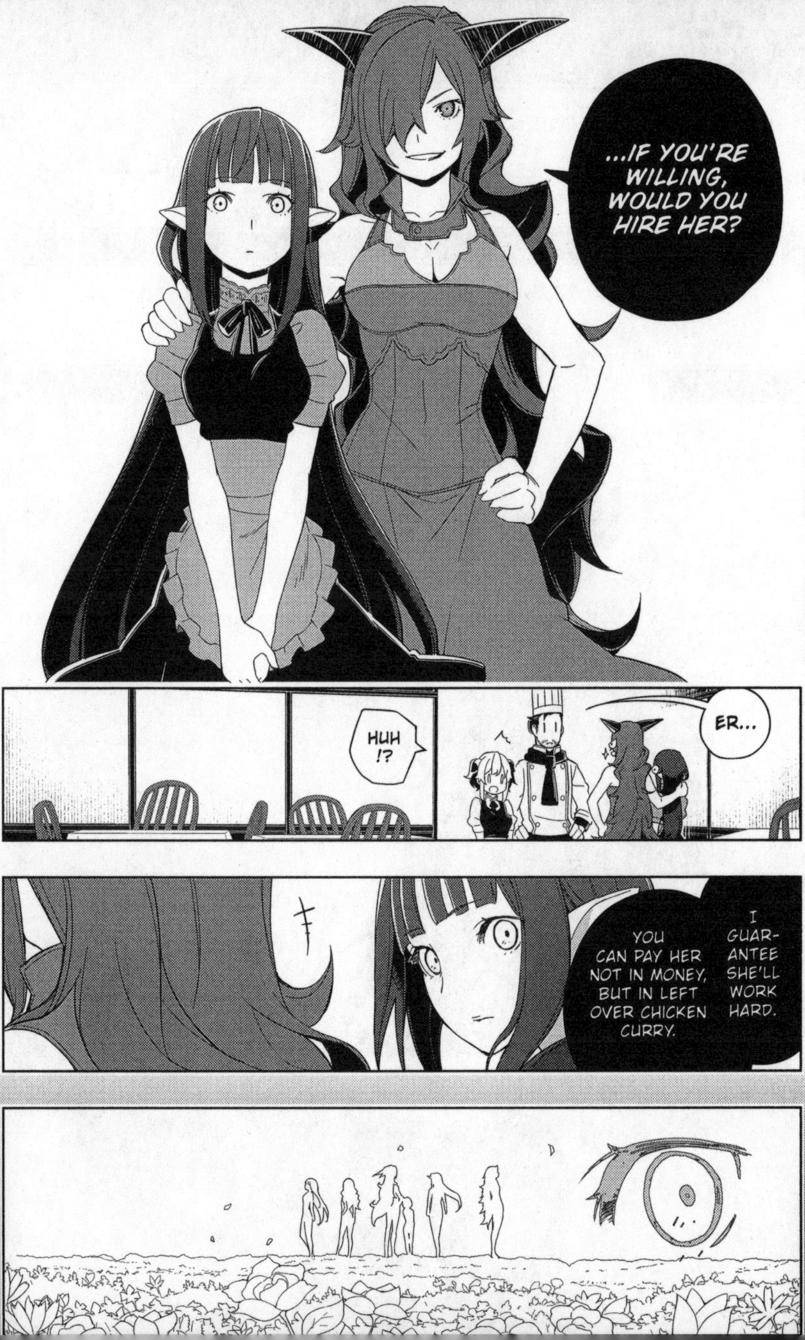
...IF YOU'RE WILLING, WOULD YOU HIRE HER?
ER...
HUH !?
I GUARANTEE SHE'LL WORK HARD.
YOU CAN PAY HER NOT IN MONEY, BUT IN LEFT OVER CHICKEN CURRY.

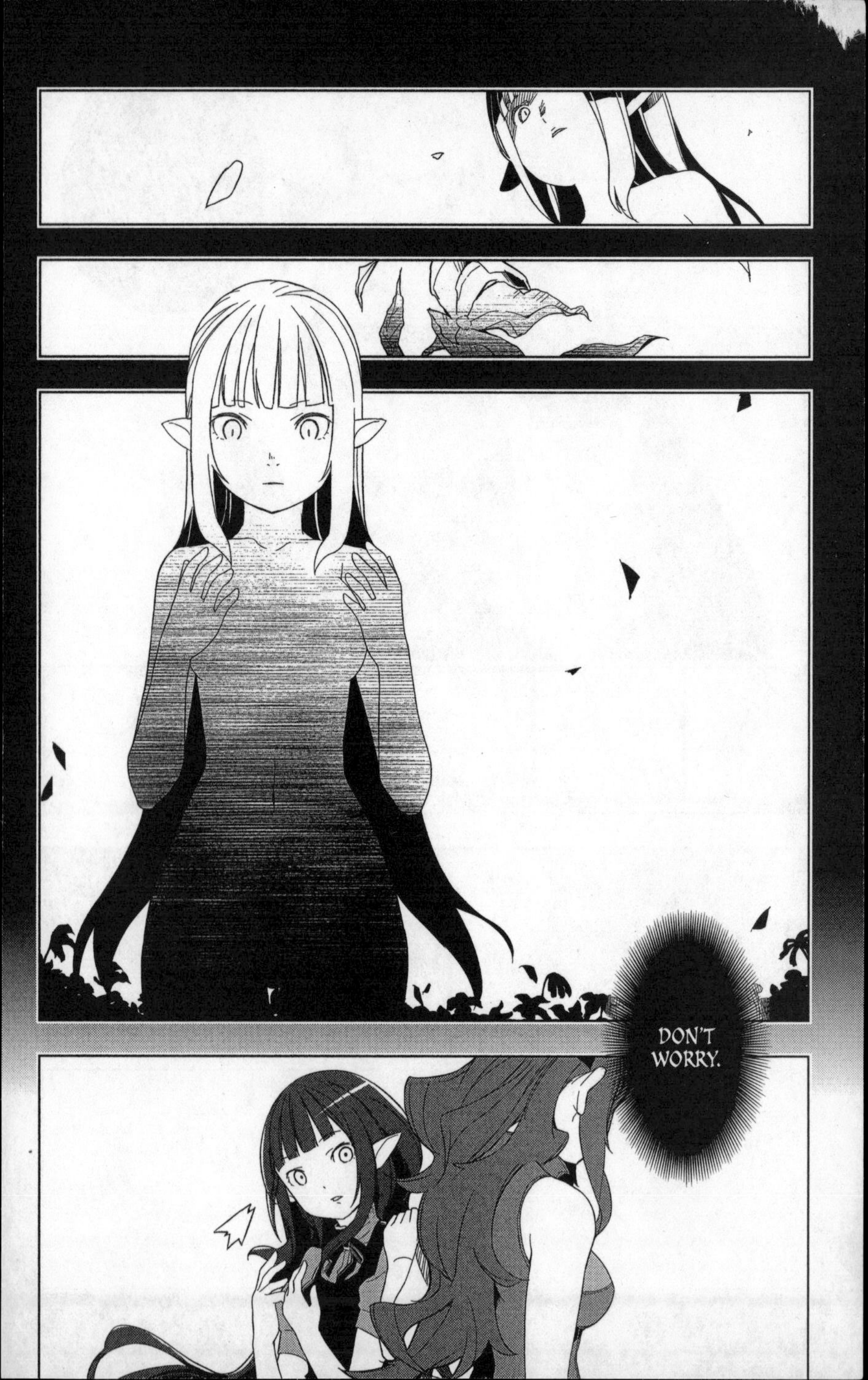
DON'T
WORRY.

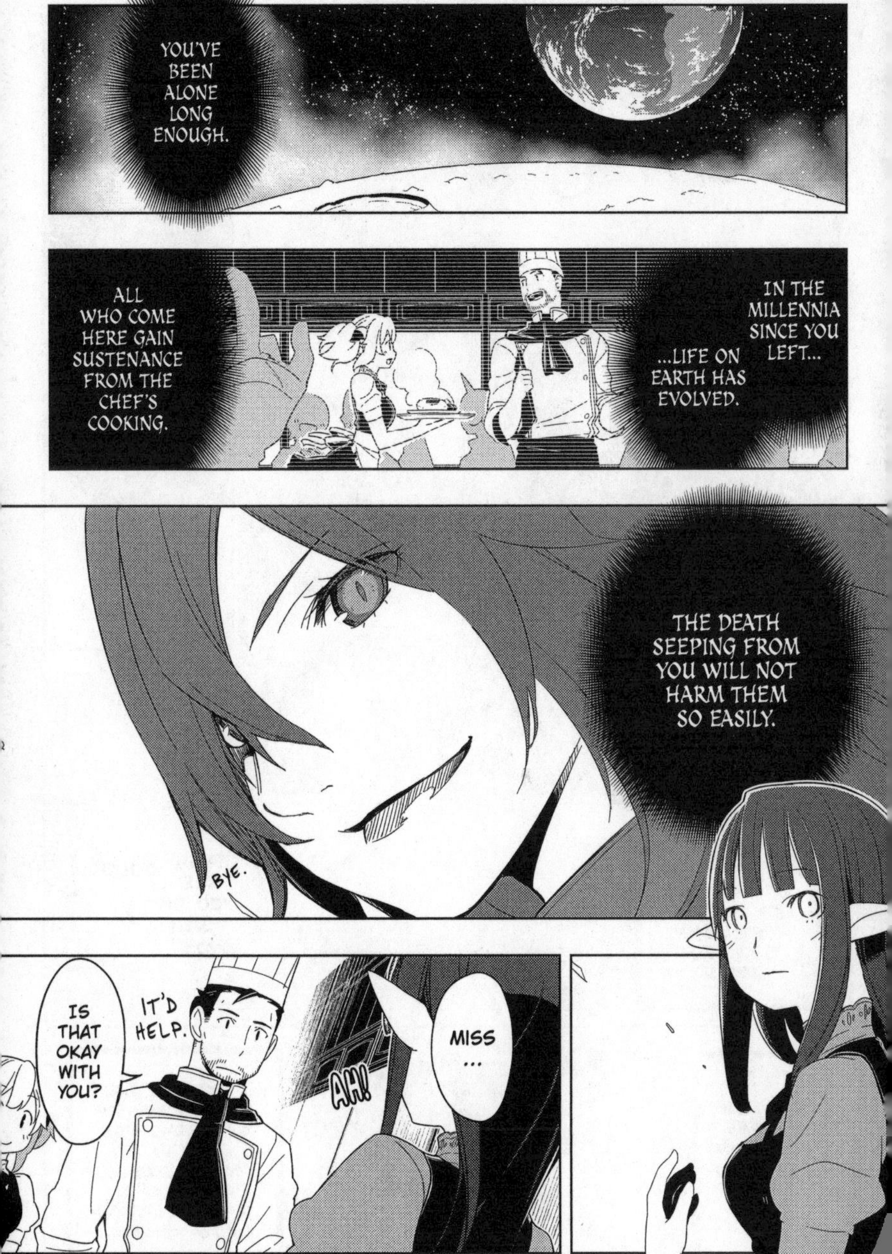
YOU'VE BEEN ALONE LONG ENOUGH.
IN THE MILLENNIA SINCE YOU LEFT...
...LIFE ON EARTH HAS EVOLVED.
ALL WHO COME HERE GAIN SUSTENANCE FROM THE CHEF'S COOKING.
THE DEATH SEEPING FROM YOU WILL NOT HARM THEM SO EASILY.
BYE.
MISS ...
AH!
IT'D HELP.
IS THAT OKAY WITH YOU?

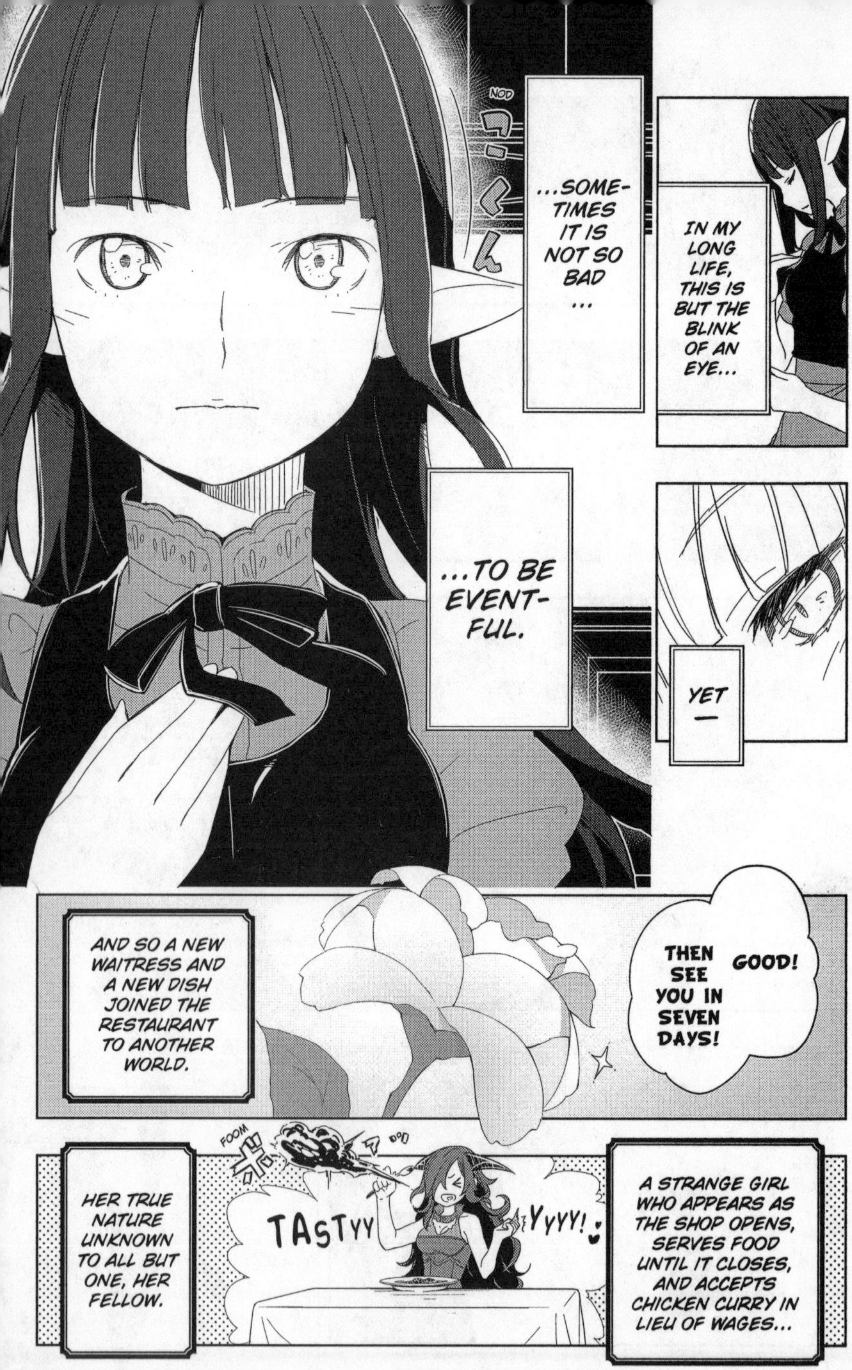
IN MY LONG LIFE, THIS IS BUT THE BLINK OF AN EYE...
YET—
NOD
...SOME-TIMES IT IS NOT SO BAD ...
...TO BE EVENT-FUL.
GOOD!
THEN SEE YOU IN SEVEN DAYS!
AND SO A NEW WAITRESS AND A NEW DISH JOINED THE RESTAURANT TO ANOTHER WORLD.
A STRANGE GIRL WHO APPEARS AS THE SHOP OPENS, SERVES FOOD UNTIL IT CLOSES, AND ACCEPTS CHICKEN CURRY IN LIEU OF WAGES...
FOOM
TASTYYYyyy!
HER TRUE NATURE UNKNOWN TO ALL BUT ONE, HER FELLOW.

RESTAURANT TO Another World

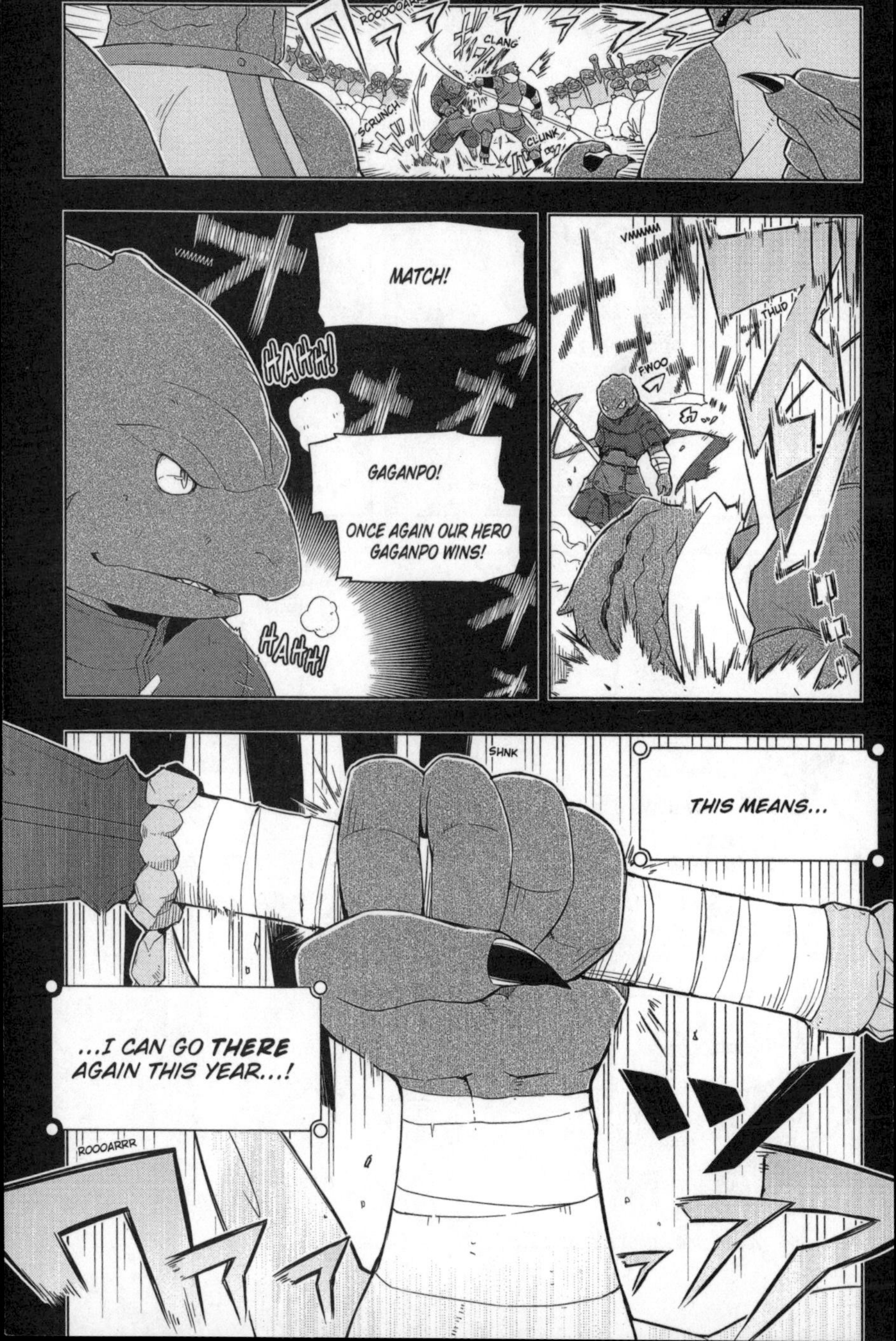
CLANG
SCRUNCH
CLUNK
THUD
FWOO
MATCH!
HAHH!
GAGANPO!
ONCE AGAIN OUR HERO GAGANPO WINS!
HAHH!
SHNK
THIS MEANS...
...I CAN GO THERE AGAIN THIS YEAR...!
ROOOARRR

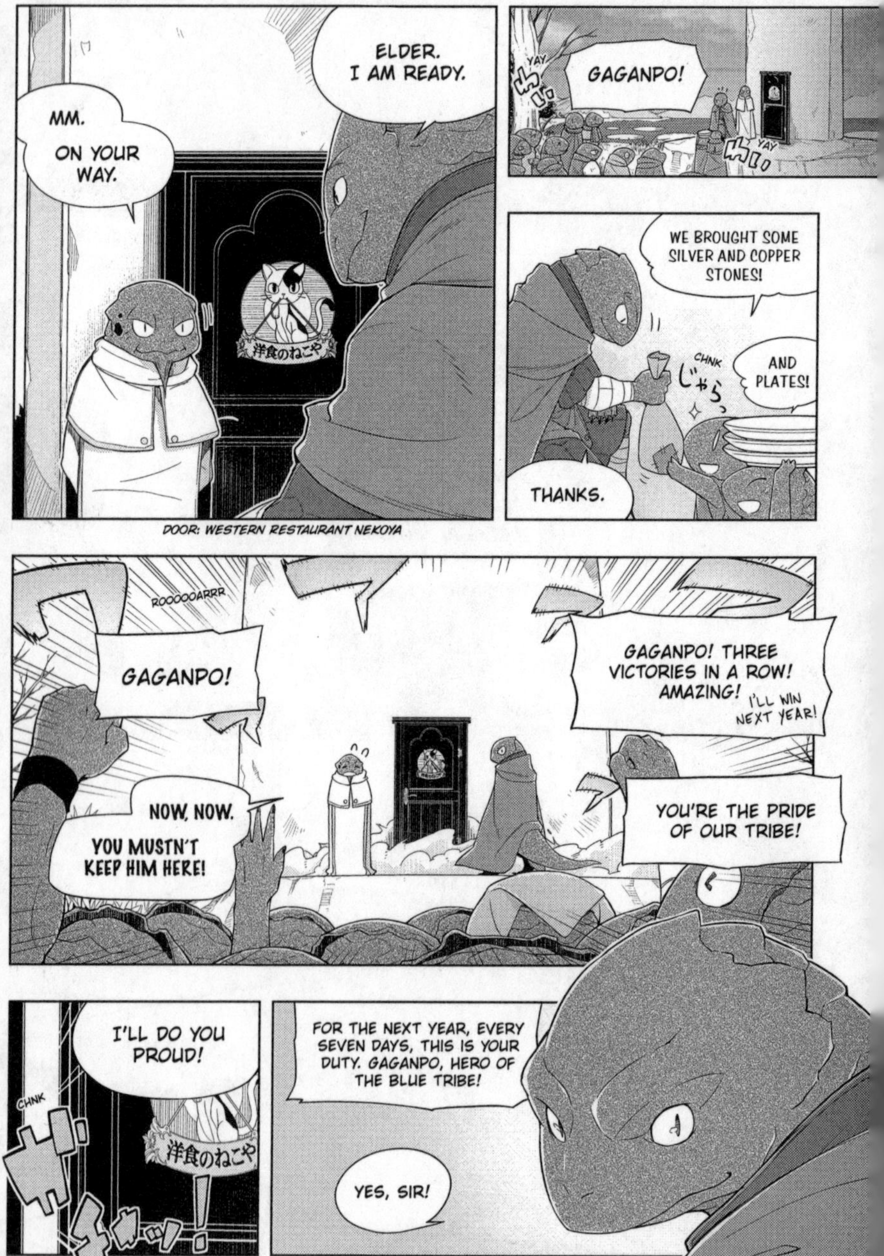
YAY
GAGANPO!
YAY
WE BROUGHT SOME SILVER AND COPPER STONES!
CHNK
AND PLATES!
THANKS.
ELDER. I AM READY.
MM. ON YOUR WAY.
洋食のねこや
DOOR: WESTERN RESTAURANT NEKOYA
GAGANPO! THREE VICTORIES IN A ROW! AMAZING!
I'LL WIN NEXT YEAR!
YOU'RE THE PRIDE OF OUR TRIBE!
ROOOOOARRR
GAGANPO!
NOW, NOW.
YOU MUSTN'T KEEP HIM HERE!
FOR THE NEXT YEAR, EVERY SEVEN DAYS, THIS IS YOUR DUTY. GAGANPO, HERO OF THE BLUE TRIBE!
YES, SIR!
I'LL DO YOU PROUD!
CHNK
洋食のねこや

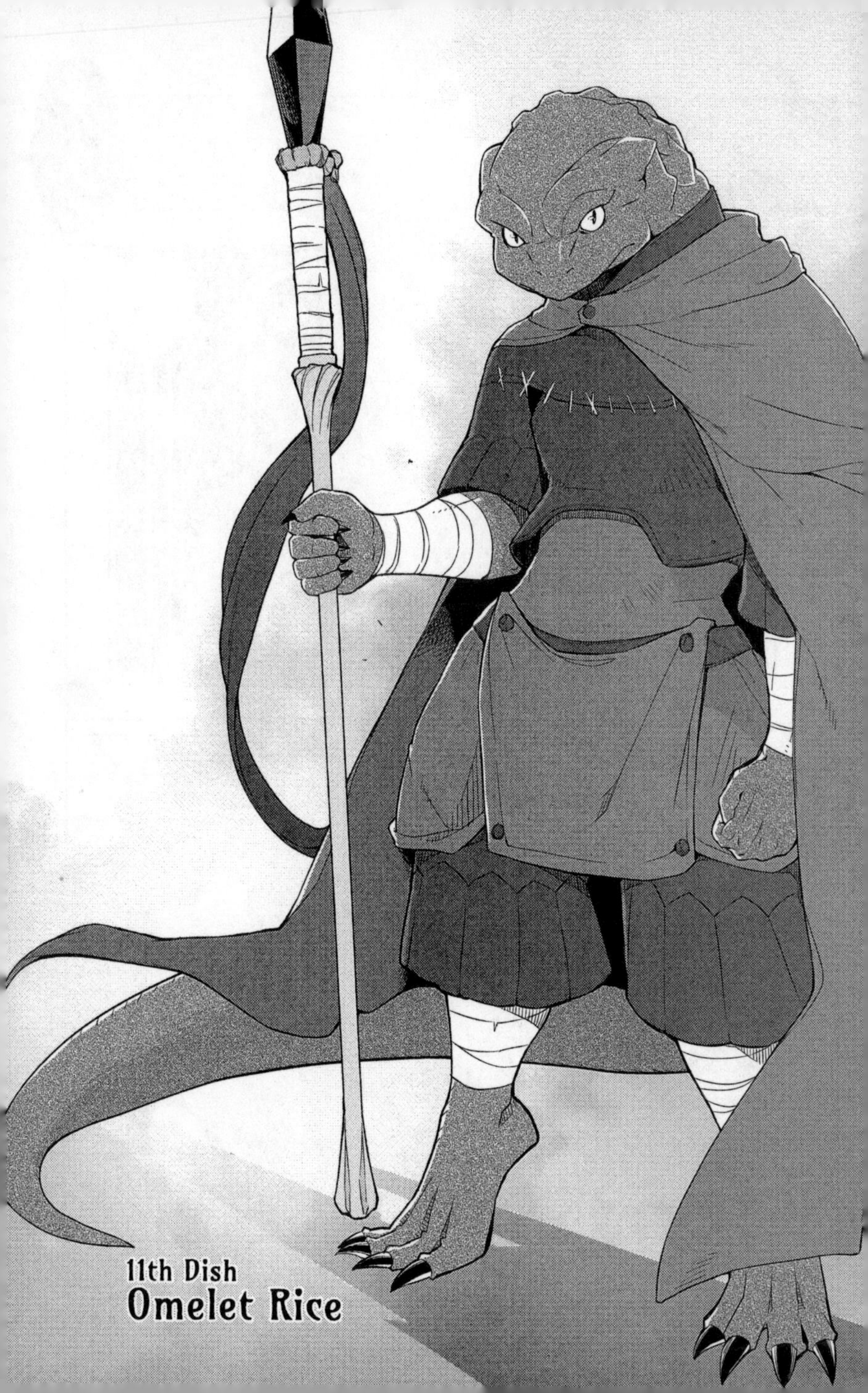

11th Dish
Omelet Rice

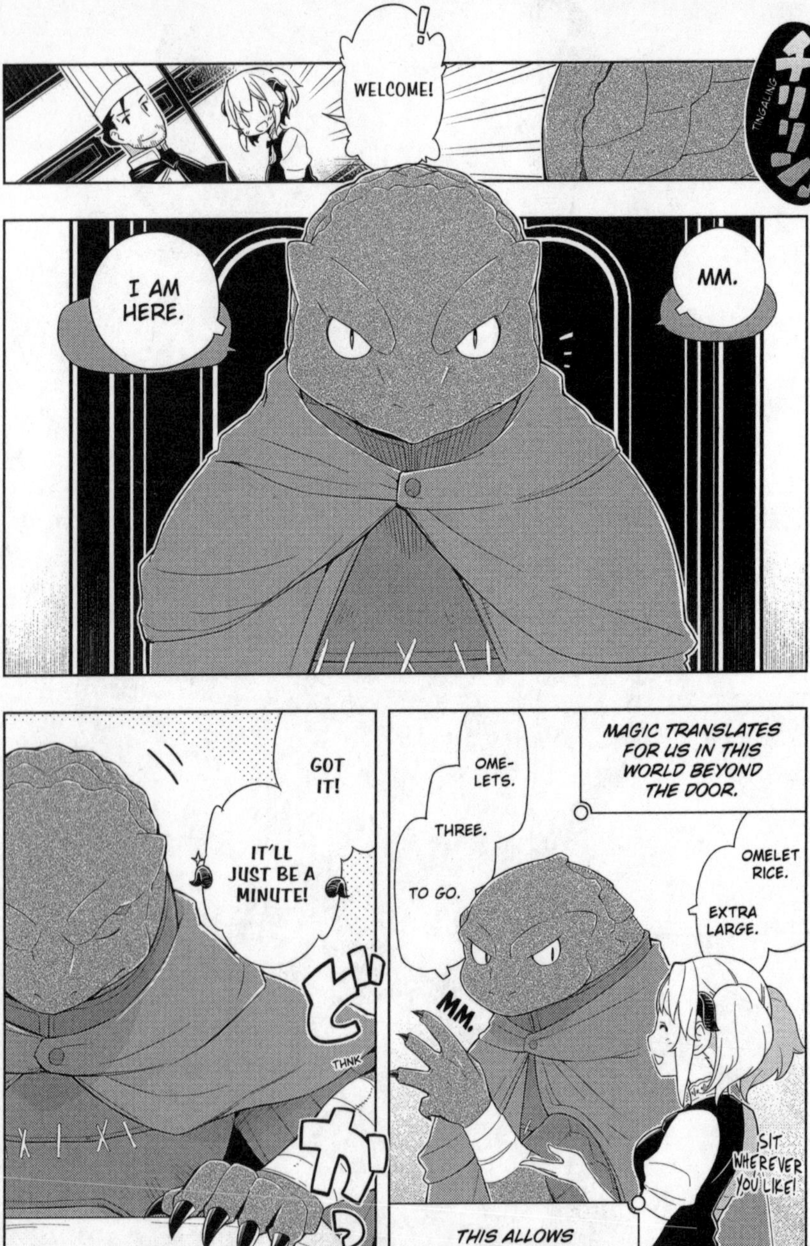
チリン
TINGALING
!
WELCOME!
MM.
I AM HERE.
MAGIC TRANSLATES FOR US IN THIS WORLD BEYOND THE DOOR.
OMELET RICE.
EXTRA LARGE.
OMELETS.
THREE.
TO GO.
SIT WHEREVER YOU LIKE!
MM.
THIS ALLOWS US LIZARDMEN TO ORDER EASILY.
GOT IT!
IT'LL JUST BE A MINUTE!
THNK

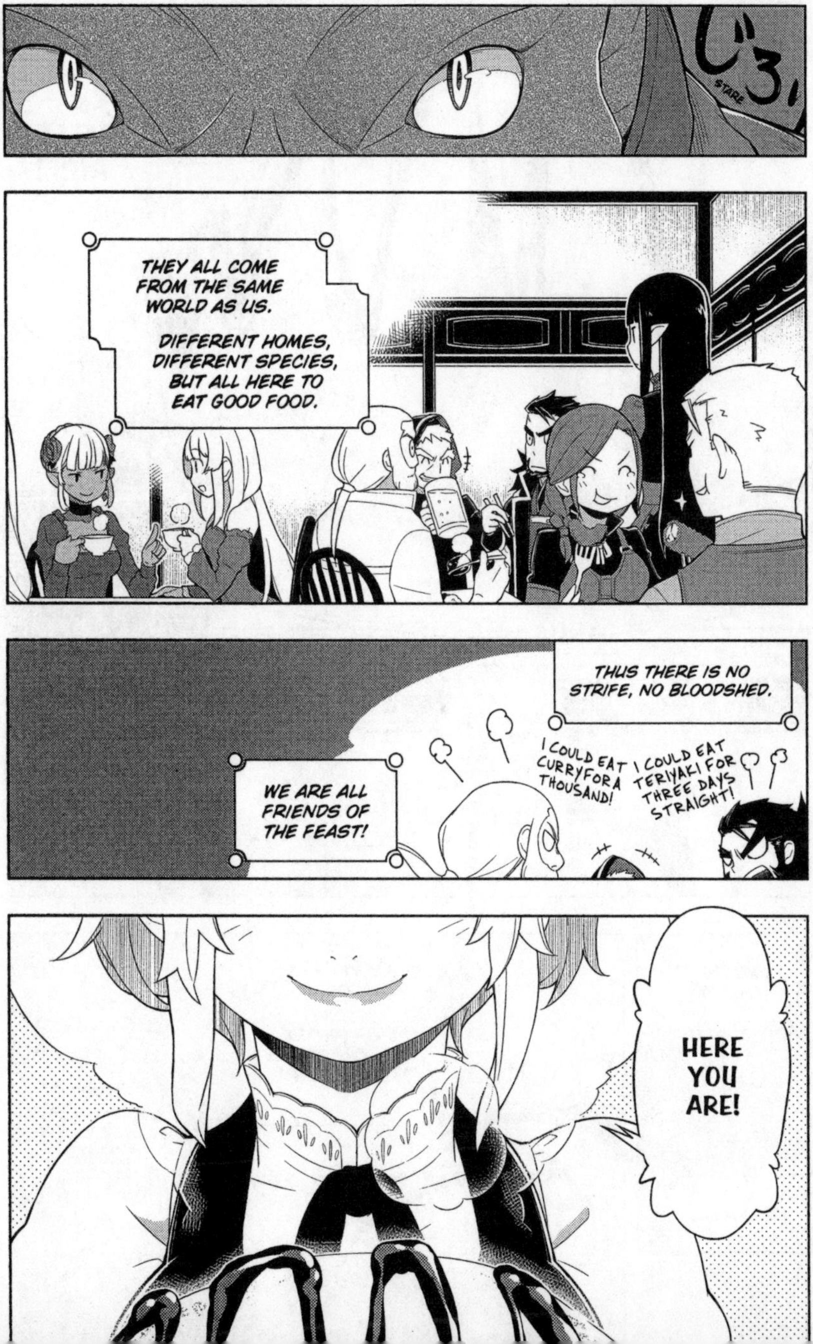
STARE
THEY ALL COME FROM THE SAME WORLD AS US.
DIFFERENT HOMES, DIFFERENT SPECIES, BUT ALL HERE TO EAT GOOD FOOD.
THUS THERE IS NO STRIFE, NO BLOODSHED.
I COULD EAT TERIYAKI FOR THREE DAYS STRAIGHT!
I COULD EAT CURRY FOR A THOUSAND!
WE ARE ALL FRIENDS OF THE FEAST!
HERE YOU ARE!

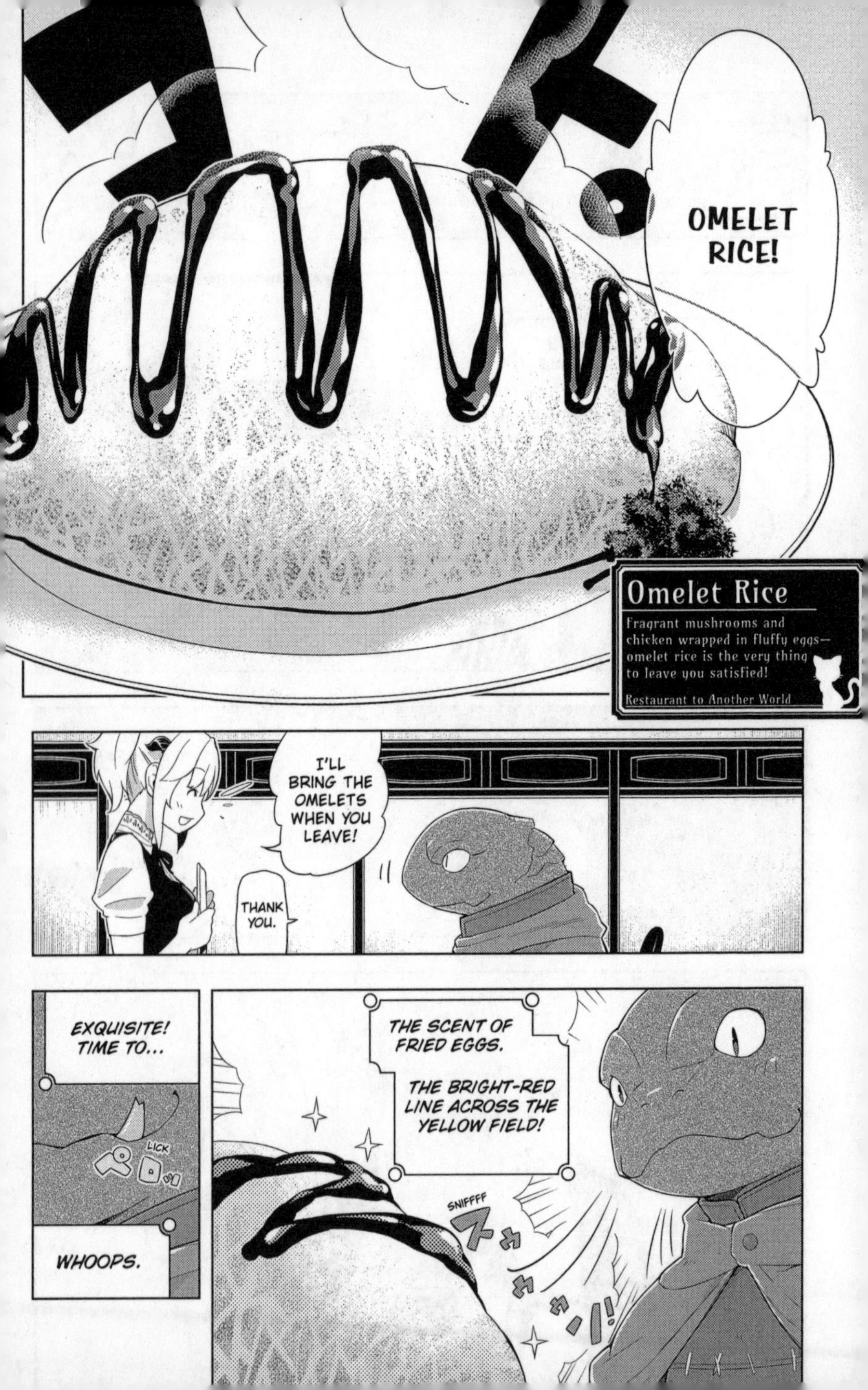
OMELET RICE!
Omelet Rice
Fragrant mushrooms and chicken wrapped in fluffy eggs—omelet rice is the very thing to leave you satisfied!
Restaurant to Another World
I'LL BRING THE OMELETS WHEN YOU LEAVE!
THANK YOU.
THE SCENT OF FRIED EGGS.
THE BRIGHT-RED LINE ACROSS THE YELLOW FIELD!
SNIFFFF
EXQUISITE! TIME TO...
LICK
WHOOPS.

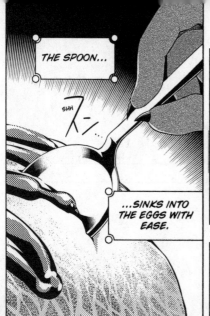

ITA-DAKI-MASU.
WHEN DINING IN ANOTHER WORLD, ONE MUST NOT FORGET TO THANK THE LOCAL GODS.
GOOD!
THE SPOON...
SHH
...SINKS INTO THE EGGS WITH EASE.
THE CONTENTS SPILL OUT, RADIATING WARMTH.
ORANGE GRAINS WITH STREAKS OF RED!
WAFT
DROOL
HOT
HOT

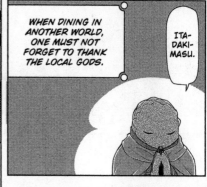

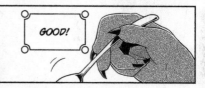

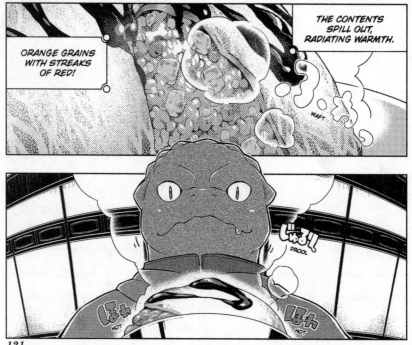

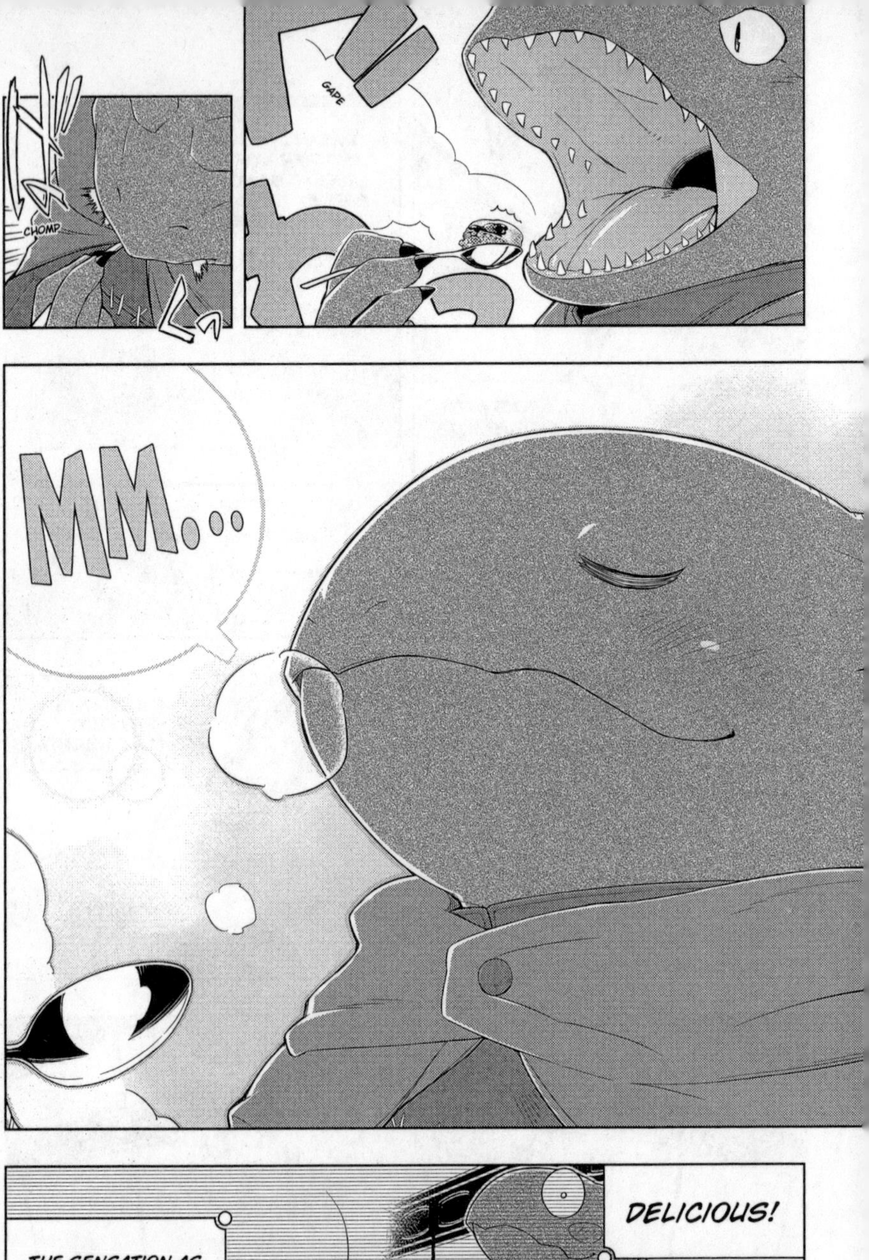
GAPE
CHOMP
MM...
DELICIOUS!
SWISH
SWISH
THE SENSATION AS VIVID AS THE FIRST DAY I ATE THIS DISH!

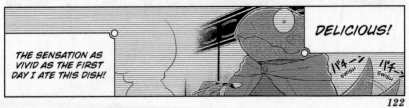

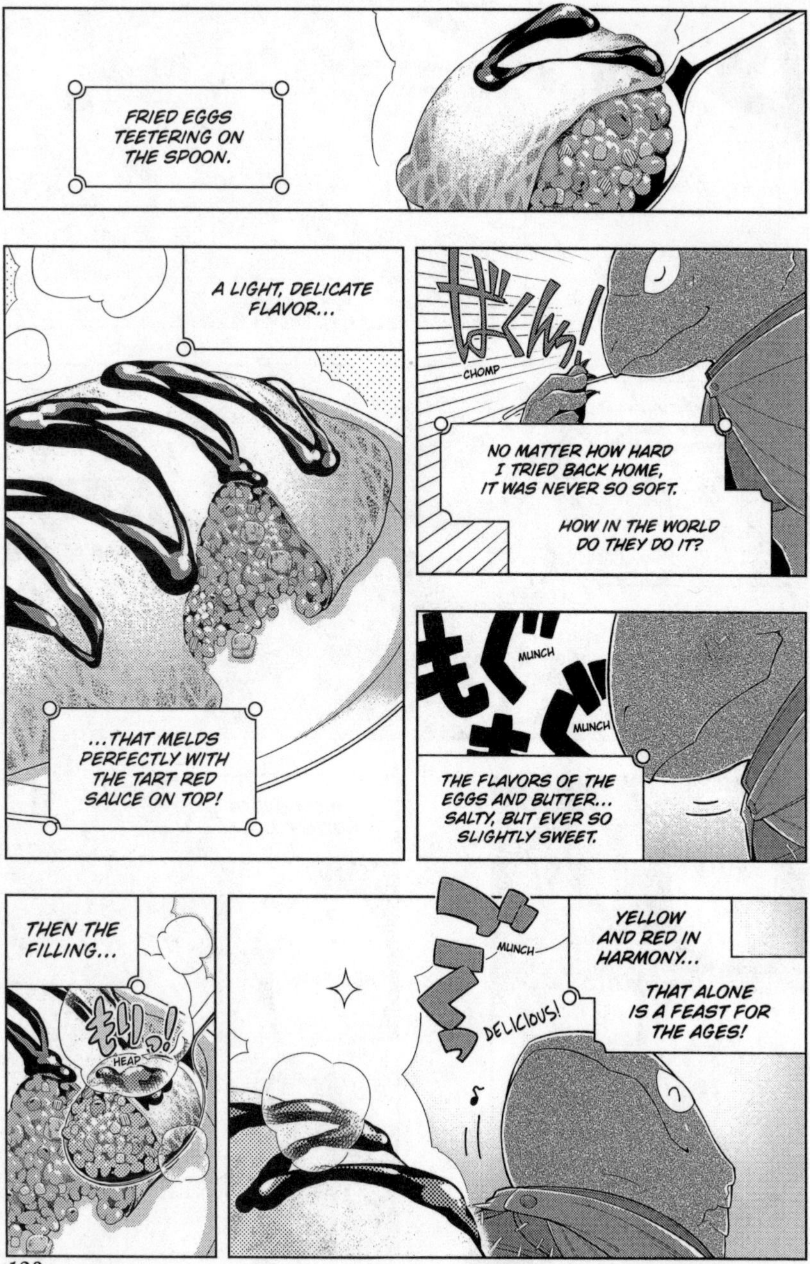

FRIED EGGS TEETERING ON THE SPOON.
CHOMP
NO MATTER HOW HARD I TRIED BACK HOME, IT WAS NEVER SO SOFT.
HOW IN THE WORLD DO THEY DO IT?
MUNCH
MUNCH
THE FLAVORS OF THE EGGS AND BUTTER... SALTY, BUT EVER SO SLIGHTLY SWEET.
A LIGHT, DELICATE FLAVOR...
...THAT MELDS PERFECTLY WITH THE TART RED SAUCE ON TOP!
YELLOW AND RED IN HARMONY...
THAT ALONE IS A FEAST FOR THE AGES!
MUNCH
DELICIOUS!
THEN THE FILLING...
HEAP

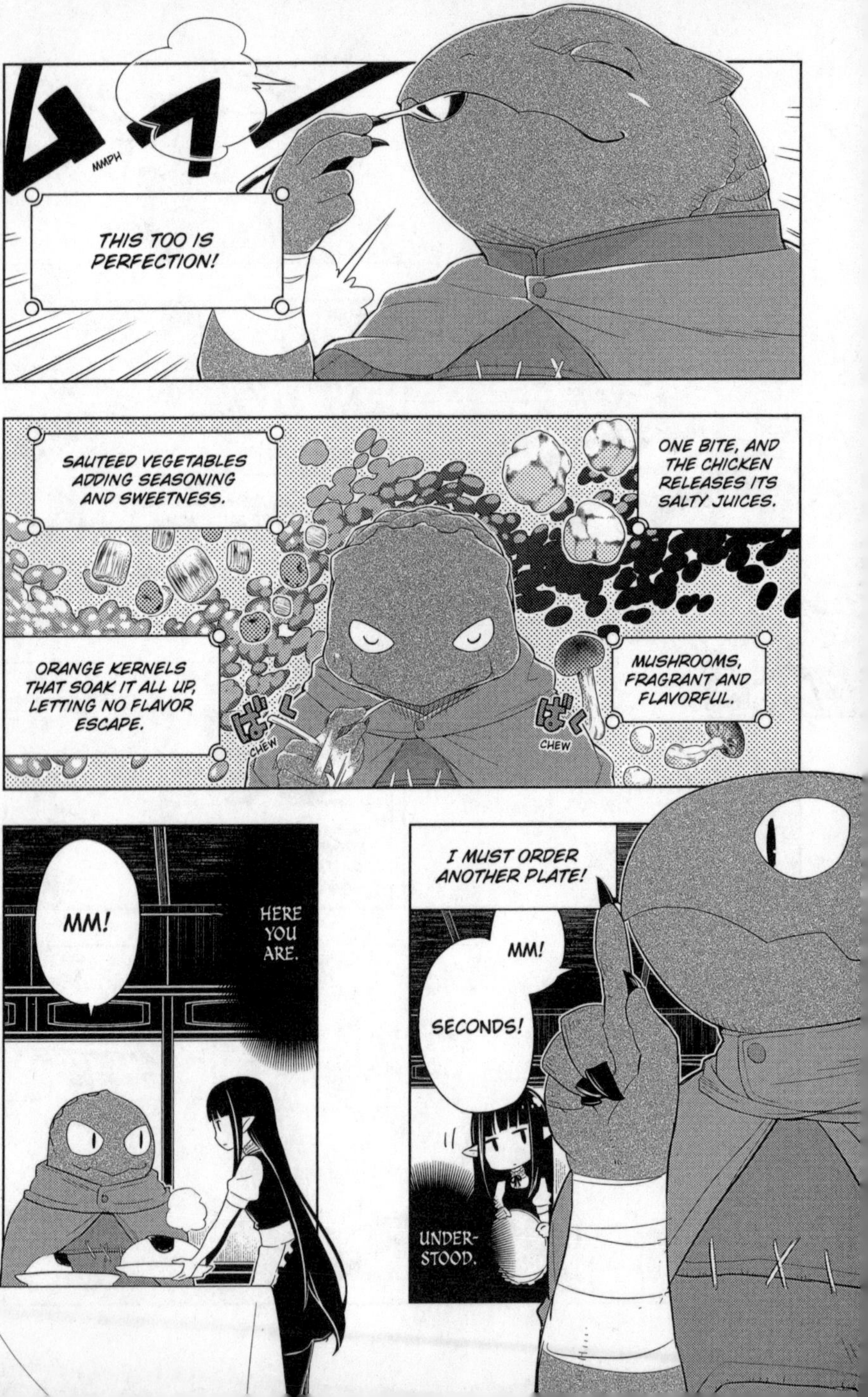

ムッ
MMPH
THIS TOO IS PERFECTION!
ONE BITE, AND THE CHICKEN RELEASES ITS SALTY JUICES.
SAUTEED VEGETABLES ADDING SEASONING AND SWEETNESS.
MUSHROOMS, FRAGRANT AND FLAVORFUL.
ぱく
CHEW
ぱく
CHEW
ORANGE KERNELS THAT SOAK IT ALL UP, LETTING NO FLAVOR ESCAPE.
I MUST ORDER ANOTHER PLATE!
MM!
SECONDS!
UNDER-STOOD.
HERE YOU ARE.
MM!

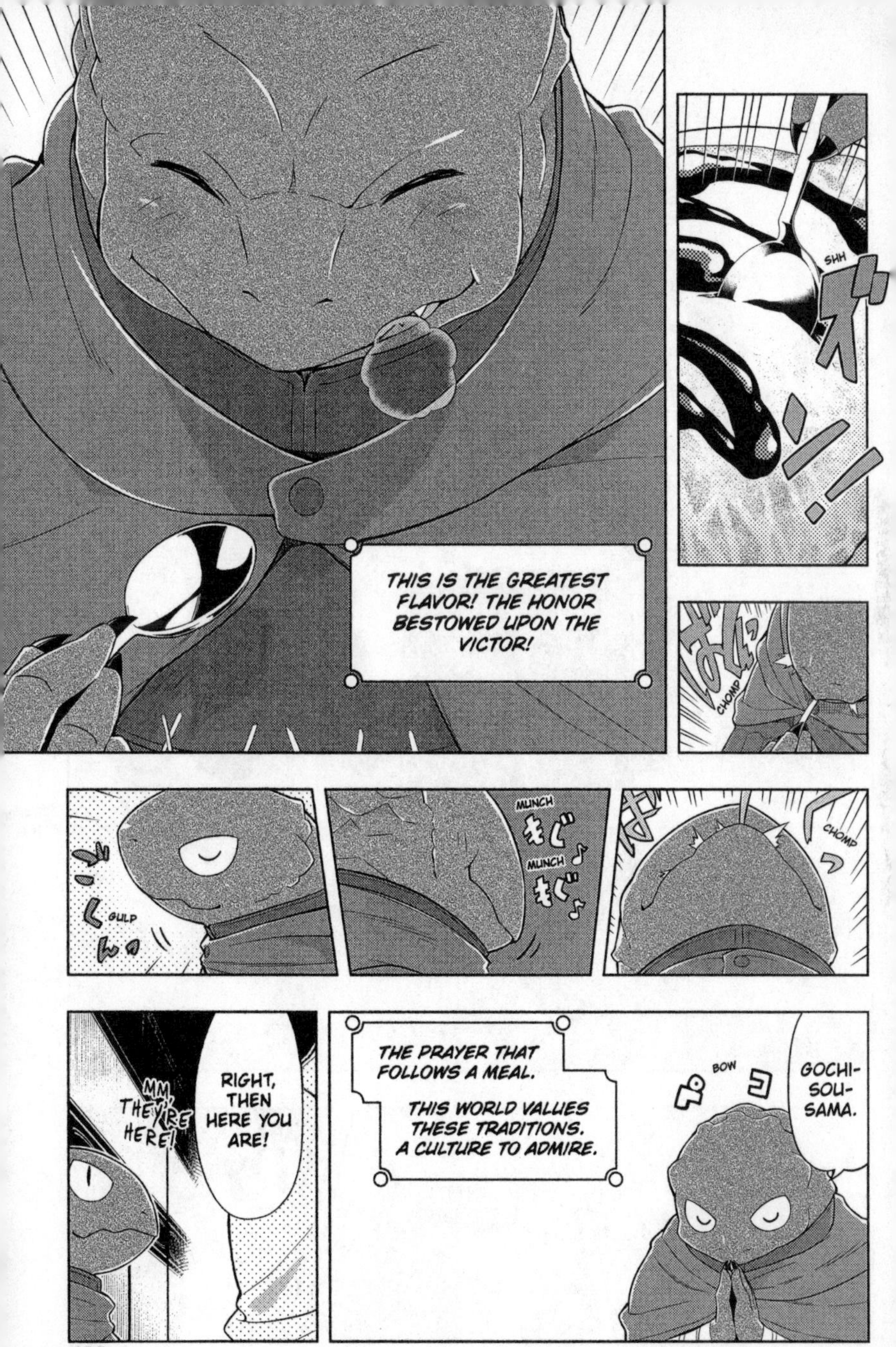
SHH
CHOMP
THIS IS THE GREATEST FLAVOR! THE HONOR BESTOWED UPON THE VICTOR!
CHOMP
MUNCH
MUNCH
GULP
GOCHI-SOU-SAMA.
BOW
THE PRAYER THAT FOLLOWS A MEAL.
THIS WORLD VALUES THESE TRADITIONS. A CULTURE TO ADMIRE.
RIGHT, THEN HERE YOU ARE!
MM, THEY'RE HERE!

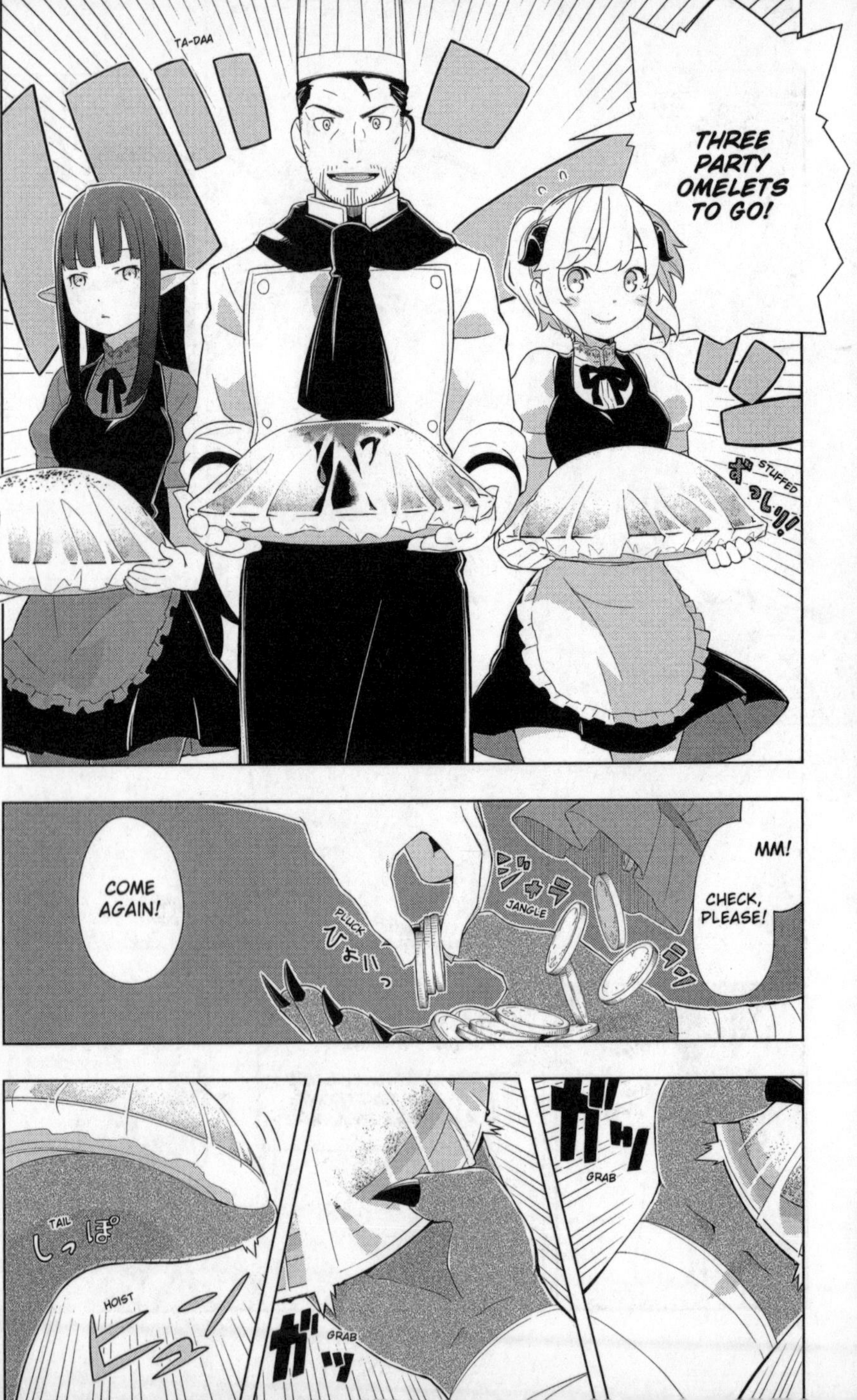
THREE PARTY OMELETS TO GO!
TA-DAA
STUFFED
MM!
CHECK, PLEASE!
JANGLE
PLUCK
COME AGAIN!
GRAB
TAIL
HOIST
GRAB

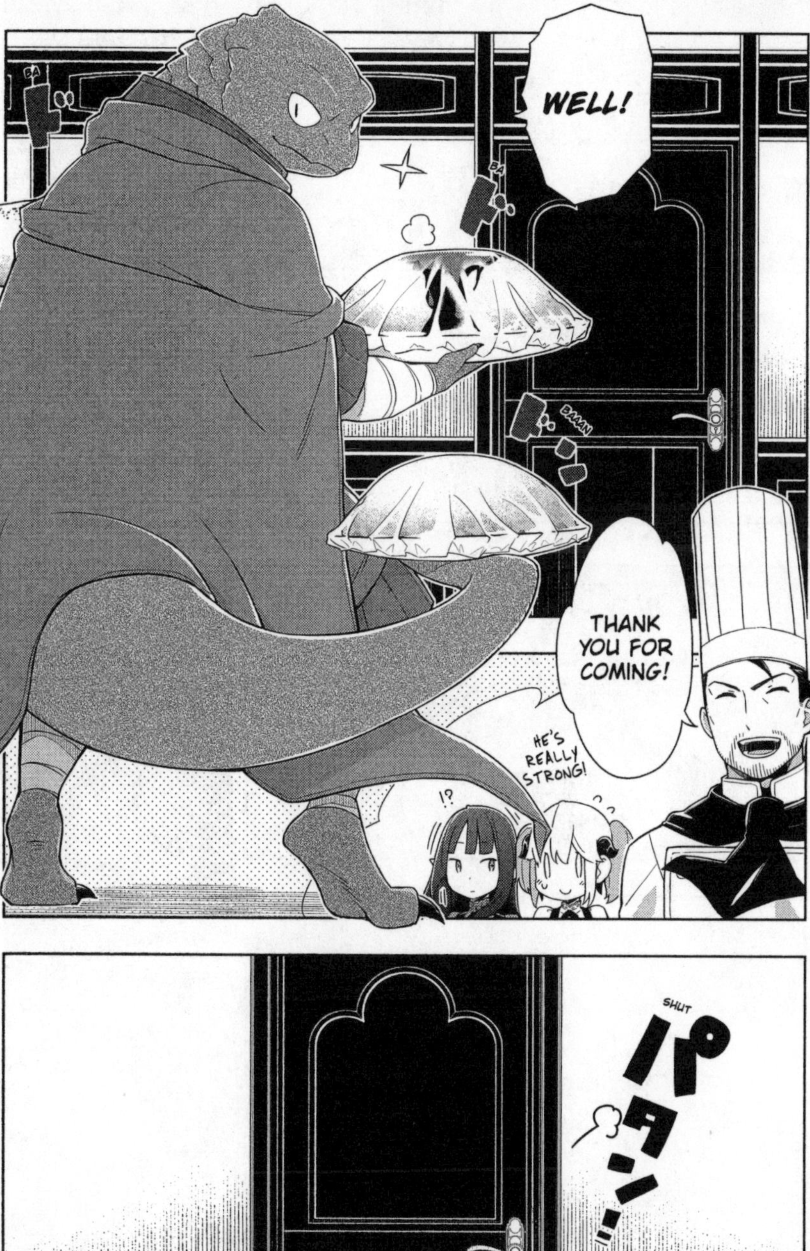
WELL!
BA
BAAN
BA
THANK YOU FOR COMING!
HE'S REALLY STRONG!
!?
SHUT
パタン!!

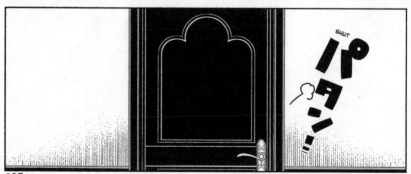

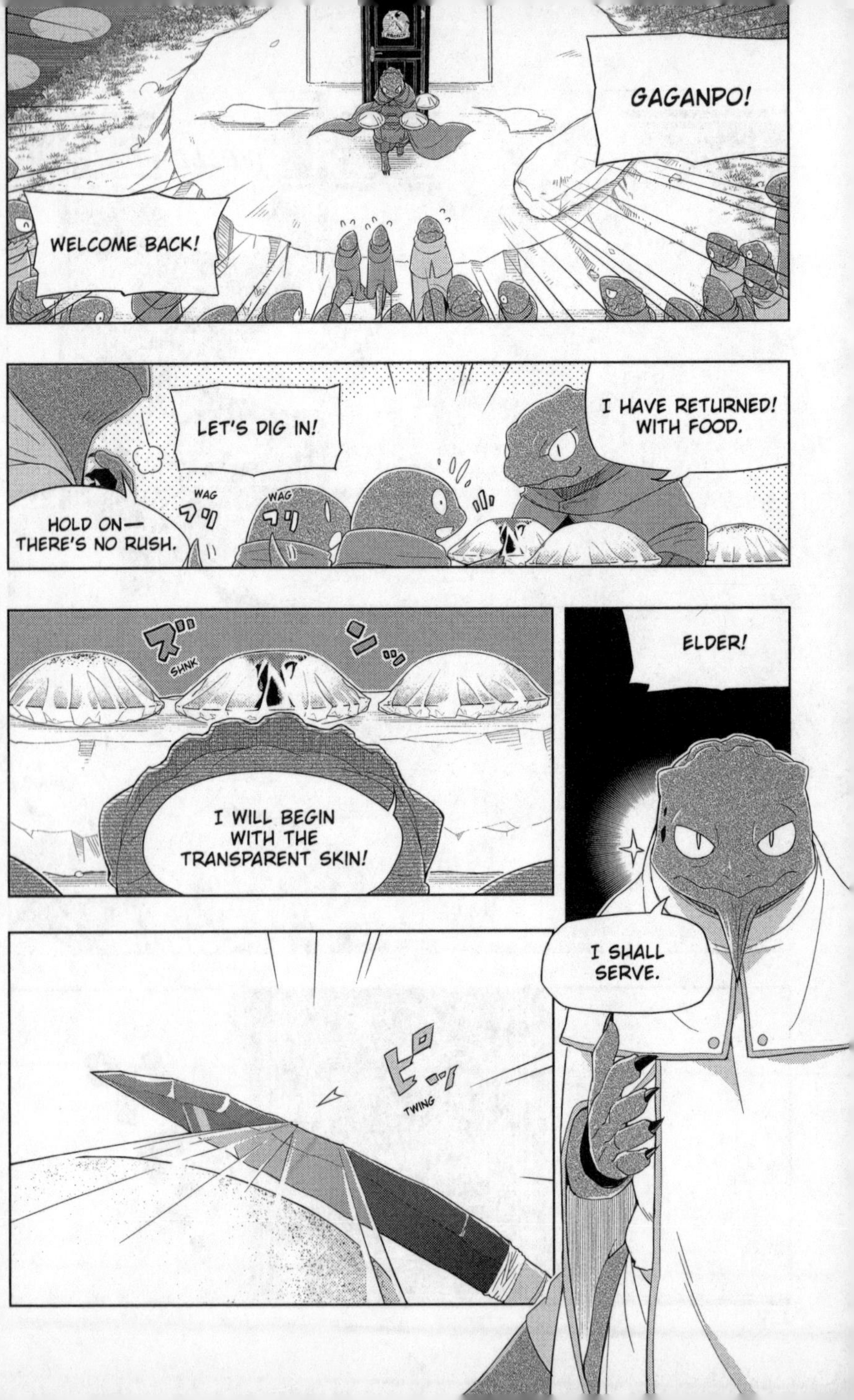
GAGANPO!
WELCOME BACK!
I HAVE RETURNED! WITH FOOD.
LET'S DIG IN!
WAG
WAG
HOLD ON— THERE'S NO RUSH.
ELDER!
I SHALL SERVE.
SHNK
I WILL BEGIN WITH THE TRANSPARENT SKIN!
TWING

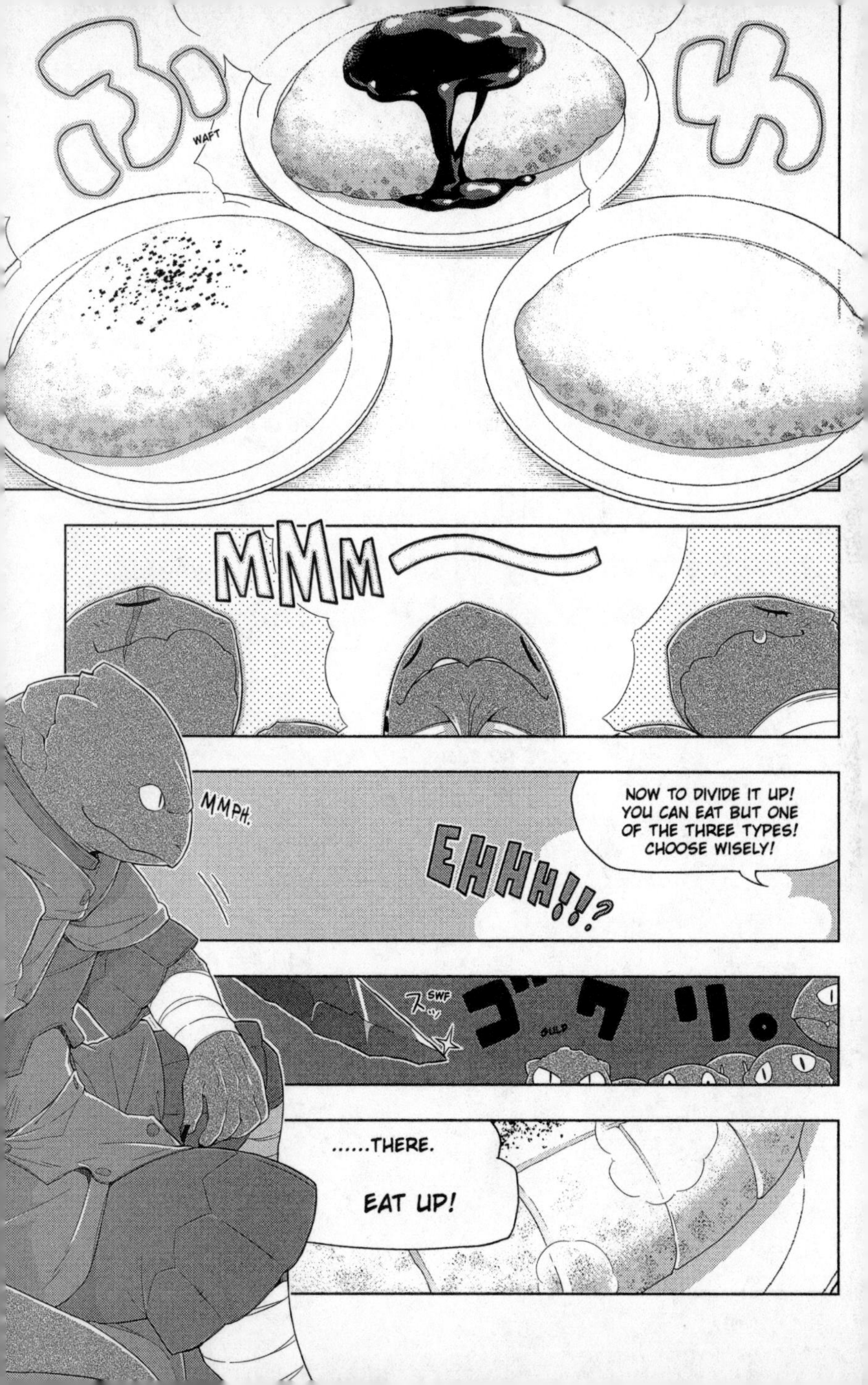
WAFT
MMM—
NOW TO DIVIDE IT UP! YOU CAN EAT BUT ONE OF THE THREE TYPES! CHOOSE WISELY!
EHHH!!?
MMPH.
GULP
SWF
......THERE.
EAT UP!

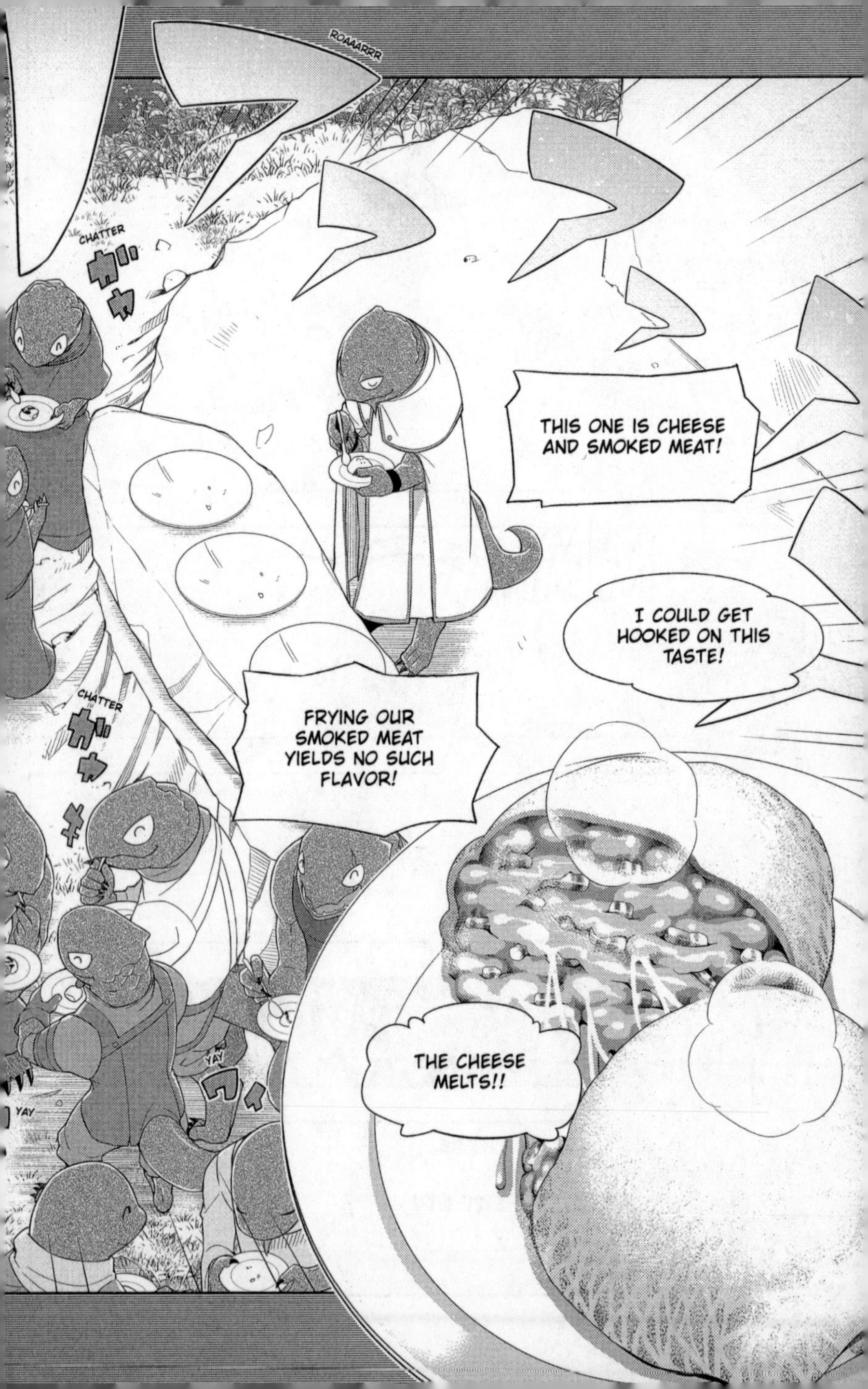
ROAAARRR
THIS ONE IS CHEESE AND SMOKED MEAT!
I COULD GET HOOKED ON THIS TASTE!
CHATTER
FRYING OUR SMOKED MEAT YIELDS NO SUCH FLAVOR!
CHATTER
THE CHEESE MELTS!!
YAY
YAY

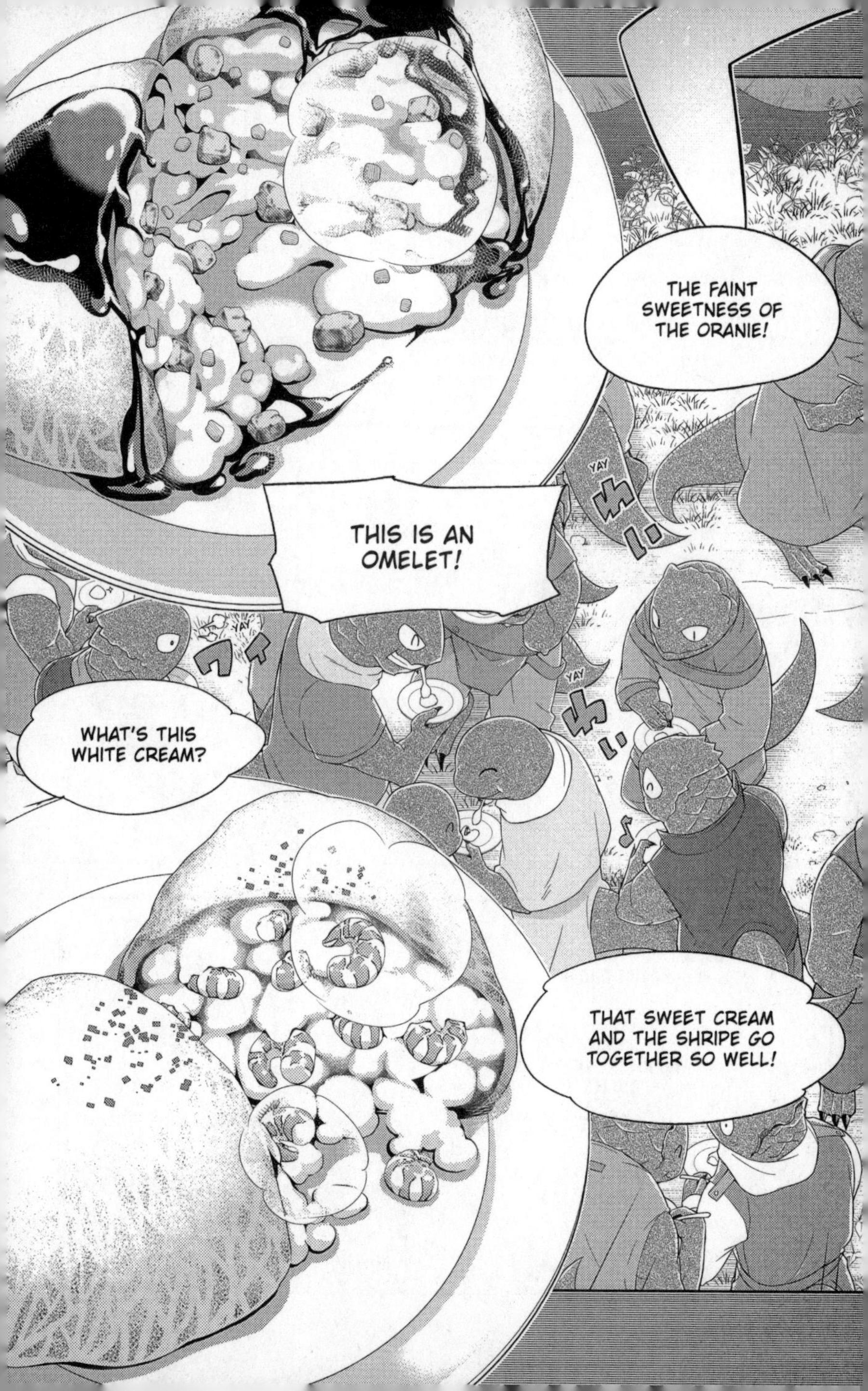
THE FAINT SWEETNESS OF THE ORANIE!
THIS IS AN OMELET!
YAY
YAY
YAY
WHAT'S THIS WHITE CREAM?
THAT SWEET CREAM AND THE SHRIPE GO TOGETHER SO WELL!

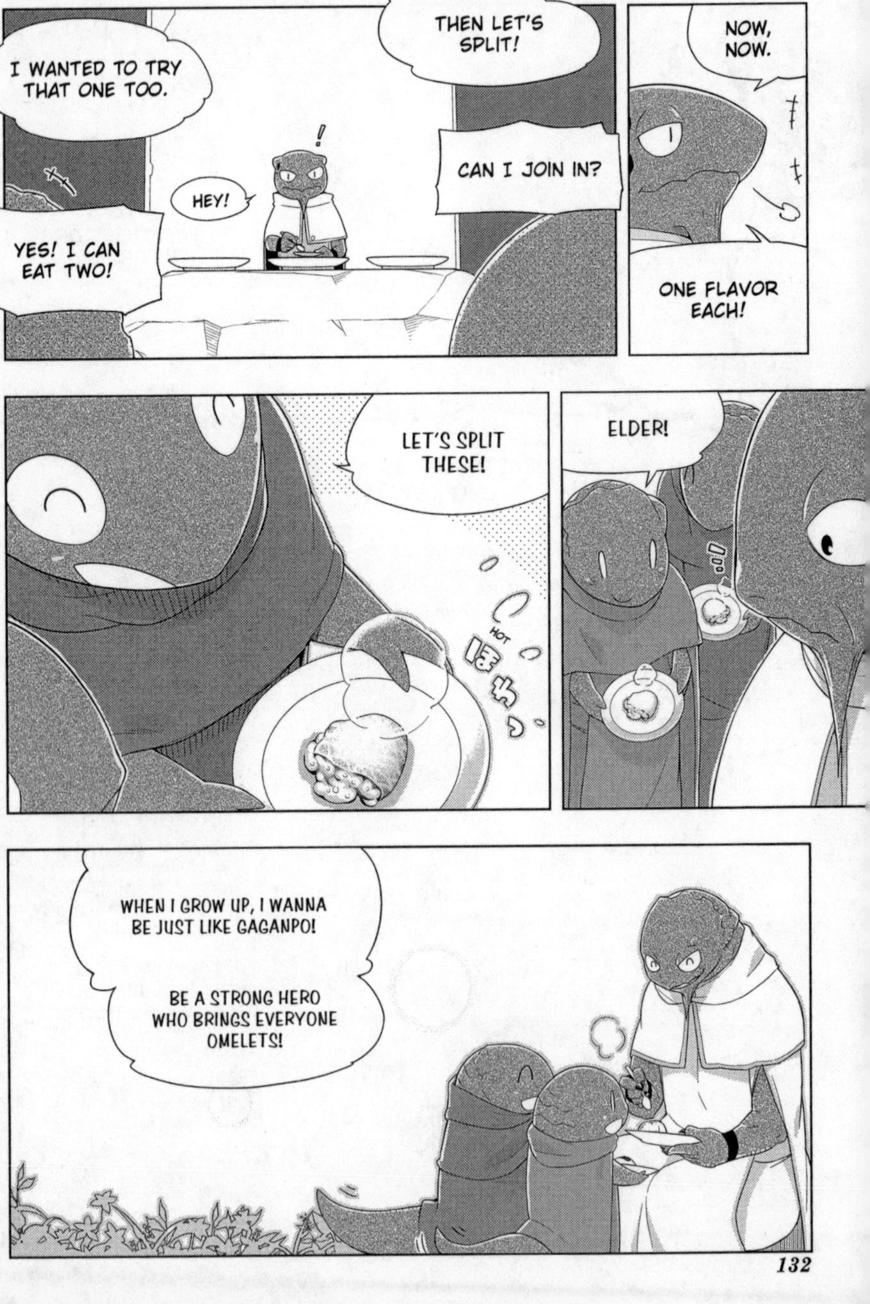
NOW, NOW.
ONE FLAVOR EACH!
THEN LET'S SPLIT!
I WANTED TO TRY THAT ONE TOO.
CAN I JOIN IN?
HEY!
YES! I CAN EAT TWO!
ELDER!
LET'S SPLIT THESE!
HOT
WHEN I GROW UP, I WANNA BE JUST LIKE GAGANPO!
BE A STRONG HERO WHO BRINGS EVERYONE OMELETS!

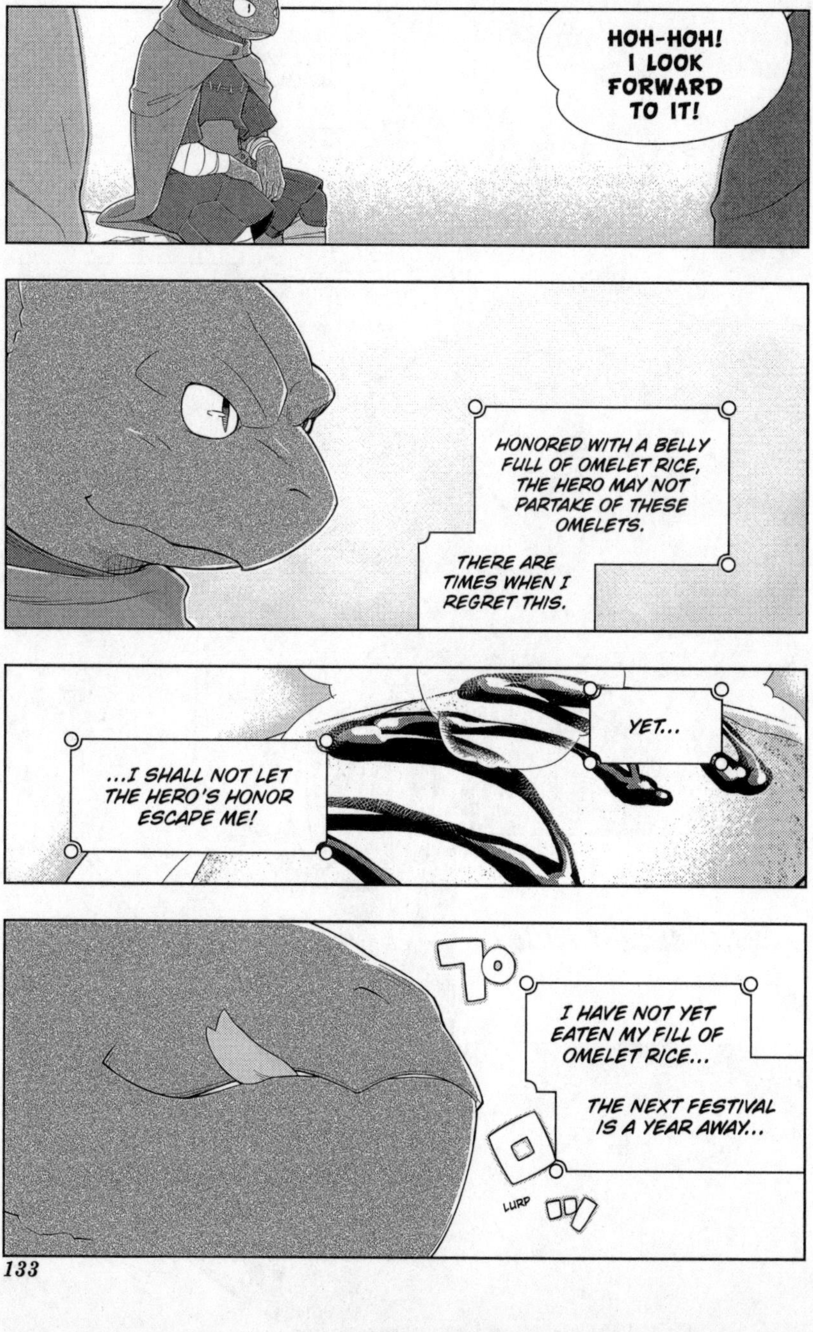
HOH-HOH! I LOOK FORWARD TO IT!
HONORED WITH A BELLY FULL OF OMELET RICE, THE HERO MAY NOT PARTAKE OF THESE OMELETS.
THERE ARE TIMES WHEN I REGRET THIS.
YET...
...I SHALL NOT LET THE HERO'S HONOR ESCAPE ME!
I HAVE NOT YET EATEN MY FILL OF OMELET RICE...
THE NEXT FESTIVAL IS A YEAR AWAY...
LURP

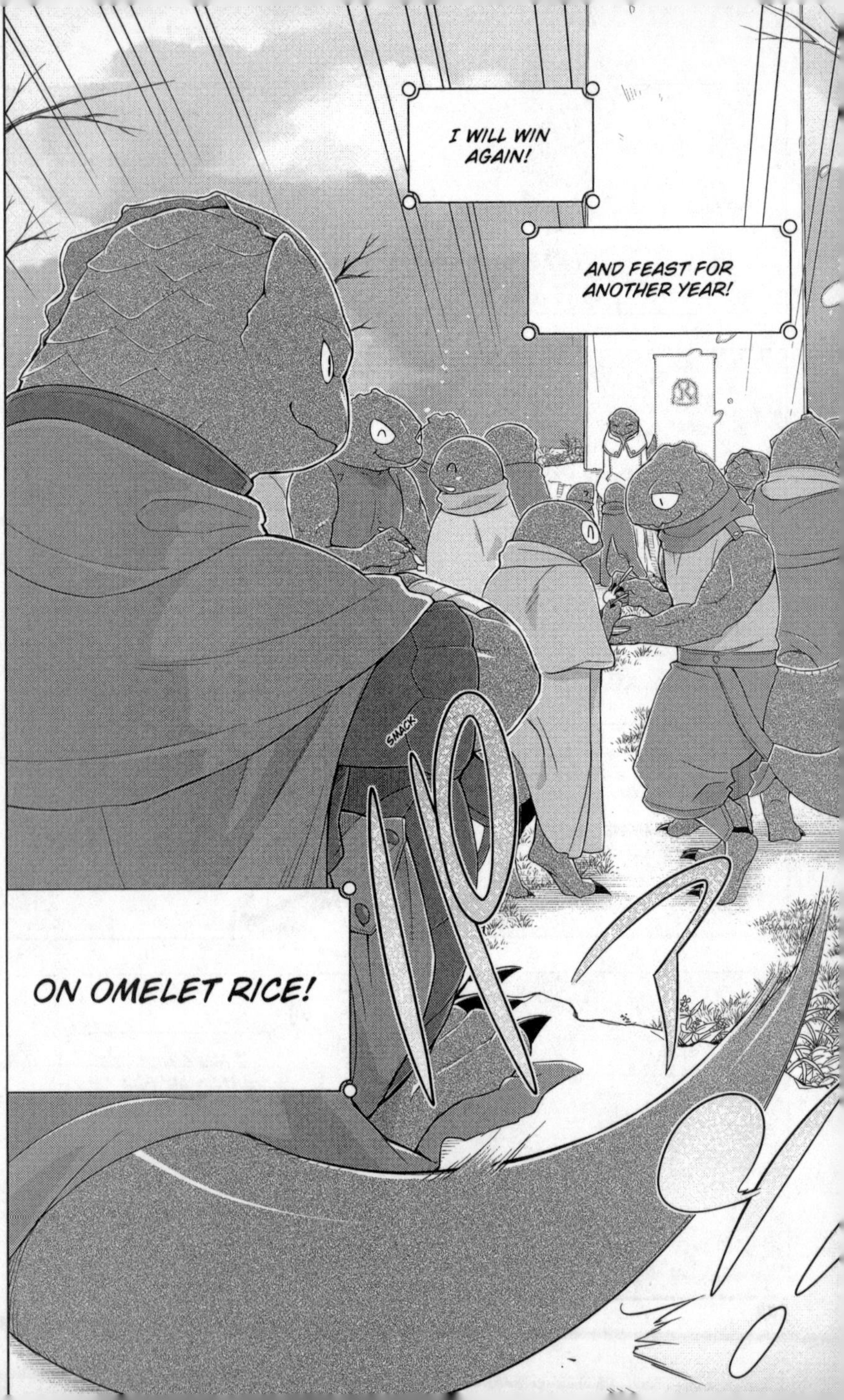
I WILL WIN AGAIN!
AND FEAST FOR ANOTHER YEAR!
SMACK
ON OMELET RICE!

RESTAURANT TO Another World

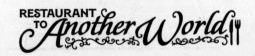

12th Dish Beef Bowl

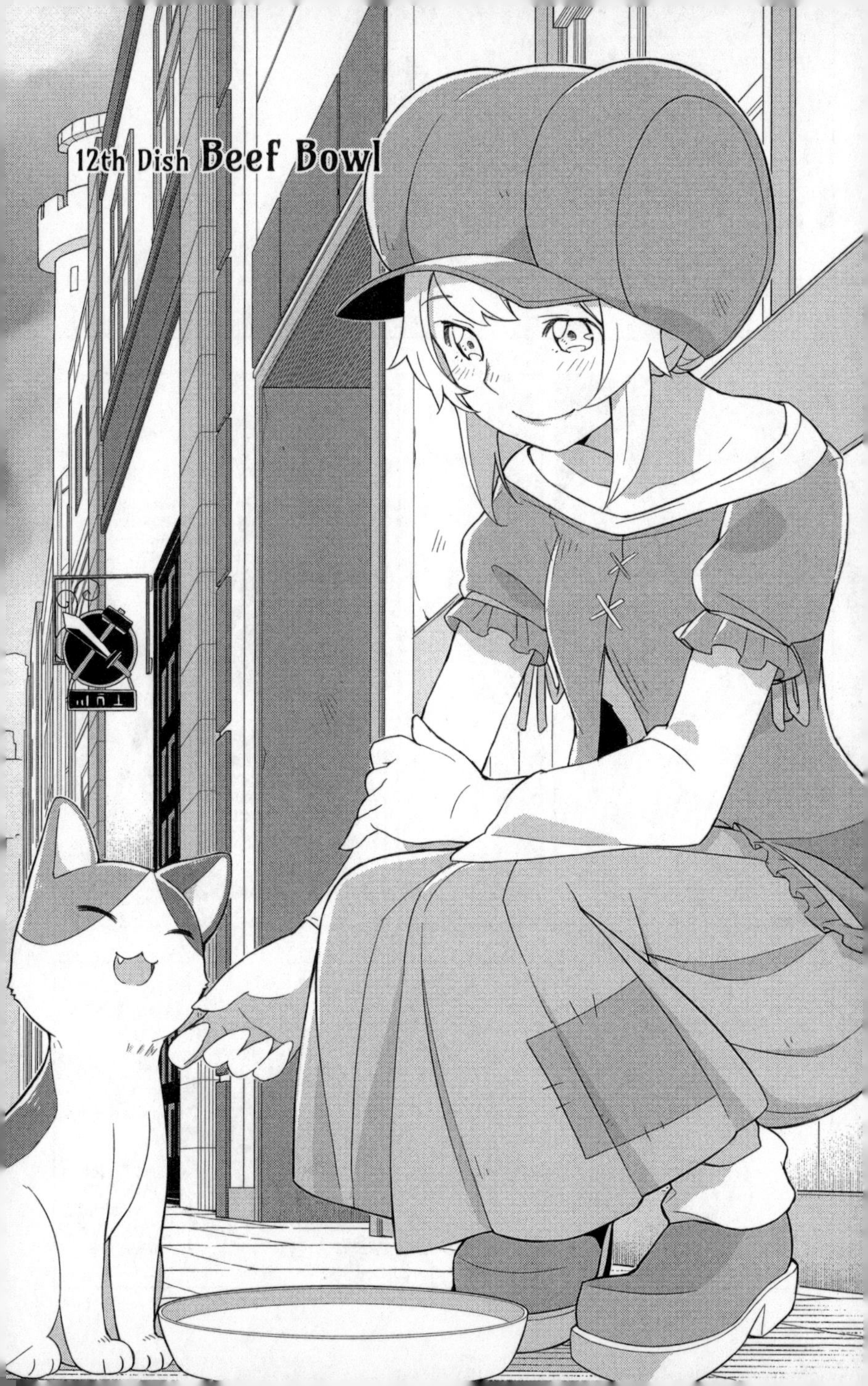

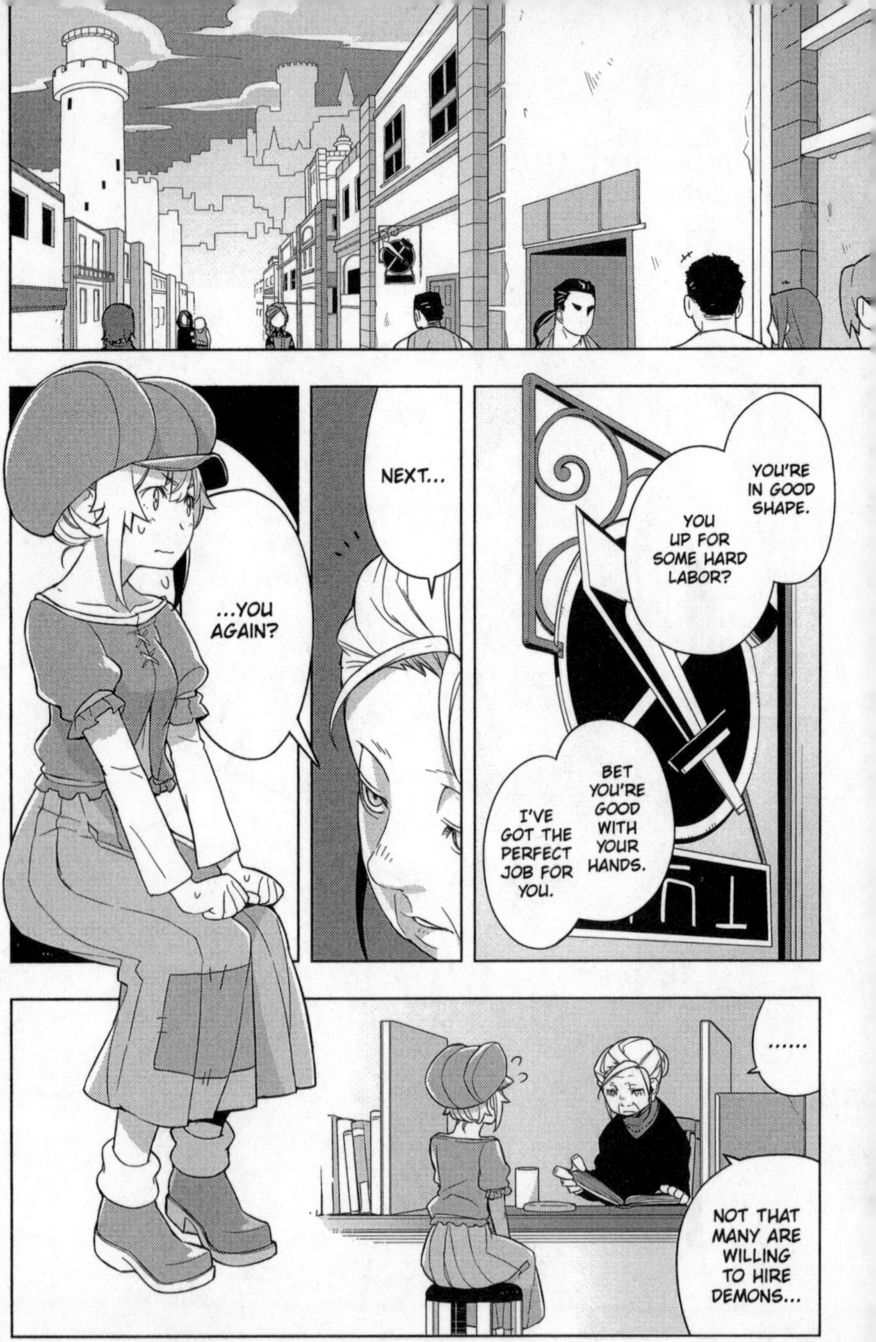
YOU'RE IN GOOD SHAPE.
YOU UP FOR SOME HARD LABOR?
BET YOU'RE GOOD WITH YOUR HANDS.
I'VE GOT THE PERFECT JOB FOR YOU.
NEXT...
...YOU AGAIN?
......
NOT THAT MANY ARE WILLING TO HIRE DEMONS...

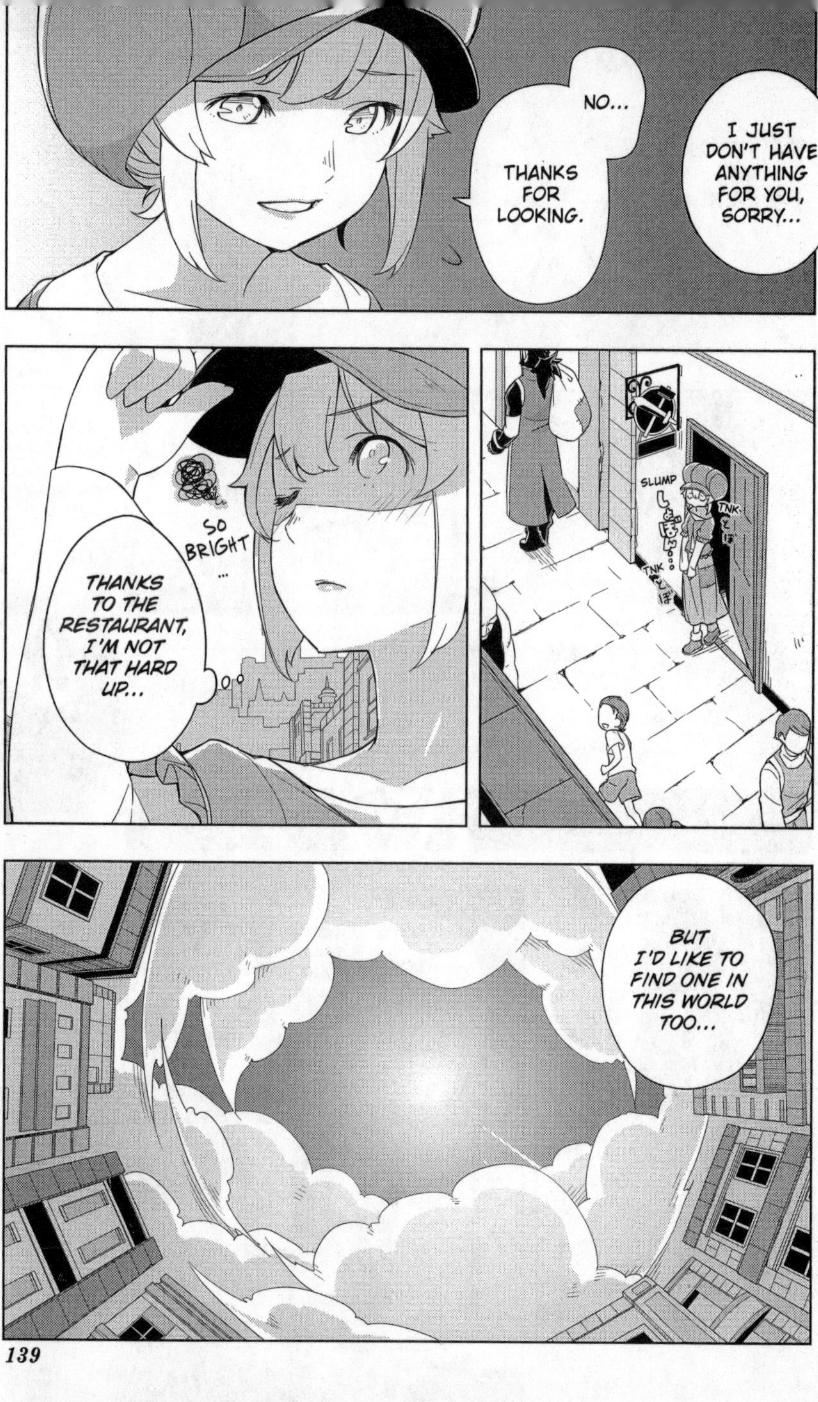
I JUST DON'T HAVE ANYTHING FOR YOU, SORRY...
NO...
THANKS FOR LOOKING.
SLUMP
しょぼん…
TNK
とぼ
TNK
とぼ
SO BRIGHT...
THANKS TO THE RESTAURANT, I'M NOT THAT HARD UP...
BUT I'D LIKE TO FIND ONE IN THIS WORLD TOO...

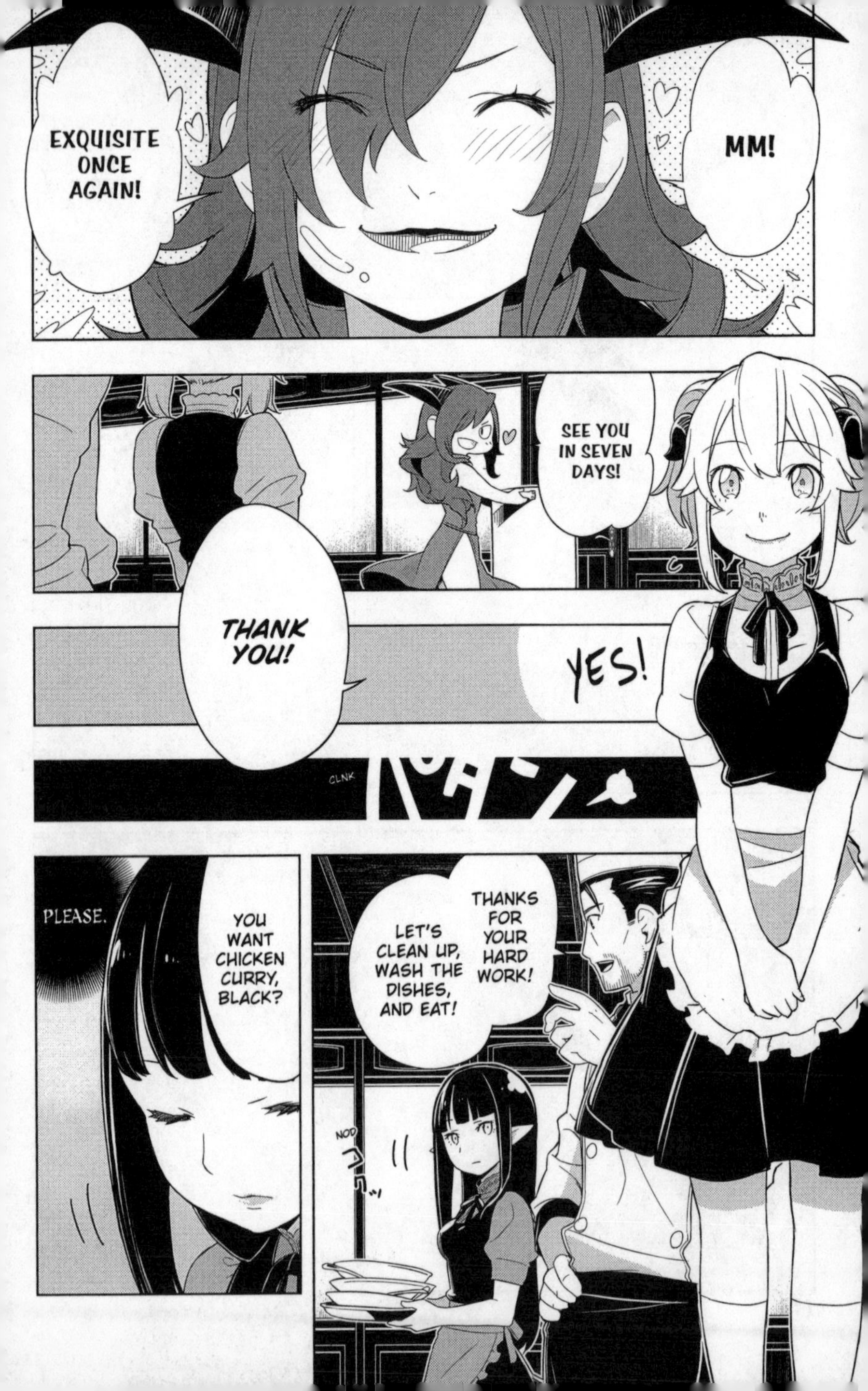
MM!
EXQUISITE ONCE AGAIN!
SEE YOU IN SEVEN DAYS!
YES!
THANK YOU!
CLNK
THANKS FOR YOUR HARD WORK!
LET'S CLEAN UP, WASH THE DISHES, AND EAT!
NOD
YOU WANT CHICKEN CURRY, BLACK?
PLEASE.

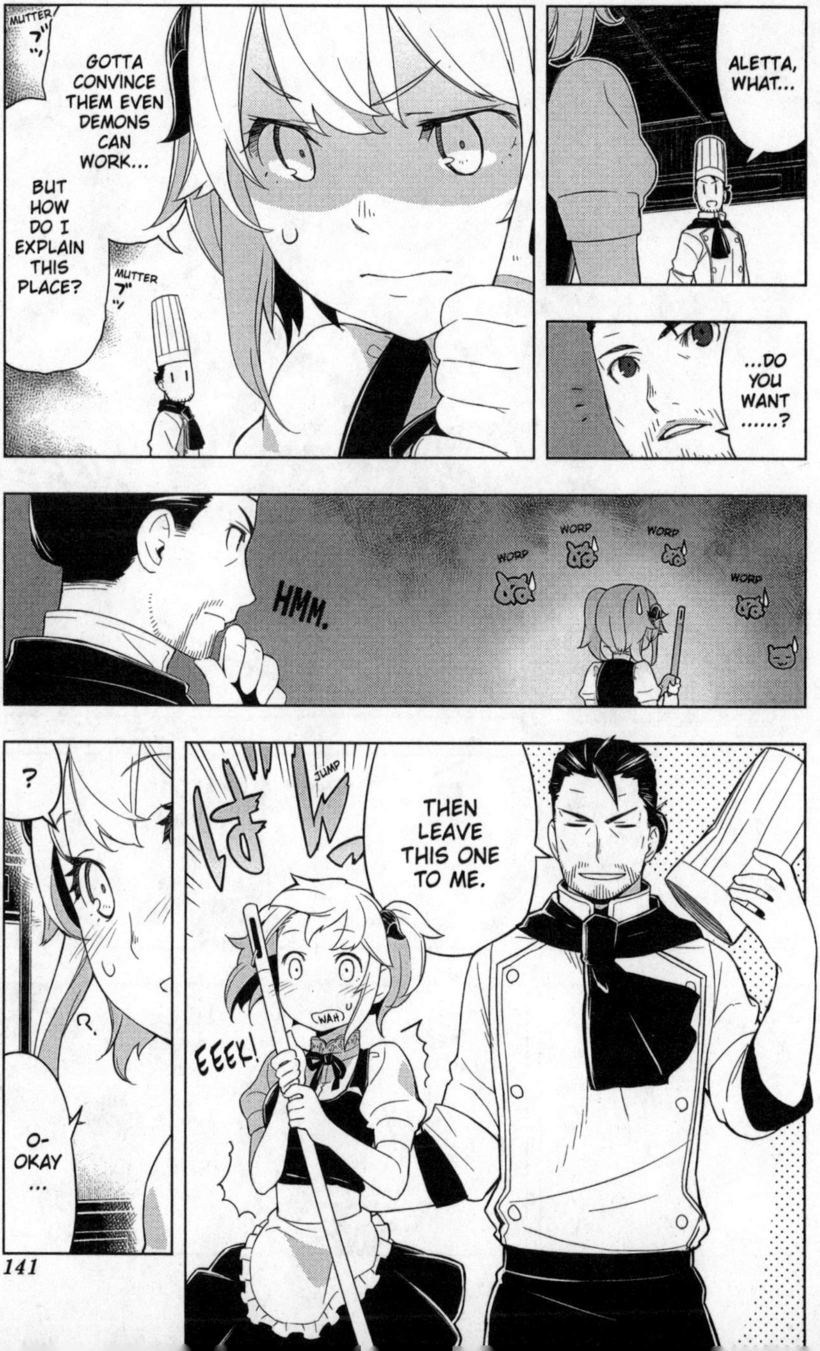
ALETTA, WHAT...
...DO YOU WANT ......?
MUTTER
ブッ
GOTTA CONVINCE THEM EVEN DEMONS CAN WORK...
BUT HOW DO I EXPLAIN THIS PLACE?
MUTTER
ブッ
HMM.
WORP
WORP
WORP
WORP
THEN LEAVE THIS ONE TO ME.
JUMP
EEEK!
WAH
?
O-OKAY ...

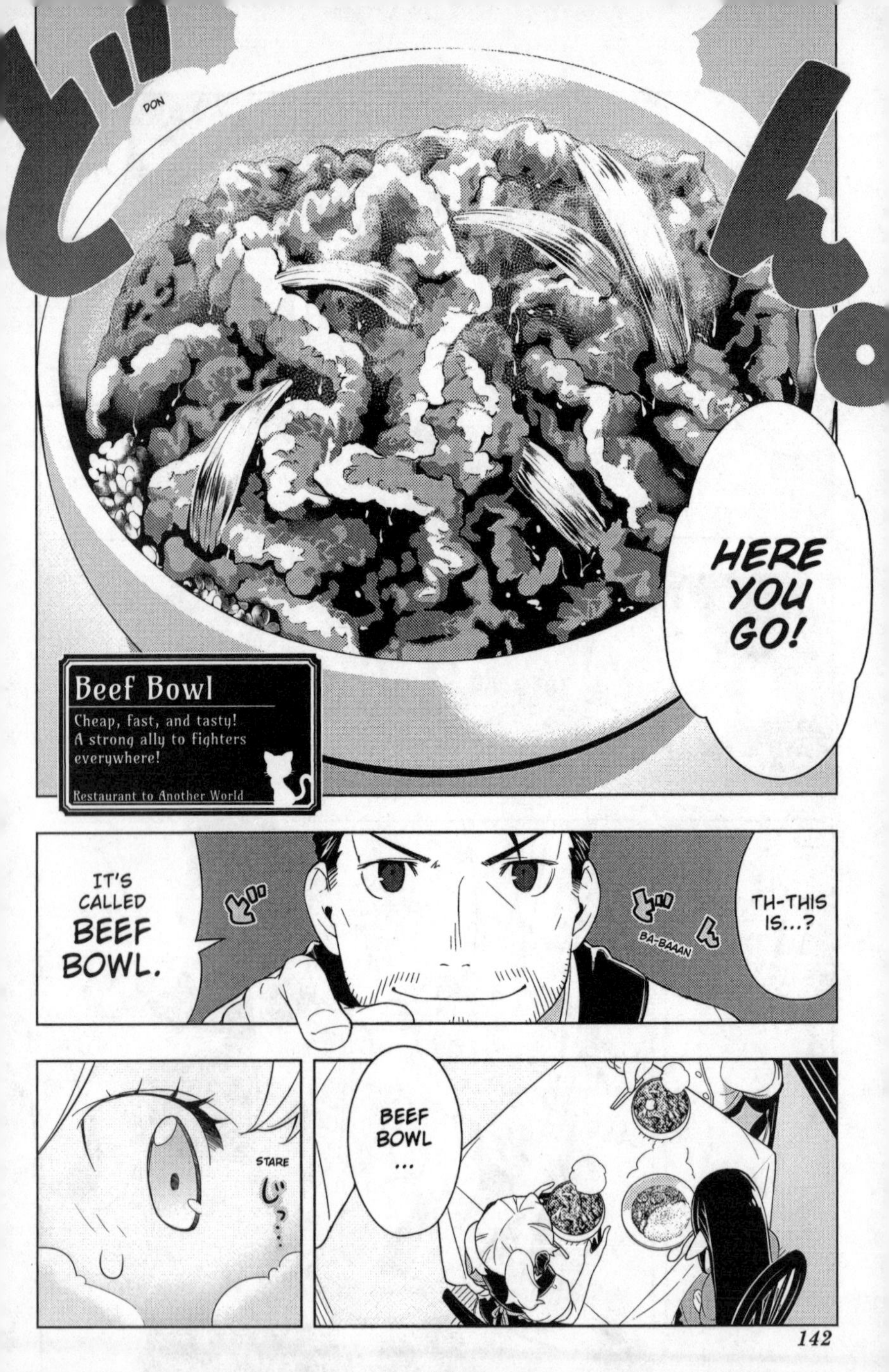
DON
HERE YOU GO!
Beef Bowl
Cheap, fast, and tasty! A strong ally to fighters everywhere!
Restaurant to Another World
TH-THIS IS...?
BA-BAAAN
IT'S CALLED BEEF BOWL.
BEEF BOWL ...
STARE

SUCH FORCE ...!!

DON
どーん

THE SWEET SCENT SOAKED INTO THE MEAT...

SNIFF

SNIFF

GROWWLLLL

...RILES UP MY BLOOD ......!

IT REALLY ...

GULP
ごくっ

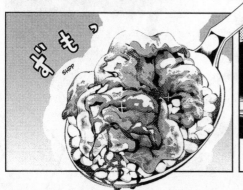

SHPP

DIG IN!

O GOD OF ALL DEMONS. THANK YOU FOR THE LIGHT OF LIFE! LET US EAT!

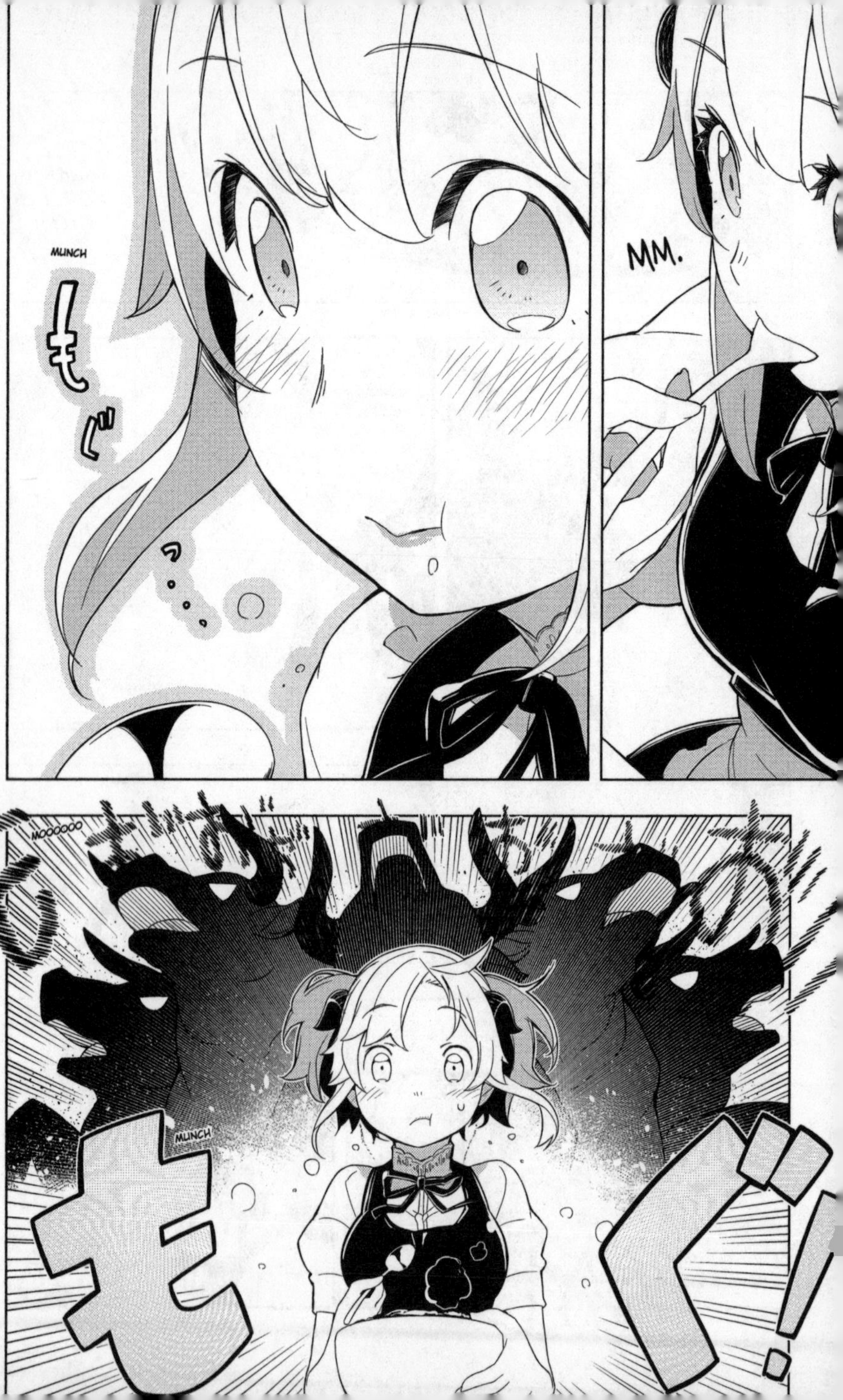
MM.
MUNCH
もぐ
MOOOOOO
MUNCH
もぐ!

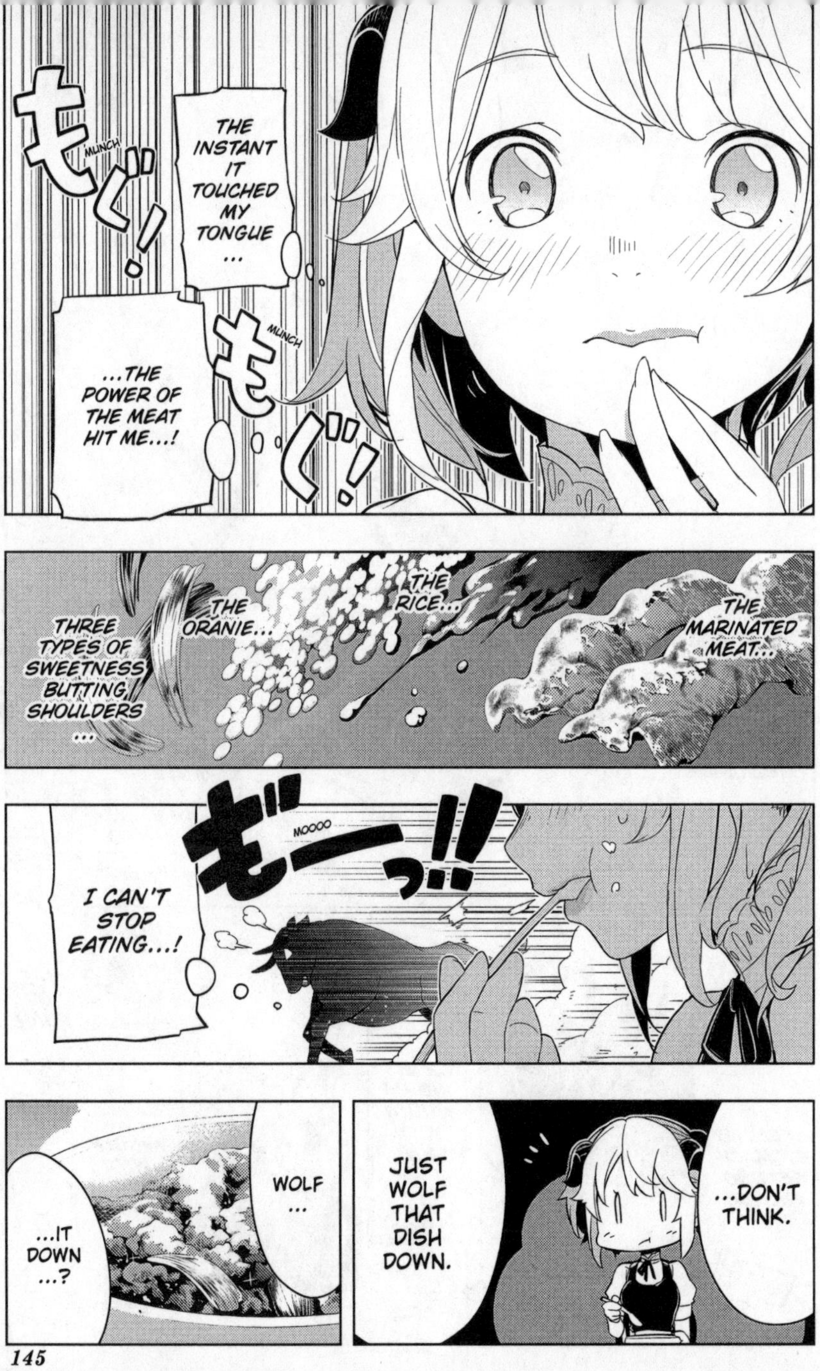
THE INSTANT IT TOUCHED MY TONGUE...
もぐ!
MUNCH
もぐ!
MUNCH
...THE POWER OF THE MEAT HIT ME...!
THE MARINATED MEAT...
THE RICE...
THE ORANIE...
THREE TYPES OF SWEETNESS BUTTING SHOULDERS...
もーっ!!
MOOOO
I CAN'T STOP EATING...!
...DON'T THINK.
JUST WOLF THAT DISH DOWN.
WOLF...
...IT DOWN...?

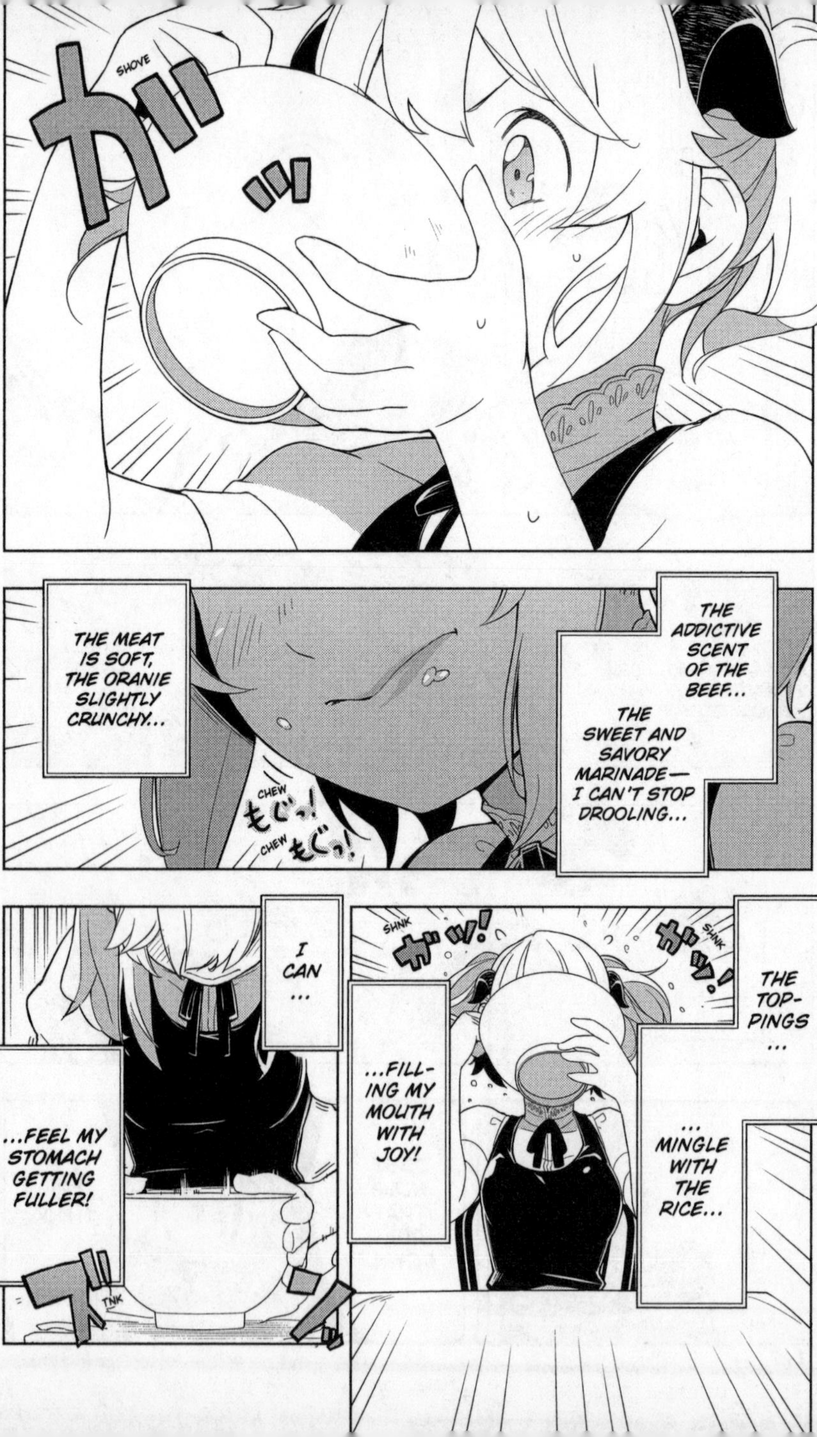

SHOVE
THE ADDICTIVE SCENT OF THE BEEF...
THE SWEET AND SAVORY MARINADE— I CAN'T STOP DROOLING...
CHEW もぐっ!
CHEW もぐっ!
THE MEAT IS SOFT, THE ORANIE SLIGHTLY CRUNCHY...
SHNK
SHNK
THE TOP-PINGS...
... MINGLE WITH THE RICE...
...FILL-ING MY MOUTH WITH JOY!
I CAN...
...FEEL MY STOMACH GETTING FULLER!
TNK

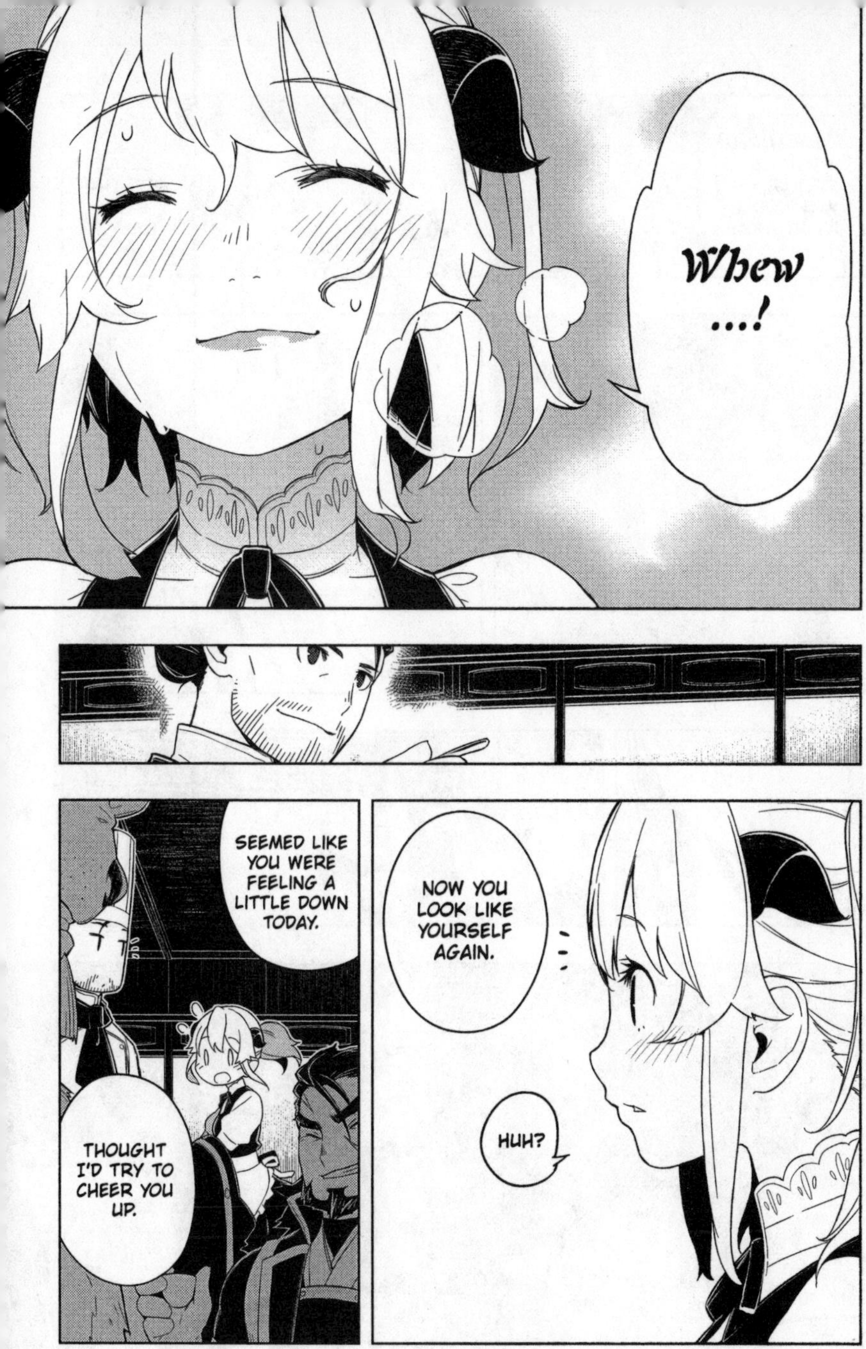
Whew ...!
NOW YOU LOOK LIKE YOURSELF AGAIN.
HUH?
SEEMED LIKE YOU WERE FEELING A LITTLE DOWN TODAY.
THOUGHT I'D TRY TO CHEER YOU UP.

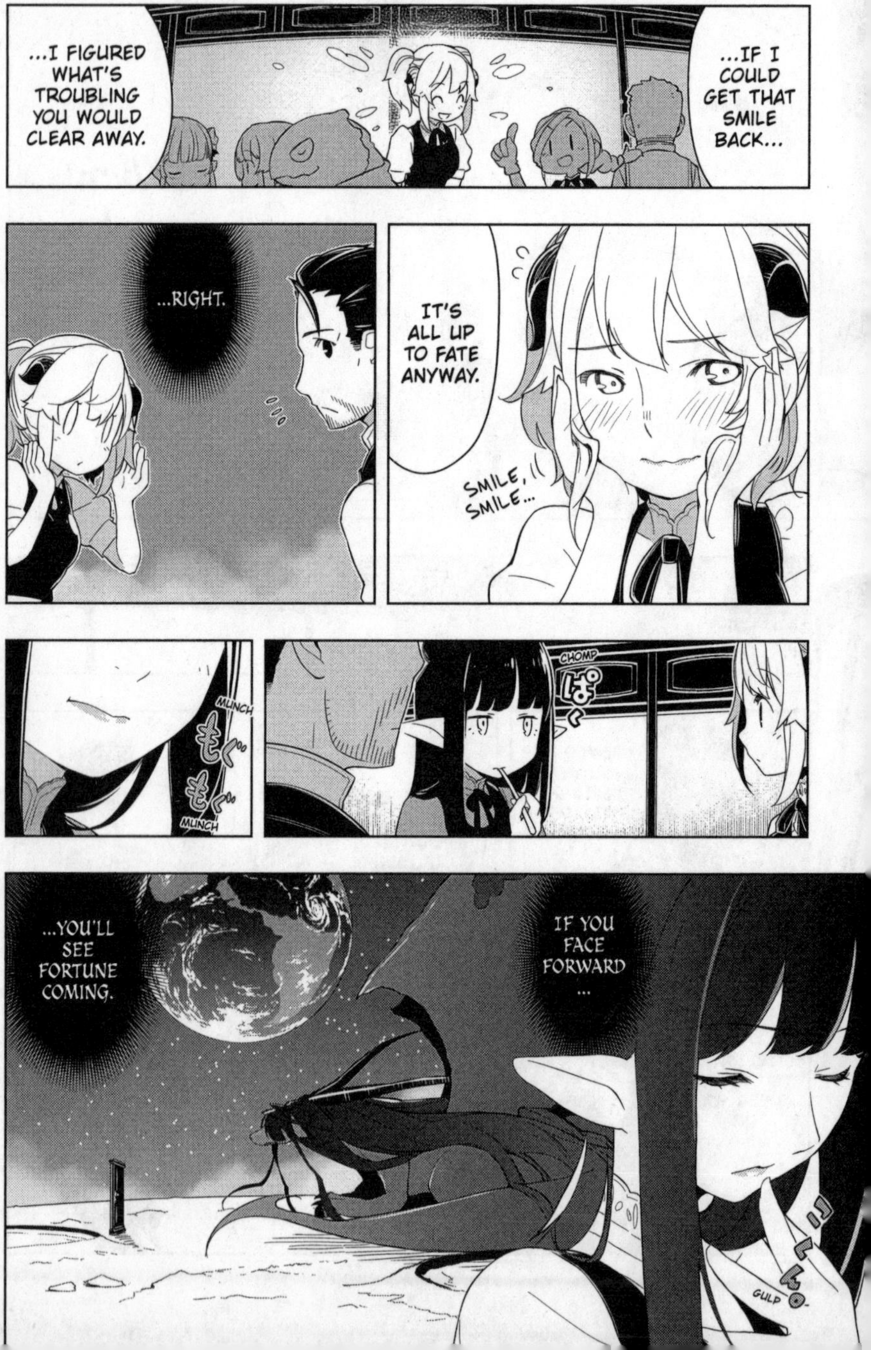
...IF I COULD GET THAT SMILE BACK...
...I FIGURED WHAT'S TROUBLING YOU WOULD CLEAR AWAY.
IT'S ALL UP TO FATE ANYWAY.
SMILE, SMILE...
...RIGHT.
CHOMP
ぱく
MUNCH
もぐ もぐ
MUNCH
IF YOU FACE FORWARD...
...YOU'LL SEE FORTUNE COMING.
GULP

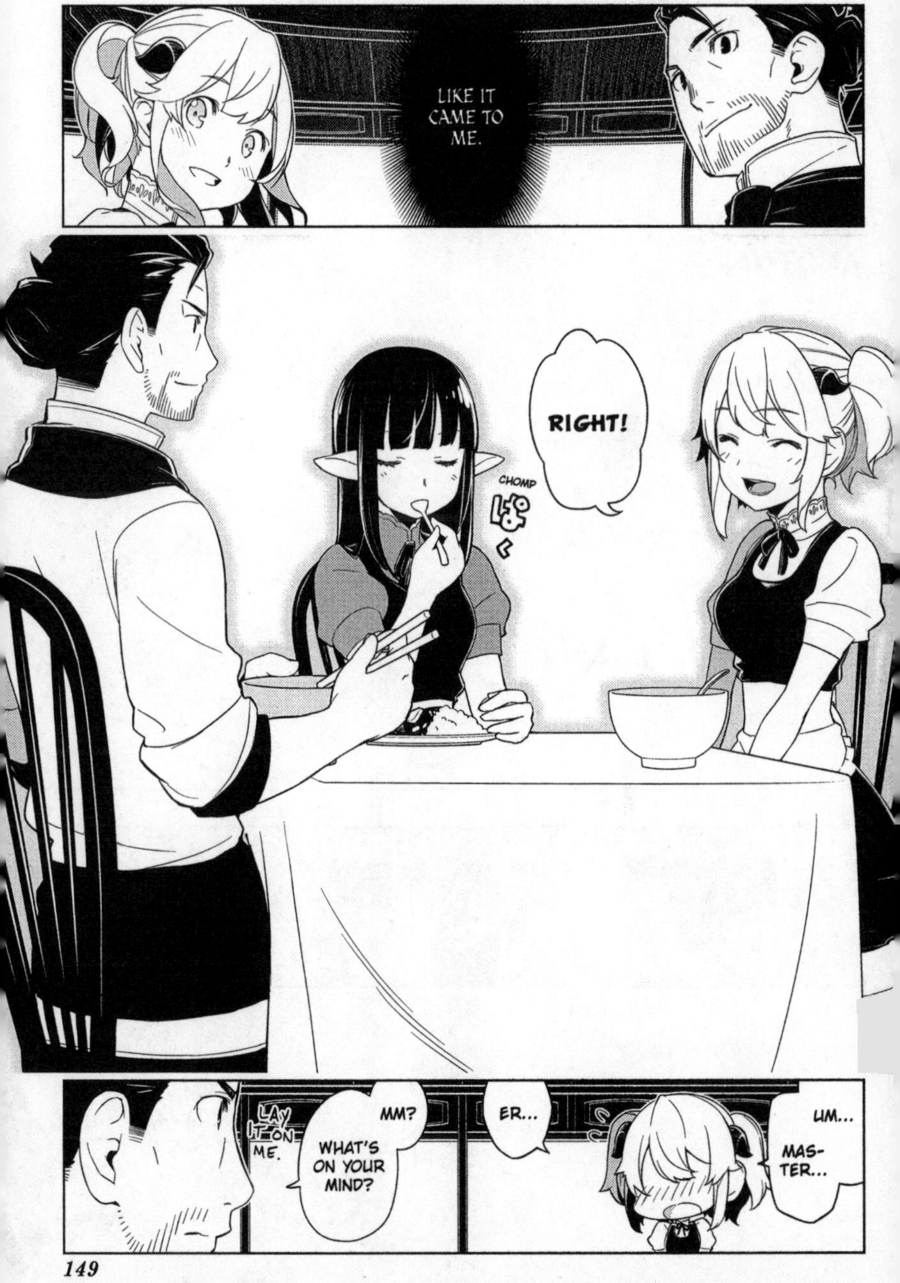
LIKE IT CAME TO ME.
RIGHT!
CHOMP
UM... MAS-TER...
ER...
MM? WHAT'S ON YOUR MIND?
LAY IT ON ME.

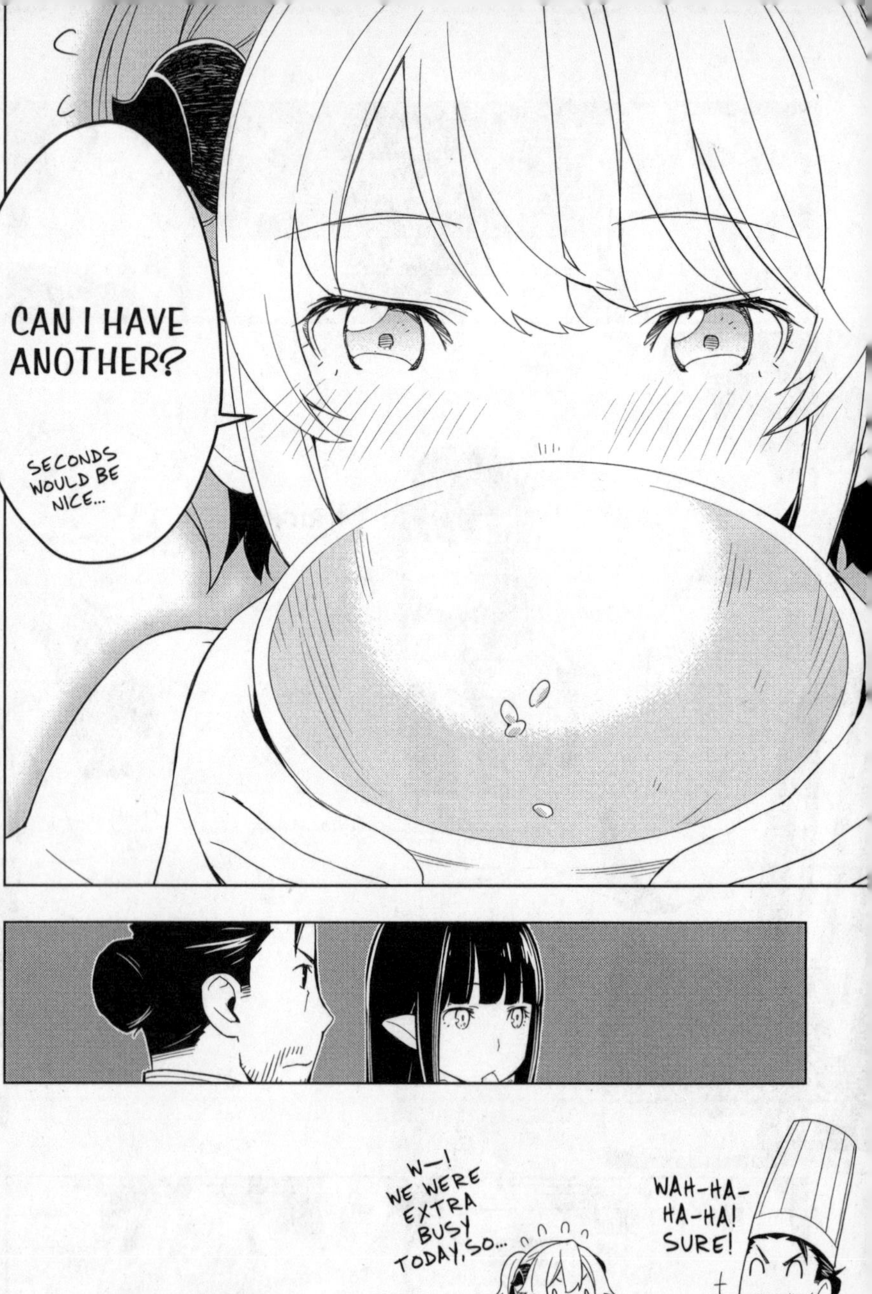
CAN I HAVE ANOTHER?
SECONDS WOULD BE NICE...
WAH-HA-HA-HA! SURE!
W—! WE WERE EXTRA BUSY TODAY, SO...

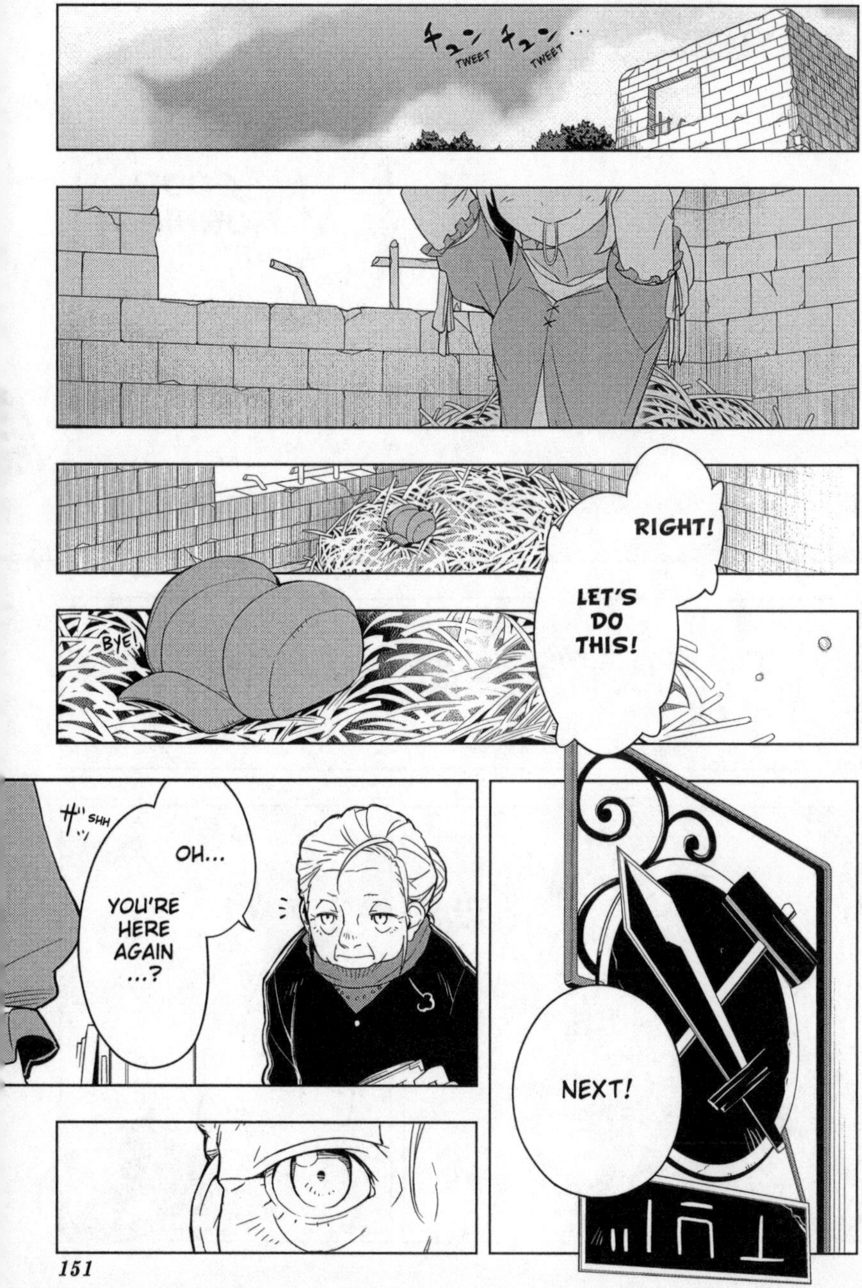
チュン TWEET チュン TWEET …
RIGHT!
LET'S DO THIS!
BYE!
NEXT!
ザッ SHH
OH…
YOU'RE HERE AGAIN …?

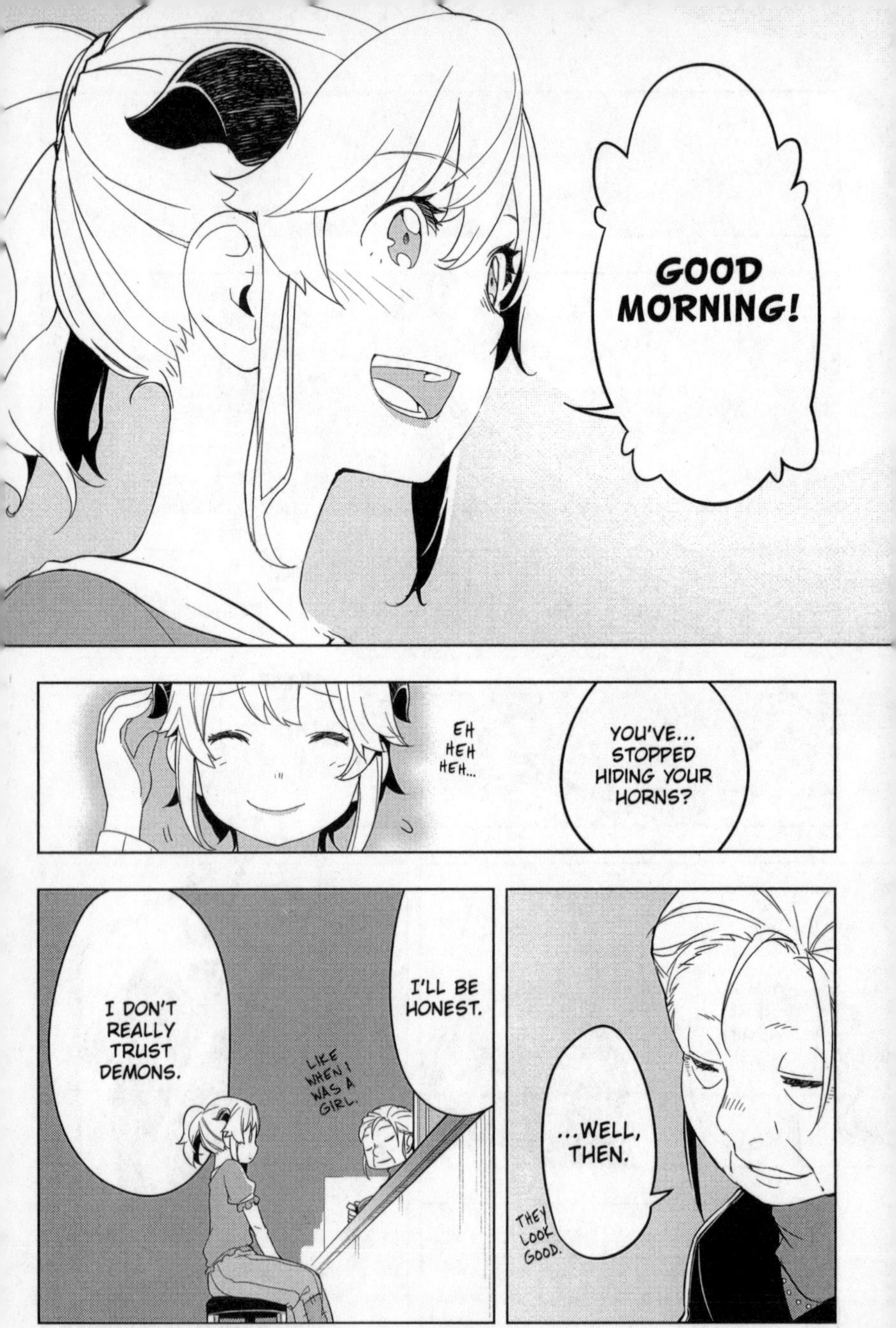
GOOD MORNING!
YOU'VE... STOPPED HIDING YOUR HORNS?
EH HEH HEH...
...WELL, THEN.
THEY LOOK GOOD.
I'LL BE HONEST.
I DON'T REALLY TRUST DEMONS.
LIKE WHEN I WAS A GIRL.

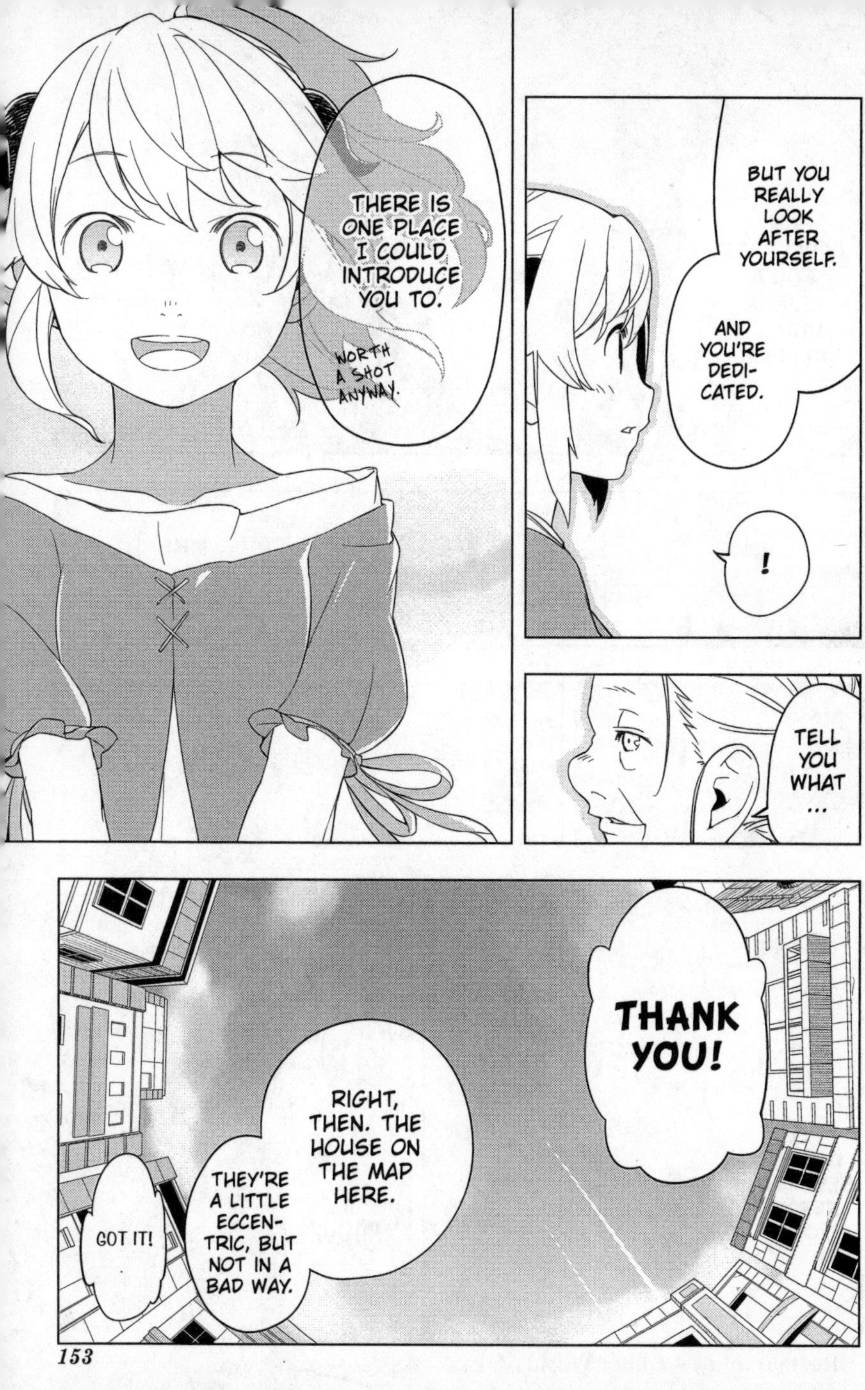
BUT YOU REALLY LOOK AFTER YOURSELF.
AND YOU'RE DEDI-CATED.
!
TELL YOU WHAT...
THERE IS ONE PLACE I COULD INTRODUCE YOU TO.
WORTH A SHOT ANYWAY.
THANK YOU!
RIGHT, THEN. THE HOUSE ON THE MAP HERE.
THEY'RE A LITTLE ECCEN-TRIC, BUT NOT IN A BAD WAY.
GOT IT!

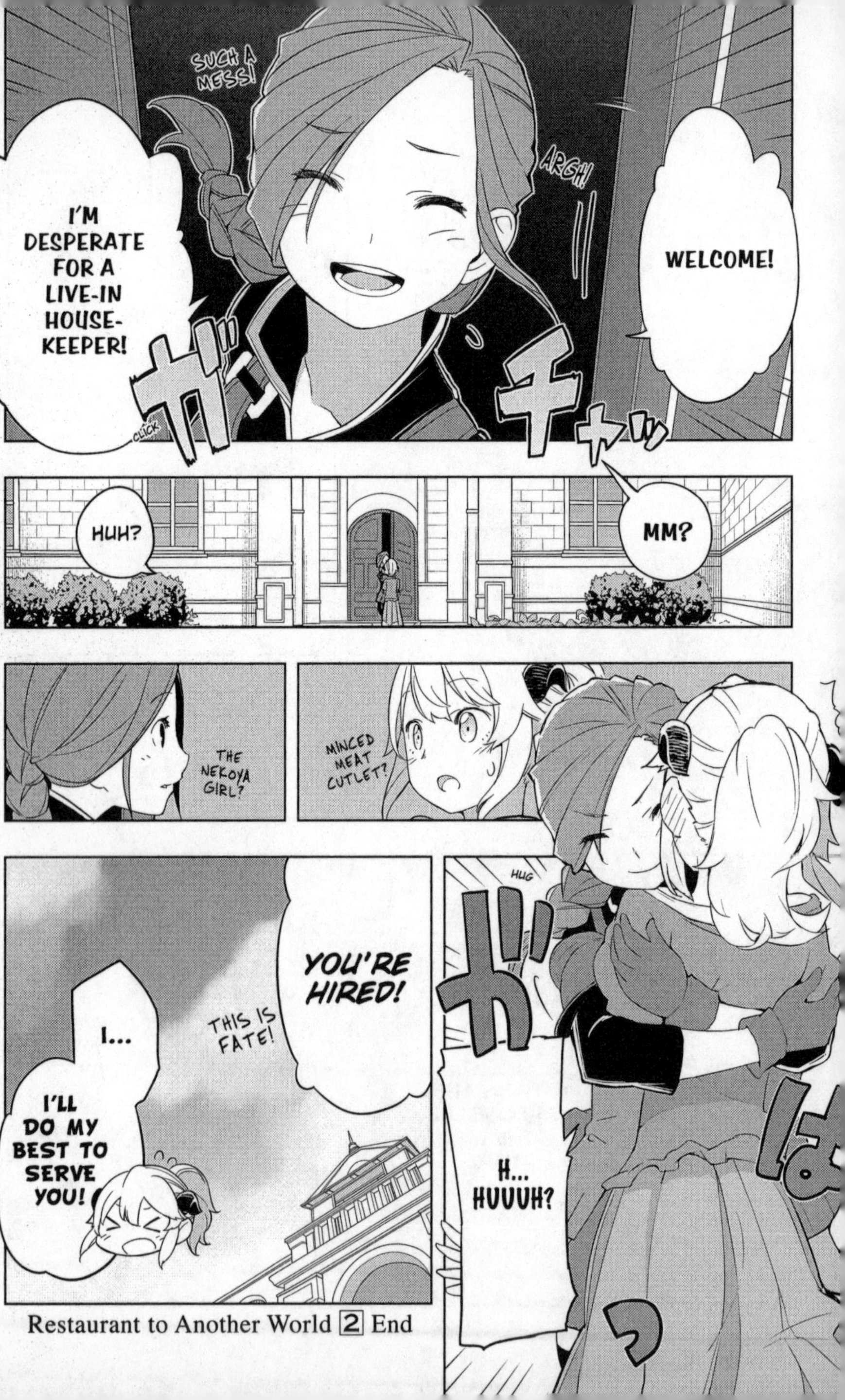
WELCOME!
ARGH!
SUCH A MESS!
I'M DESPERATE FOR A LIVE-IN HOUSE-KEEPER!
CLICK
MM?
HUH?
HUG
H... HUUUH?
MINCED MEAT CUTLET?
THE NEKOYA GIRL?
YOU'RE HIRED!
THIS IS FATE!
I...
I'LL DO MY BEST TO SERVE YOU!

Restaurant to Another World 2 End

RESTAURANT TO Another World

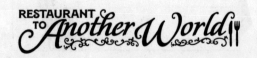

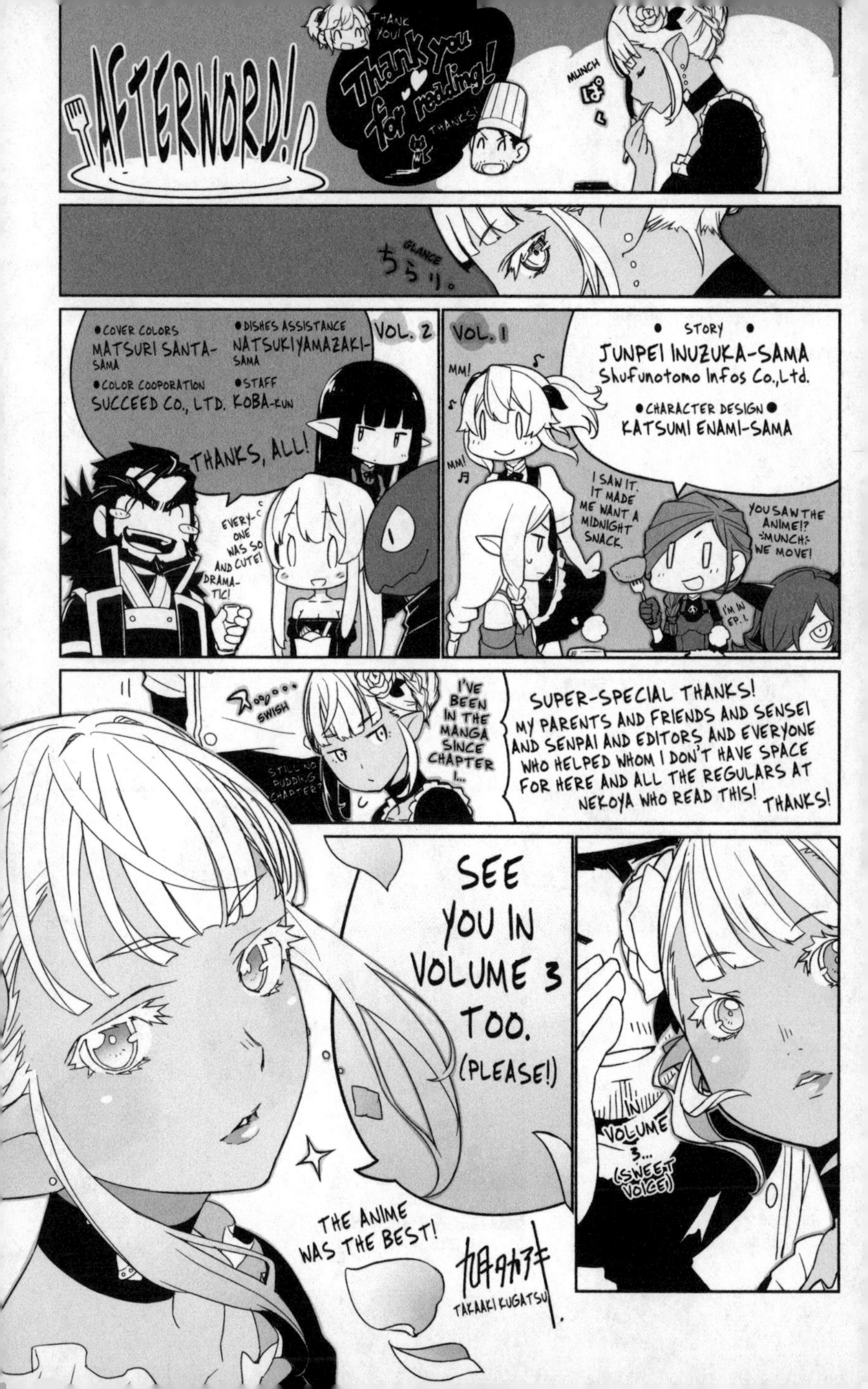MUNCH
ぽ
THANK YOU!
Thank you for reading!
THANKS!
AFTERWORD!
GLANCE
ちらり。
VOL. 1
• STORY •
JUNPEI INUZUKA-SAMA
Shufunotomo Infos Co., Ltd.
• CHARACTER DESIGN •
KATSUMI ENAMI-SAMA
MM! ♪
MM! ♪
YOU SAW THE ANIME!? MUNCH WE MOVE!
I SAW IT. IT MADE ME WANT A MIDNIGHT SNACK.
I'M IN EP. 1
VOL. 2
• DISHES ASSISTANCE
NATSUKI YAMAZAKI-SAMA
• STAFF
KOBA-KUN
• COVER COLORS
MATSURI SANTA-SAMA
• COLOR COOPORATION
SUCCEED CO., LTD.
THANKS, ALL!
EVERYONE WAS SO DRAMATIC!
AND CUTE!
SUPER-SPECIAL THANKS! MY PARENTS AND FRIENDS AND SENSEI AND SENPAI AND EDITORS AND EVERYONE WHO HELPED WHOM I DON'T HAVE SPACE FOR HERE AND ALL THE REGULARS AT NEKOYA WHO READ THIS! THANKS!
I'VE BEEN IN THE MANGA SINCE CHAPTER 1...
STILL NO PUDDING CHAPTER?
SWISH
IN VOLUME 3...
(SWEET VOICE)
SEE YOU IN VOLUME 3 TOO. (PLEASE!)
THE ANIME WAS THE BEST!
九月タカアキ
TAKAAKI KUGATSU

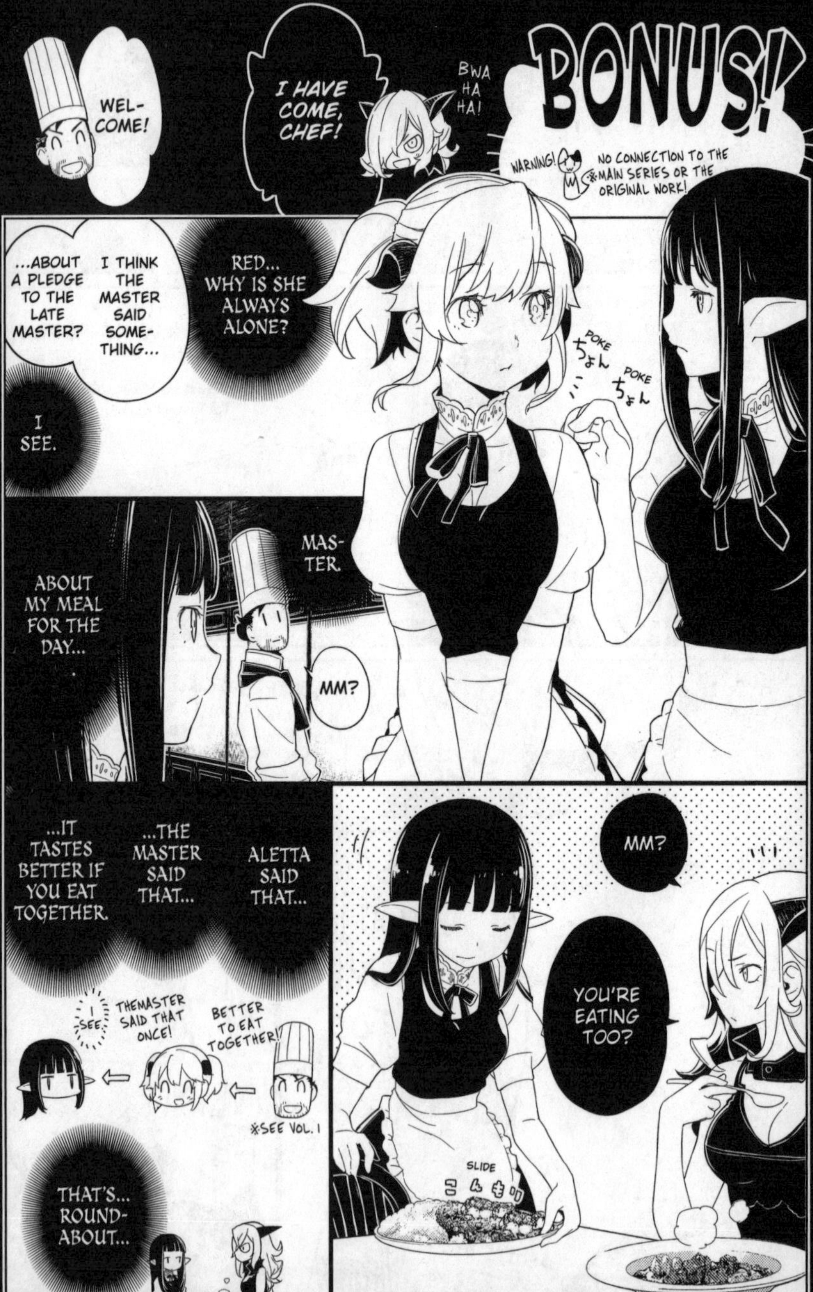
BONUS!
WARNING! ※NO CONNECTION TO THE MAIN SERIES OR THE ORIGINAL WORK!
BWA HA HA!
I HAVE COME, CHEF!
WEL-COME!
POKE ちょん
POKE ちょん
RED... WHY IS SHE ALWAYS ALONE?
I THINK THE MASTER SAID SOME-THING...
...ABOUT A PLEDGE TO THE LATE MASTER?
I SEE.
MAS-TER.
MM?
ABOUT MY MEAL FOR THE DAY...
MM?
YOU'RE EATING TOO?
SLIDE
ALETTA SAID THAT...
...THE MASTER SAID THAT...
...IT TASTES BETTER IF YOU EAT TOGETHER.
BETTER TO EAT TOGETHER!
THEMASTER SAID THAT ONCE!
I SEE.
※SEE VOL. 1
THAT'S... ROUND-ABOUT...

RESTAURANT TO Another World

STORY:
JUNPEI INUZUKA
(Shufunotomo Infos Co.,Ltd.)

ART:
TAKAAKI KUGATSU

CHARACTER DESIGN:
KATSUMI ENAMI

TRANSLATION: **ANDREW CUNNINGHAM**

LETTERING: **LYS BLAKESLEE AND RACHEL J. PIERCE**

ISEKAI SHOKUDO vol. 2
© 2017 Junpei Inuzuka/Shufunotomo Infos Co.,Ltd.
© 2017 Takaaki Kugatsu/SQUARE ENIX CO., LTD.
First published in Japan in 2017 by SQUARE ENIX CO., LTD.
English translation rights arranged with SQUARE ENIX CO., LTD. and Yen Press, LLC
through Tuttle-Mori Agency, Inc.

English translation © 2020 by SQUARE ENIX CO., LTD.

Yen Press
150 West 30th Street, 19th Floor
New York, NY 10001

Visit us at yenpress.com
facebook.com/yenpress
twitter.com/yenpress
yenpress.tumblr.com
instagram.com/yenpress

Yen Press is an imprint of Yen Press, LLC.
The Yen Press name and logo are trademarks of Yen Press, LLC.

The publisher is not responsible for websites (or their content) that are
not owned by the publisher.

First Yen Press Edition: September 2020

Library of Congress Control Number: 2020933606

ISBNs: 978-1-9753-0906-0 (paperback)
978-1-9753-0907-7 (ebook)

10 9 8 7 6 5 4 3 2 1

BVG

Printed in the United States of America

Somewhere, today, the chime on that door is ringing—

Restaurant to Another World, over-flowing with smiles and flavors.

RESTAURANT TO Another World

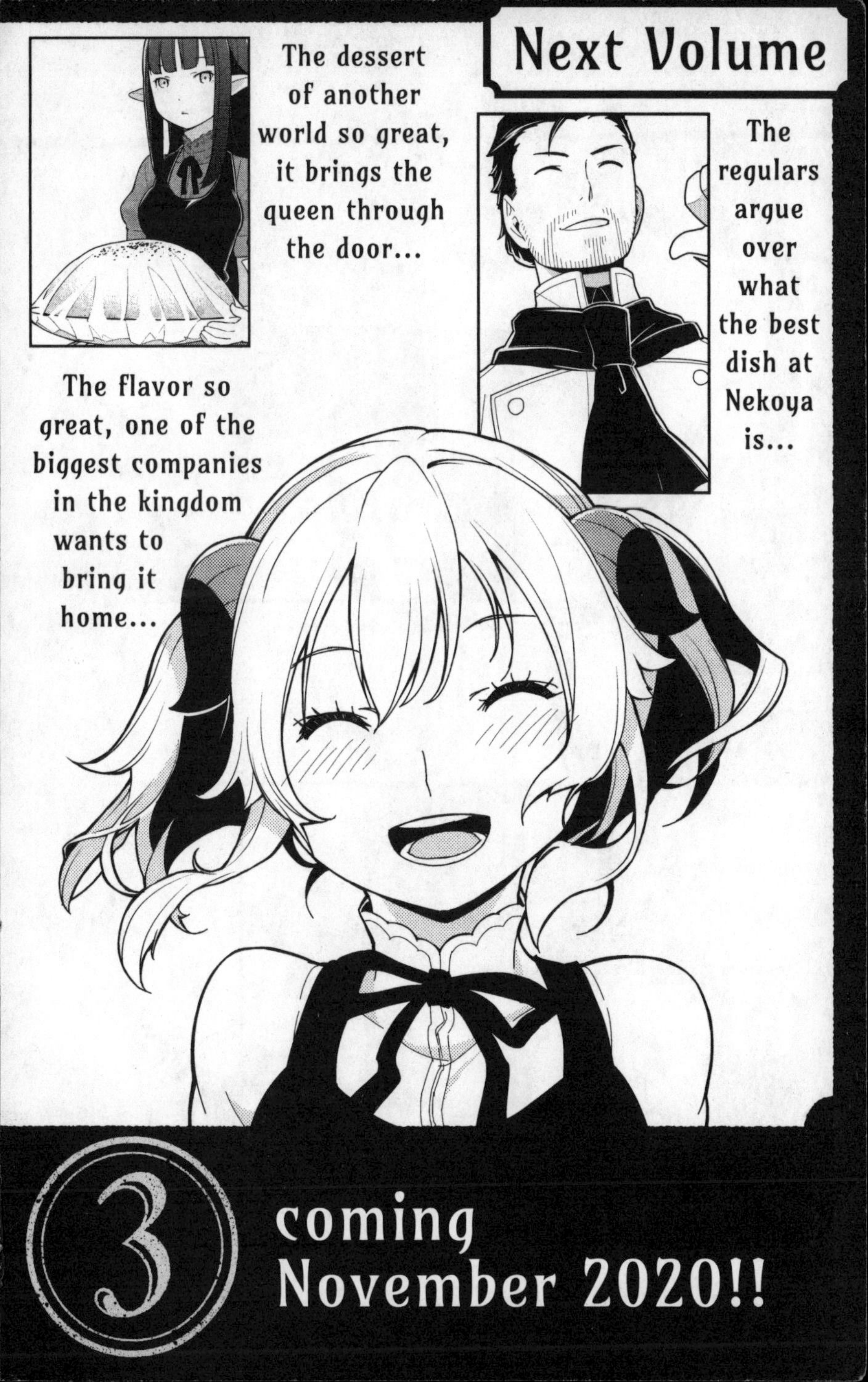
Next Volume
The dessert of another world so great, it brings the queen through the door...
The regulars argue over what the best dish at Nekoya is...
The flavor so great, one of the biggest companies in the kingdom wants to bring it home...
3
coming November 2020!!

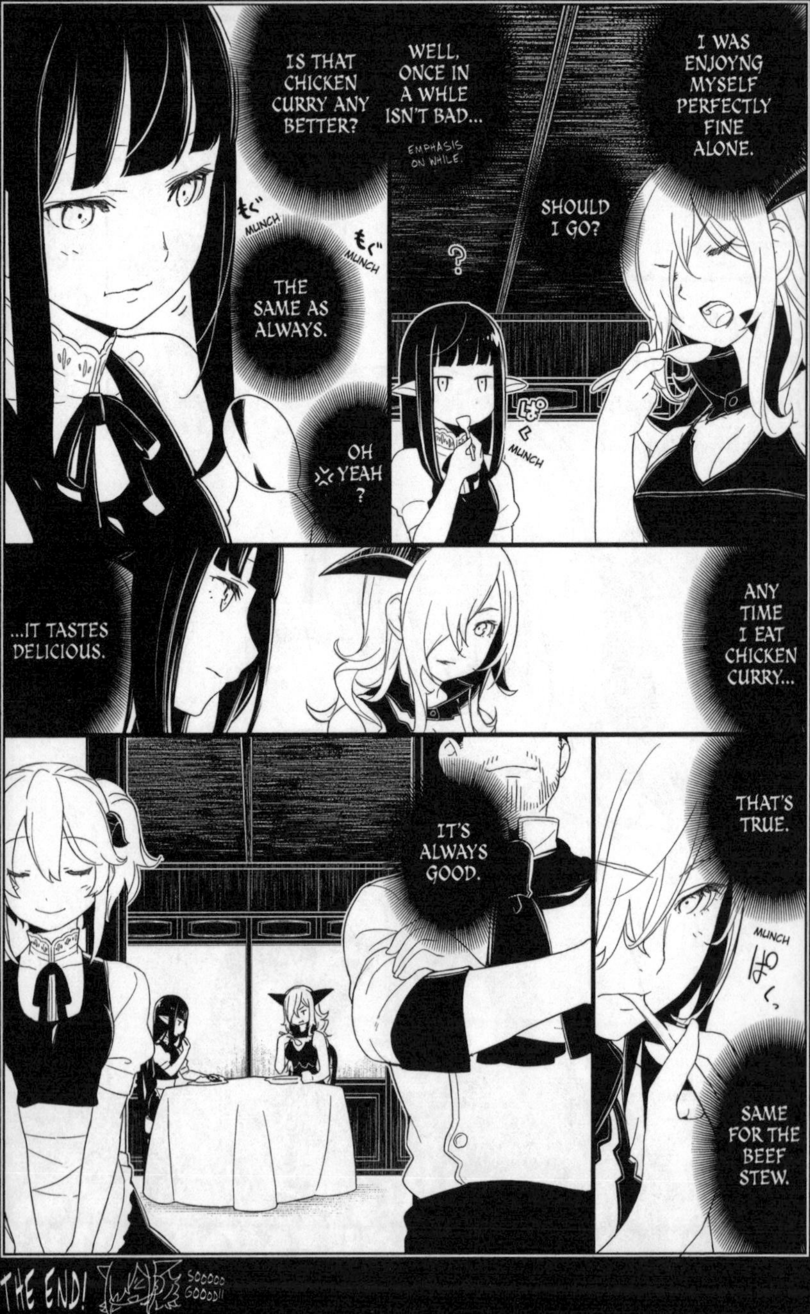
I WAS ENJOYNG MYSELF PERFECTLY FINE ALONE.
SHOULD I GO?
WELL, ONCE IN A WHLE ISN'T BAD...
EMPHASIS ON WHILE.
?
ぱく
MUNCH
IS THAT CHICKEN CURRY ANY BETTER?
もぐ
MUNCH
もぐ
MUNCH
THE SAME AS ALWAYS.
OH YEAH?
ANY TIME I EAT CHICKEN CURRY...
...IT TASTES DELICIOUS.
THAT'S TRUE.
MUNCH
ぱく
SAME FOR THE BEEF STEW.
IT'S ALWAYS GOOD.
THE END!
SOOOOO GOOOD!!